3

Love & Blessing

Zi Leonard

Srimad Bhagavad Gita

Srimad Bhagavad Gita

The Song Celestial

The dialogue between Arjuna, son of Pandu
and the Supreme Being in His incarnation as
Sri Krishna Vaasudeva, Prince of the Yadavas

Recorded by

Krishna Dwaipayana Vyasa

Text in Sanskrit as given in

The Mahabharatha

English transliteration and translation by

Vanamali

Aryan Books International

New Delhi

Srimad Bhagavad Gita

ISBN: 978-81-7305-109-8

First Published: 1997

Reprinted in **2013** by:

Aryan Books International
Pooja Apartments, 4B, Ansari Road, New Delhi-110 002 (India)
Tel.: 23287589, 23255799; Fax: 91-11-23270385
E-mail: aryanbooks@gmail.com
www.aryanbooks.co.in

Computer Typeset and Printed in India at
ABI Prints & Publishing Co., New Delhi

CONTENTS

NOTE BY TRANSLATOR

The Srimad Bhagavad Gita is a spiritual dialogue between Lord Krishna and Arjuna. It is ranked among the Upanishads, which are the great storehouse of Vedantic teachings. It comes in the middle portion of the great epic, the Mahabharatha written by the sage, Vyasa. Lord Krishna was the *avatar* or the incarnation of the Supreme Being into the form of a human being whereas Arjuna typifies the ordinary man, faced with one of the most difficult problems which any one could conceive —the killing of his own kinsmen. The whole dialogue is placed in the middle of the battlefield of Kurukshetra amidst the din and clamour of a fratricidal war. Arjuna's problem was a particular one related to his particular need. Lord Krishna's answer is the whole of the Bhagavad Gita, and cuts at the root of the human problem—which is one of ignorance. Ignorance of the nature of our own selves, ignorance of the nature of the Supreme Being and ignorance of the nature of the universe which we inhabit. This is the Srimad Bhagavad Gita. It needs no introduction to any one either in or outside of India. It has been translated hundreds of times not only in English but also in many different languages. Then why another translation? The answer is I do not know. Only He— the Eternal Charioteer, Lord Krishna, seated within the hearts of all, knows the answer. He commands and I obey, a puppet, a perfect instrument. I offer no apologies. I have no excuses. He commanded and I obeyed. My beloved Vanamali. To Thee the credit or the blame. To Thee the glory or the shame. I am Thine alone. Thy humble maid. What can I offer Thee but another *tulsi* leaf in Thy unfading garland of wild flowers!

ॐ

INTRODUCTION

The Srimad Bhagavad Gita is one of the most well known of the Hindu scriptures. It comes in the middle portion of the great epic called the Mahabharatha, composed by the sage Vyasa. All the names which appear in the first chapter of the Bhagavad Gita are prominent characters in the epic. The Mahabharatha is a voluminous treatise dealing with the fortunes of the Kuru dynasty which ruled over India, or Bharathavarsha as it was called then, about five thousand years ago.

Bhishma is the grandsire of the Kuru clan who in earlier years had abdicated the throne in favour of his step-brother. Dritarashtra (the first character to appear in the first chapter of the Gita), was Bhishma's eldest nephew. Since he was born blind, the kingdom went to his younger brother Pandu. Dritarashtra had a hundred sons who were collectively known as the Kauravas. Duryodana was the eldest of the Kauravas. Sanjaya, the second character to appear in the Gita, was Dritarashtra's companion.

Pandu the younger nephew who inherited the throne of the Kurus had five sons who were collectively known as the Pandavas. Yudhistira was the eldest, Bhima was the second, the twins, Nakula and Sahadeva were the fourth and fifth, and Arjuna, known by many names (refer glossary of names), was the third or middle Pandava, to whom the discourse of the Gita was given.

Drona was the preceptor of both the Pandavas and the Kauravas. After the death of his father, Pandu, Yudhistira was proclaimed as heir apparent to the throne of the Kurus. This aroused the animosity of the Kauravas who plotted to seize the kingdom using unfair means if necessary. Their many plots to kill the Pandavas did not succeed but eventually they managed to banish the Pandavas and grab the kingdom for themselves. When the Pandavas returned they demanded half the kingdom which was theirs by right but Duryodana refused. The bitter animosity which had sprung up between the cousins from childhood could no longer be contained with reasonable counsel and eventually culminated in the great Mahabharatha war, in which Bhishma and Drona were forced to side with the wicked Kauravas despite their partiality for the noble Pandavas. However, the Pandavas were helped by Lord Krishna who was not only their cousin but also the incarnation of Lord Vishnu, the preserver in the Hindu Trinity.

On the morn of the fateful day of the battle, the two armies arrayed themselves on opposite sides of the battlefield of the Kurus known as Kurukshetra. Dritarashtra, the father of the Kauravas was unable to participate in the battle due to his disability. He was very anxious to know of the happenings on the battlefield. The sage Vyasa gave the power of television to his Prime Minister, Sanjaya, who described the whole battle to the blind king in graphic detail.

The first chapter of the Gita starts with Dritarashtra's opening words to Sanjaya, asking him to describe the scene of battle. The rest of the chapter is Sanjaya's description of the battle and the names of the various heroes who participated. Lord Krishna had opted to be Arjuna's charioteer in the battle since he had promised Duryodana not to take up arms. On the morn of the fateful day, just before the commencement of the battle, Arjuna asked Lord Krishna to drive his chariot between the two armies so that he could observe the opposite ranks. However, the sight of his beloved grandsire Bhishma, and his revered preceptor Drona, completely unnerved him and shocked him into a realisation of the enormity of the crime he was about to commit—the slaughter of his own kith and kin in order to gain a kingdom. This thought totally demoralised the mighty hero so that he became a nervous wreck. He threw down his arms and refused to fight. The discourse of the Srimad Bhagavad Gita is given to the dejected Arjuna by Lord Krishna on the battlefield of Kurukshetra just before the commencement of the war.

To understand the Bhagavad Gita more fully we recommend reading the companion volume to this, called, **"Nitya Yoga"** which is a commentary on the eighteen chapters of the Gita. It is also a Vanamali publication.

Hari Aum Tat Sat.

GITA DHYANAM

(Invocatory Meditation on the Gita)

GITA DHYANAM

(Invocatory Meditation on the Gita)

ॐ पार्थाय प्रतिबोधितां भगवता नारायणेन स्वयं
        व्यासेन ग्रथितां पुराण मुनिना मध्ये महाभारतम् ।
अद्वैतामृतवर्षिणीं   भगवतीमष्टादशाध्यायिनी–
        मंब त्वामनुसंदधामि भगवद्गीते भवदवेषिणीम् ।।१।

*Om Paarthaaya pratibhodhitam bhagavataa naaraayanena
swayam*

*Vyaasena grathitaam puraanamuninaa madhye mahaabhaa-
ratam*

*Adwaitaamritavarshineem bhagavateem ashtaadashaadh-
yayineem*

*Amba twaamanusandadhaami bhagavadgeete bhavadwes-
hineem.*

1. Aum. The Bhagavad Gita by whom Arjuna
became illumined by Lord Narayana Himself, is
contained within the Mahabharatha and is composed by the ancient sage—Vyasa. She is the bestower
of the nectar of non-duality and the destroyer of
rebirth and consists of eighteen chapters. Upon
Thee, O Mother Bhagavad Gita do I meditate!

नमोऽस्तु ते व्यास विशालबुद्धे फुल्लारविंदायतपत्रनेत्र
येन त्वया भारततैलपूर्णः प्रज्वालितो ज्ञानमयः प्रदीपः ।।

*Namostute vyaasa vishaala buddhe phullaaravindaa-
yatapatra netra
Yena twayaa bhaaratatailapoornah prajwaalito jnaana-
maya pradeepah.*

2.   Salutations unto Thee O Vyasa of broad intellect,
whose eyes are like the petals of full blown lotuses;
by whom was lighted this lamp of wisdom, filled
with the oil of the Mahabharatha.

प्रपन्नपारिजाताय तोत्रवेत्रैकपाणये ।
ज्ञानमुद्राय कृष्णाय गीतामृतदुहे नमः ।।३।।

ॐ

*Prapanna paarijaataaya totravetraikapaanaye;
Jnaanamudraaya krishnaaya geetaamritaduhe   namah.*

3.   Salutations to Krishna, who is the wish-fulfilling
tree of those who take refuge in Him. He holds the
whip in one hand and the symbol of knowledge in
the other and He is the one who milks the nectar of
the Gita.

सर्वोपनिषदो   गावो   दोग्धा   गोपालनन्दनः
पार्थो वत्सः सुधीर्भोक्ता दुग्धं गीतामृतं महत् ।।४।।

*Sarvopanishado gaavo dogdhaa gopalanandanah;
Paartho vatsah sudheerbhokta dugdham geetaamritam mahat*

4. All the Upanishads are the cows while Krishna, the cowherd boy is the milker. Arjuna is the calf, while the men of purified intellect are the ones who drink the milk. The milk itself is the ambrosia of the Gita.

वसुदेवसुतं देवं कंसचाणूरमर्दनम् ।
देवकीपरमानन्दं कृष्णं वंदे जगद्गुरुम् ।

Vasudevasutam devam kamsachaanooramardanam;
Devakee paramaanandam krishnam vande jagadgurum.

5. I offer adorations to Lord Krishna, the preceptor of the universe, the son of Vasudeva, the destroyer of evil forces and the Supreme bliss of his mother, Devaki.

भीष्मद्रोणतटा जयद्रथजला गांधारनीलोत्पला
शल्यग्राहवती कृपेण वहनी कर्णेन वेलाकुला ।
अश्वत्थामविकर्णघोर मकरा दुर्योधनावर्तिनी
सोत्तीर्णा खलु पांडवै रणनदी कैवर्तकः केशवः ।।

Bheeshmadronatataa jayadrathajalaa gandhaaraneelotpala
Shalyagraahavatee kripena vahanee karnena velaakulaa;
Ashwatthaama vikarnaghoramakaraa duryodhanaavartinee
Sotteernaa khalu pandavairananadee kaivartakah keshavah

6. With Lord Krishna as their boatman, the Pandavas crossed over with great ease, the great

river of the Mahabharata. Its banks were Bhishma
and Drona, its water, Jayadratha and its deceptive
blue lotus was the Prince of Gandhara. The river's
shark was Shalya. The current was Kripa and the
tidal wave Karna. Ashwatthama and Vikarna were
its two terrible crocodiles and Duryodhana, its
whirlpool.

पाराशर्यवचः सरोजममलं गीतार्थगन्धोत्कटं
नानाख्यानककेसरं हरिकथा संबोधनाबोधितम् ।
लोके सज्जनषट्पदैरहरहः पेपीयमानं मुदा
भूयाद्भारतपंकजं कलिमलप्रध्वंसि नः श्रेयसे ॥७॥

*Paaraasharyavachah sarojamamalam geetaarthagandhot-
katam
Naanaakhyaanakakesaram harikathaasambodhanaabod-
hitam;
Loke sajjanshatpadairaharahah pepeeyamaanam mudaa,
Bhooyaadbhaaratapankajam kalimalapradhwamsinah
sreyase*

7. May this spotless lotus of the Mahabharata, born
in the lake of the words of the sage Vyasa, sweet
with the fragrance of the essence of the Gita, with
many narratives as its filaments, fully opened by the
discourses on Hari, the destroyer of the sins of the
Kali Yuga and imbibed joyously day after day by the
bees of the good and noble people, become the
bestower of auspiciousness on all of us?

ॐ

मूकं करोति वाचालं पंगुं लंघयते गिरिम्।
यत्कृपा तमहं वंदे परमानन्द माधवम् ॥८॥

Mookam karoti vaachaalam pangum langhayate girim;
Yatkripaa tamaham vande paramaanandamaadhavam.

8. I salute Lord Krishna, the embodiment of Supreme Bliss, whose grace makes the mute eloquent and the lame scale mountains.

यं ब्रह्मा वरुणेन्द्ररुद्रमरुतः स्तुन्वंति दिव्यैः स्तवै–
र्वेदैः सांगपदक्रमोपनिषदैर्गायन्ति यं सामगाः।
ध्यानावस्थिततद्गतेन मनसा पश्यन्ति यं योगिनो
यस्यान्तं न विदुःसुरासुरगणा देवाय तस्मै नमः ॥९॥

Yam brahmaavarunendrarudramarudah stunwanti divyaih stavair
Vedaih saangapadakramopanishadaih gaayanti yam saamagaah;
Dhyaanaavasthitatadgatenamanasaa pashyanti yam yogino;
Yasyaantam na viduh suraasuraganaah devaaya tasmai namah.

9. Adorations to that God whom Brahma, Varuna, Indra, Rudra and the Maruts praise with divine hymns; whom the singers of the Sama Veda invoke by various methods; whom yogis behold with their minds absorbed in Him through meditation and whose limits the hosts of the Devas and Asuras know not.

अथ प्रथमोऽध्यायः
Atha Prathamo'dhyaayah

CHAPTER I
ARJUNA VISHADA YOGA
The Yoga of the Despondency of Arjuna

धृतराष्ट्र उवाच

धर्मक्षेत्रे कुरुक्षेत्रे समवेता युयुत्सवः।
मामकाः पाण्डवाश्चैव किमकुर्वत संजय ।।१।।

Dhritaraashtra uvaacha
Dharmakshetre kurukshetre samavetaa yuyutsavah;
Maamakaah paandavaaschaiva kimakurvata sanjaya.

Thus spoke Dritarashtra:

1.   O Sanjaya, tell me, what did they do—my sons
and the sons of Pandu, when they assembled on the
field of Righteousness, the battlefield of the Kurus,
in their eagerness to fight?

संजय उवाच

दृष्टवा तु पाण्डवानीकं व्यूढं दुर्योधनस्तदा।
आचार्यमुपसंगम्य राजा वचनमब्रवीत् ।।२।।

Sanjaya uvaacha
Drishtwaa tu paandavaaneekam vyudham duryodha-
nastadaa;
Aachaaryam upasamgamya raajaa vachanam abraveet

Thus spoke Sanjaya:

2.   Seeing the Pandava army arrayed in battle formation, Prince Duryodana approached his preceptor
and spoke thus.

पश्यैतां पाण्डुपुत्रणामाचार्य महतीं चमूम् ।
व्यूढां द्रुपदपुत्रेण तव शिष्येण धीमता ।।३।।

Pasyaitaam paanduputraanaam aachaarya mahateem chamoom;
Vyudhaam drupadaputrena tava sishyena dheemataa.

3.   Behold O Master, this mighty army of the Pandavas arrayed in battle formation by your talented pupil, the son of King Drupada.

अत्र   शूरा महेष्वासा भीमार्जुनसमा युधि ।
युयुधानो विराटश्च द्रुपदश्च महारथः ।।४।।

Atra sooraa maheshwaasaa bheemaarjuna samaa yudhi;
Yuyudhano viraatascha drupadascha mahaarathah.

4.   They have many heroes and mighty archers like Yuyudhana and Virata as well as Drupada, skilled in chariot warfare and equal in combat to Bhima and Arjuna.

धृष्टकेतुश्चेकितानः काशिराजश्च वीर्यवान् ।
पुरुजित्कुन्तिभोजश्च शैब्यश्च नरपुंगवः ।।५।।

Drishtaketuschekitaanah kaasiraajascha veeryavaan;
Purujit kuntibhojascha saibhyascha narapungavah

5.   Drishtaketu, Chekitana and the heroic King of Kashi as well as Purujit, Kuntibhoja and Shaibya who are all foremost among men.

युधामन्युश्च विक्रान्त उत्तमौजाश्च वीर्यवान्।
सौभद्रो द्रौपदेयाश्च सर्व एव महारथाः ।।६।।

Yudhaamanyuscha vikraanta uttamaujaaschaveeryavaan;
Saubhadro draupadeyaascha sarva eva mahaarathaah.

6. The powerful Yudhamanyu and the valorous Uttamaujas, Subhadra's son as well as the sons of Draupadi—all experts in chariot warfare.

अस्माकं तु विशिष्टा ये तान्निबोध द्विजोत्तम।
नायका मम सैन्यस्य संज्ञार्थ तान्ब्रवीमि ते ।।७।।

Asmaakam tu visishtaa ye taannibodha dwijjottama;
Naayakaa mama sainyasya samjnaartham taan braveemi te.

7. O Best of Brahmins, let me draw your attention to our own principal warriors—the generals of my army.

भवान्भीष्मश्च कर्णश्च कृपश्च समितिंजयः।
अश्वत्थामा विकर्णश्च सौमदत्तिस्तथैव च ।।८।।

Bhavaan bheeshmascha karnascha kripascha samitinjayah;
Aswaththaamaa vikarnascha saumadattistathaiva cha

8. Your venerable self, Bhishma, Karna, the ever-victorious Kripa, Ashwatthama, Vikarna and Saumadatti.

ॐ

अन्ये च बहवः शूरा मदर्थे त्वक्तजीविताः।
नानाशस्त्रप्रहरणाः सर्वे युद्धविशारदाः ।।६।।

Anye cha bahavah sooraa madarthe tyaktajeevitaah;
Naanaasastrapraharanaah sarve yuddhavisaaradah.

9.   There are yet many other heroes armed with
diverse weapons and skilled in warfare who are all
ready to lay down their lives for my sake.

अपर्याप्तं तदस्माकं बलं भीष्माभिरक्षितम्।
पर्याप्तं त्विदमेतेषां बलं भीमाभिराक्षितम् ।।१०।।

Aparyaaptam tadasmaakam balam bheeshmabhirakshitam
Paryaaptam twidametesham balam bheemaabhirakshitam

10. Unequalled is this army of ours protected by
Bhishma, while their army which is under the protection of Bhima is insufficient (vulnerable).

अयनेषु च सर्वेषु यथाभागमवस्थिताः।
भीष्ममेवाभिरक्षन्तु भवन्तः सर्व एव हि ।।११।।

Ayaneshu cha sarveshu yathaabhaagamavasthitah;
Bheeshmamevaabhirakshantu bhavantah sarva eva hi.

11. Therefore all of you should guard Bhishma from
all sides, while standing firm in your respective
battle fronts.

तस्य संजनयन्हर्षं कुरुवृद्धः पितामहः ।
सिंहनादं विनद्योच्चैः शङ्खं दध्मौ प्रतापवान् ।।१२।।

Thasya sanjanayan harsham kuruvriddhah pitaamahah;
Simhanaadam vinadyocchaih sankham dadhmau
prataapavaan.

12. Then the aged grand-sire of the Kuru clan glad-
dened Duryodana's heart with his battle cry resembling the roar of a lion and blew his conch with great
power.

ततः शङ्खाश्च भेर्यश्च पणवानकगोमुखाः ।
सहसैवाभ्यहन्यन्त स शब्दस्तुमुलोऽभवत् ।।१३।।

Tatah sankhaascha bheryascha panavaanakagomukhaah;
Sahasaivabhyahanyanta sa sabdastumuloÆbhavat.

13. Thereupon the tumultuous sound of conches,
kettledrums, tabors, drums and trumpets blared
forth simultaneously.

ततः श्वेतैर्हयैर्युक्ते महति स्यन्दने स्थितौ ।
माधवः पाण्डवश्चैव दिव्यौ शङ्खौ प्रदध्मतुः ।।१४।।

Tatah svetair hayair yukte mahati syandane sthitau;
Maadhavah paandavaschaiva divyau sankhau
pradadhmatuh.

ॐ

14. At this Krishna (Madhava) and Arjuna (Pandava), seated in their magnificent chariot drawn by white steeds, blew their celestial conches.

पाञ्चजन्यं हृषीकेशो देवदत्तं धनंजयः।
पौण्ड्रं दध्मौ महाशङ्खं भीमकर्मा वृकोदरः ।।१५।।

Paanchajanyam hrishikeso devadattam dhananjaya;
Paundramdadhmau mahaasankham bheemakarmaa
vrikodharah

15. Krishna (Hrishikesha) blew His conch, the Panchajanya while Arjuna (Dhananjaya) blew his conch, the Devadutta. At this Bhima (Vrikodara), of mighty deeds, blew his huge conch—the Paundra.

अनन्तविजयं राजा कुन्तीपुत्रो युधिष्ठिरः।
नकुलः सहदेवश्च सुघोषमणिपुष्पकौ ।।१६।।

Anantavijayam rajaa kuntee-putro yudhishthirah;
Nakulah sahadevascha sughoshamanipushpakau.

16. Now King Yudhishtira, the son of Kunti blew his conch, the Anantavijaya while Nakula and Sahadeva blew their respective conches, the Sughosha and the Manipushpaka.

काश्यश्च परमेष्वासः शिखण्डी च महारथः।
धृष्टद्युम्नो विराटश्च सात्यकिश्चापराजितः ।।१७।।

Kaasyascha parameshwasah sikhandee cha mahaarathah;
Drishtadyumno viraatascha satyakischaaparaajitah.

द्रुपदो द्रौपदेयाश्च सर्वशः पृथिवीपते ।
सौभद्रश्च महाबाहुः शङ्खान्दध्मुः पृथक्पृथक् ।।१८।।

Drupado draupadeyaascha saravasah prithiveepate;
Saubhadrascha mahaabaahuh sankhaan dadhmuh
prithakprithak

17&18. Then O Lord of the Earth (Dritarashtra), the
King of Kashi who was a mighty bowman, the great
chariot-warrior, Shikandin, the invincible Satyaki,
Drishtadyumna, Virata, Drupada, Draupadi's sons
as well as the mighty armed son of Subhadra, each
in turn sounded their conches.

स घोषो धार्तराष्ट्राणां हृदयानि व्यदारयत् ।
नभश्च पृथिवीं चैव तुमुलो व्यनुनादयन् ।।१९।।

Sa ghosho dhaartaraashtraanaam hridayaani vyadaarayat;
Nabhascha prithiveem chaiva tumulo vyanunaadayan.

19. That tumultuous uproar resounded through the
sky and earth and rent the hearts of Dritarashtra's
sons.

अथ व्यवस्थितान्दृष्ट्वा धार्तराष्ट्रान् कपिध्वजः ।
प्रवृत्ते शस्त्रसंपाते धनुरुद्यम्य पाण्डवः ।।२०।।
हृषीकेशं तदा वाक्यमिदमाह महीपते ।

Atha vyavasthithaan drishtwaa dhaartharaashtraan kapidhwajah;
Pravritee sastrasampaate dhanurudyamya paandavah.
Hrisheekesam tadaa vaakyamidamaaha maheepate;

20. Then, O Lord of the Earth (Dritarashtra), beholding the host of the sons of Dritarashtra standing in
battle formation, ready to discharge their missiles,
the ape-bannered Arjuna (Pandava) lifted up his
bow and spoke thus to Krishna (Hrishikesha).

अर्जुन उवाच
सेनयोरुभयोर्मध्ये रथं स्थापय मेऽच्युत ।।२१।।
यावदेतान्निरीक्षेऽहं योद्धुकामानवस्थितान् ।
कैर्मया सह योद्धव्यमस्मिन्रणसमुद्यमे ।।२२।।

Arjuna uvaacha
Senayor ubhayormadhye ratham sthaapaya me Achyuta.
Yaavadetaan nireeksheham yoddhukaamaan avasthitaan;
Kairmayaa saha yodhavyam asmin ranasamudyame.

योत्स्यमानानवेक्षेऽहं य एतेऽत्र समागताः ।
धार्तराष्ट्रस्य दुर्बद्धेर्युद्धे प्रियचिकीर्षवः ।।२३।।

Yotsyamaanaanavekshe Æham ya eteÆtra samaagataah;
Dhartaraashtrasya durbuddhe yuddhe priyachikeershavah.

Thus spoke Arjuna:

21, 22&23. O Krishna (Achyutha)! Please place my
chariot between the two armies so that I can observe

these battle-hungry warriors with whom I have to fight, who have assembled here in their eagerness to champion the cause of the evil-minded son of Dritarashtra.

संजय उवाच

एवमुक्तो हृषीकेशो गुडाकेशेन भारत।
सेनयोरुभयोर्मध्ये स्थापयित्वा रथोत्तमम् ।।२४।।

Sanjaya uvaacha
Evamukto hrishikeso gudaakesena bharata;
Senayor ubhayormadhye sthaapayitwa rathottamam.

भीष्मद्रोणप्रमुखतः सर्वेषां च महीक्षिताम्।
उवाच पार्थ पश्यैतान्समवेतान्कुरुनिति ।।२५।।

Bheeshmadronapramukhatah sarveshaam cha maheeks-hitaam;
Uvaacha paartha pasyaitaan samavetaan kurooniti.

Thus spoke Sanjaya:

24&25. O Dritarashtra (Bharatha)! When Krishna (Hrishikesha) heard these words of Arjuna (Gudakesha), He stationed their magnificent chariot between the two armies right in front of Bhishma, Drona and the other rulers of the world, and then said, "O Arjuna (Partha)! Behold these Kurus who have assembled here!"

तत्रापश्यत्स्थितान्पार्थः पितॄनथ पितामहान् ।
आचार्यान्मातुलान्भ्रातॄन्पुत्रान्पौत्रान्सखींस्तथा ।।२६।।

Tatraapasyat sthitaan paarthah pitrinatha pitaamahaan;
Aachaaryaan maatulaan bhraatrun   putraan pautraan
sakhimstatha.

श्वशुरान्सुहृदश्चैव   सेनयोरुभयोरपि ।
तान्समीक्ष्य स कौन्तेयः सर्वान्बन्धूनवस्थितान् ।।२७।।
कृपया परयाविष्टो विषीदन्निदमब्रवीत् ।

Svasuraan suhridaschaiva senayor ubhayor api;
Taan sameekshya sa kaunteyah sarvaan bandhoon
avasthitaan.
Kripayaa parayaavishto visheedannidam abraveet;

26&27. Standing before him Arjuna (Partha) saw in
both armies, paternal uncles, grand sires, teachers,
maternal uncles, brothers, cousins, sons, grand-sons,
fathers-in-law and friends. Seeing all these kinsmen
arrayed before him, Arjuna (Kaunteya) was filled
with sorrow and spoke with a voice choking with
compassion.

अर्जुन उवाच
दृष्टवेमं स्वजनं कृष्ण युयुत्सुं समुपस्थितम् ।।२८।।
सीदन्ति मम गात्राणि मुखं च परिशुष्यति ।
वेपथुश्च शरीरे मे रोमहर्षश्च जायते ।।२९।।

Arjuna uvaacha

Drishtwemam swajanam krishna yuyutsum samupas-thitam
Seedanti mama gaatraani mukham chaparisushyati;
Vepathuscha shareere me romaharshascha jaayete.

Thus spoke Arjuna:

28&29. O Krishna! At the sight of my kinsmen
gathered here ready for battle, my limbs give way,
my mouth is parched, my body trembles and my
hair stands on end.

गाण्डीवं स्रंसते हस्तात्त्वक्चैव परिदह्यते।
न च शक्नोम्यवस्थातुं भ्रमतीव च मे मनः ।।३०।।

*Gaandeevam sramsate hastaat twak chaiva paridahyate;
Na cha saktnomyavasthaatum bhramateeva cha me manah.*

30. My bow—Gandiva, slips from my hand and my
skin burns. My mind reels and I am unable to stand.

निमित्तानि च पश्यामि विपरीतानि केशव।
न च श्रेयोऽनुपश्यामि हत्वा स्वजनमाहवे ।।३१।।

*Nimittaani chapasyaami vipareetaani kesava;
Na cha sreyoÆnupasyaami hatwaa swajanamaahave.*

31. O Krishna (Keshava)! I see only inauspicious
omens and fail to see what good can accrue from
killing my own people in battle.

ॐ

न काङ्क्षे विजयं कृष्ण न च राज्यं सुखानि च।
किं नो राज्येन गोविन्द किं भोगैर्जीवितेन वा ।।३२।।

Na kangkshe vijayam krishna na cha rajyam sukhaani cha;
Kim no raajyena govinda kim bhogair jeevitena vaa.

येषामर्थे काङ्क्षितं नो राज्यं भोगाः सुखानि च।
त इमेऽवस्थिता युद्धे प्राणांस्त्यक्त्वा धनानि च ।।३३।

Yeshaam arthe kaangkshitam no raajyam bhogaah
sukhaani cha;
Ta ime avasthitaa yuddhe praanaamstyaktwaa
dhanaani cha

32&33. O Krishna! I covet not victory or kingdom or
pleasures. What is the use of an empire or of
enjoyment or even life itself O Krishna (Govinda),
when those for whose sake we desire a kingdom,
pleasures and enjoyments are standing here on the
battlefield, staking their wealth and their very lives!

आचार्याः पितरः पुत्रास्तथैव च पितामहाः।
मातुलाः श्वशुराःपौत्राः श्यालाःसम्बन्धिनस्तथा ।।३४।।

Aachaaryah pitarah putraasthathaiva cha pitaamahaah;
Maatulaah swasuraah pautraah syaalaah sambandh-
inastathaa.

एतान्न हन्तुमिच्छामि घ्नतोऽपि मधुसूदन।
अपि त्रैलोक्यराज्यस्य हेतोः किं नु महीकृते ।।३५।।

Etaan na hantum icchaami ghnatoÆpi madhusoodhana;
Api trailokyaraajyasya hetoh kim nu maheekrite.

34&35. O Krishna (Madhusudana)! I do not wish to
slay my teachers, fathers, sons, grand sires, maternal
uncles, fathers-in-law, grandsons, brothers-in-law
and other relations even though they may slay me.
No! Not even for the sovereignty of the three worlds,
how much less for an earthly kingdom!

निहत्य धार्तराष्ट्रान्नः का प्रीतिः स्याज्जनार्दन। पापमेवाश्रयेदस्मान्हत्वैतानाततायिनः ।।३६।।

Nihatya dhaartaraashtraanah ka preetih syaajjanaardana;
Paapam evaa srayed asmaan hatwaitaan aatataayinah.

36. O Krishna (Janardana)! What joy can we derive
from killing the sons of Dritarashtra? Sin alone will
accrue to us if we slay them, evil though they are.

तस्मान्नार्हा वयं हन्तुं धार्तराष्ट्रान्स्वबान्धवान्। स्वजनं हि कथं हत्वा सुखिनः स्याम माधव ।।३७।।

Tasman naarhaa vayam hantum dhaartraashtraan
swbaandhavaan;
Swajanam hi katham hatwaa sukhinah syaama maadhava.

37. Therefore O Krishna (Madhava) it is not correct
on our part to kill the sons of Dritarashtra who are
our kinsmen. What happiness can we hope to get by
slaying our relations?

यद्यप्येते न पश्यन्ति लोभोपहतचेतसः।
कुलक्षयकृतं दोषं मित्रद्रोहे च पातकम् ।।३८।।

Yadyapyete na pasyanti lobhopahatachetasah;
Kulakshayakritam dosham mitradrohe cha paatakam.

कथं न ज्ञेयमस्माभिः पापादस्मान्निवर्तितुम्।
कुलक्षयकृतं दोषं प्रपश्यद्भिर्जनार्दन ।।३९।।

Katham na jneyam asmaabhih paapaad asmaan nivartitum;
Kulakshayakritam dosham prapasyadbhir janaardana.

38&39. Even if they, with minds overcome by greed,
see no evil in the destruction of a family and no
crime in treachery to friends, why should we not
draw back from such an outrage O Krishna
(Janardana)—we who can well perceive the evil
which will accrue from the annihilation of a dynasty.

कुलक्षये प्रणश्यन्ति कुलधर्माः सनातनाः।
धर्मे नष्टे कुलं कृत्स्नमधर्मोऽभिभवत्युत ।।४०।।

Kulakshaye pranasyanti kuladharmaah sanaatanaah;
Dharme nashte kulam kritsnam adharm o'bhibhavatyuta.

40. With the destruction of a family its ancient traditions will be lost and with the collapse of these customs,
unrighteousness will overcome the entire family.

अधर्माभिभवात्कृष्ण प्रदुष्यन्ति कुलस्त्रियः।
स्त्रीषु दुष्टासु वार्ष्णेय जायते वर्णसंकरः ।।४१।।

Adharmaabhibhavaat krishna pradushyanti kulastriyah;
Streeshu dushtaasu vaarshneya jaayate varnasankarah.

41. O Krishna! When unrighteousness prevails, the
women of the family will lose their chastity, and
when women become corrupt O Krishna (Varshneya),
it will lead to an intermixture of castes.

संकरो नरकायैव कुलघ्नानां कुलस्य च।
पतन्ति पितरो ह्येषां लुप्तपिण्डोदकक्रियाः ।।४२।।

Sankaro narakaayaiva kulaghnaanaam kulasya cha;
Patanti pitaro hyeshaam luptapindodakakriyaah.

42. This admixture will drag both the family mem-
bers and their destroyers to Hell. Deprived of their
libations the ancestors of the race will also fall.

दोषैरेतैः कुलघ्नानां वर्णसंकरकारकैः।
उत्साद्यन्ते जातिधर्माः कुलधर्माश्च शाश्वताः ।।४३।।

Doshair etaih kulaghnaanaam varnasankarakaarakaih;
Utsaadyante jaatidharmaah kuladharmaascha saaswataah.

43. The evil done by the destroyers of the family,
which has brought about the intermixture of castes
(resulting in the confusion of the social order), will

ॐ

in turn lead to the fall of the age-old caste and moral traditions of the family.

उत्सन्नकुलधर्माणां मनुष्याणां जनार्दन।
नरकेऽनियतं वासो भवतीत्यनुशुश्रुम ॥४४॥

Utsanna kuladharmaanaam manushyaanaam janaardana;
Narake niyatam vaaso bhavateetyanususruma.

44. We have often heard O Krishna (Janardana), that those whose family code of morals has been corrupted will have to abide indefinitely in Hell.

अहोबत महत्पापं कर्तुं व्यवसिता वयम्।
यद्राज्यसुखलोभेन हन्तुं स्वजनमुद्यताः ॥४५॥

Aho bata mahat paapam kartum vyavasitaa vayam;
Yadraajya sukha lobhena hantum swajanam udyataah.

45. Alas! Goaded by greed for a kingdom and the pleasures thereof, we are on the brink of committing the heinous crime of killing our own kith and kin.

यदि मामप्रतीकारमशस्त्रं शस्त्रपाणयः।
धार्तराष्ट्रा रणे हन्युस्तन्मे क्षेमतरं भवेत् ॥४६॥

Yadi maam aprateekaaram asastram sastrapaanayah;
Dhaartaraashtraa rane hanyus taanme kshemataram
bhavet.

46. Indeed, it would give me greater happiness if the sons of Dritarashtra, fully armed, slay me, unarmed and unresisting in battle.

संजय उवाच
एवमुक्त्वार्जुनः संख्ये रथोपस्थ उपाविशत् ।
विसृज्य सशरं चापं शोकसंविग्नमानसः ।।४७।।

Sanjaya uvaacha
Evamuktwaarjunah sankhye rathopastha upaavishat;
Visrijya sasaram chaapam sokasamvignamaanasah.

Thus spoke Sanjaya:

47. Lamenting thus on the battlefield, Arjuna flung his bow and arrows aside and sank to the seat of the chariot, his mind filled with anguish.

ॐ तत्सदिति श्रीमद्भगवद्गीतासूपनिषत्सु ब्रह्मविद्यायां
योगशास्त्रे श्रीकृष्णार्जुनसंवादेऽर्जुनविषाद—
योगो नाम प्रथमोऽध्यायः ।।१।।

Om tat sat iti srimad bhagavad gitaasoopanishatsu
brahmavidyaayaam yogashaastre sri krishnaarjunasa-
mvaade arjunavishaadayogo naama prathamo'dhyaayah.

Aum Tat Sat:

Thus in the Upanishad of the Bhagavad Gita, the Knowledge of Supreme Brahman, the Scripture of

Yoga, the dialogue between Sri Krishna and Arjuna, ends the first chapter entitled, "The Yoga of the Despondency of Arjuna."

ॐ

Aum Sri Krishnaya Paramatmane Namah!
Aum Sri Parthasarathaye Namah!

अथ द्वितीयोऽध्यायः
Atha Dwithiyo'dhyaayah.

CHAPTER II
SANKHYA YOGA
The Yoga of the Wisdom of Sankhya

तं तथाकृपयाविष्टम् श्रुपूर्णाकुलेक्षणम् ।
विषीदन्तमिदं वाक्यमुवाच मधुसूदनः ।।१।।

Sanjaya uvaacha
Tam tatha kripayaavishtam asrupoornaakulekshanam;
Visheedantam idam vaakyam uvaacha madhusoodanah.

Thus spoke Sanjaya:

1. Then Krishna (Madhusudana) spoke these words to him who was overwhelmed with compassion and sorrow and whose eyes were brimming over with tears.

श्रीभगवानुवाच
कुतस्त्वा कश्मलमिदं विषमे समुपस्थितम् ।
अनार्यजुष्टमस्वर्ग्यमकीर्तिकरमर्जुन ।।२।।

Sree Bhagavaan uvaacha
Kutastwa kasmalam idam vishame samupasthitam;
Anaaryajushtam aswargyam akeertikaram arjuna.

Thus spoke the Blessed Lord:

2. O Arjuna! Whence has this timidity overcome you in this hour of trial? It is un-befitting a noble soul. It will not lead to heaven and will bring disgrace on you.

ॐ

क्लैब्यं मा स्म गमः पार्थ नैतत्त्वय्युपपद्यते।
क्षुद्रं हृदयदौर्बल्यं त्यक्त्वोत्तिष्ठ परंतप ।।३।।

Klaibyam ma sma gamah paartha naitat twayyupapadyate;
Kshudram hridaya daurbalyam tyaktwottishtha paramtapa.

3.   Yield not to unmanliness O Arjuna (Partha)! It
ill befits you. Shake off this paltry faint-heartedness
and arise O Arjuna (Paramtapa)!

अर्जुन उवाच
कथं भीष्ममहं संख्ये द्रोणं च मधुसूदन।
इषुभिः प्रति योत्स्यामि पूजार्हावरिसूदन ।।४।।

Arjuna uvaacha
Katham bheeshmam aham sankhye dronam cha
madhusoodana;
Ishubhih pratiyotsyaami poojaarhaavarisoodana.

Thus spoke Arjuna:

4.   O Krishna (Madhusudana, Arisudana)! How can
I shoot arrows at Bhishma and Drona in battle—they
who are worthy of worship?

गुरूनहत्वा हि महानुभावान्
        श्रेयो भोक्तुं भैक्ष्यमपीह लोके।
हत्वार्थकामांस्तु   गुरूनिहैव
        भुञ्जीय भोगान्रुधिरप्रदिग्धान् ।।५।।

Guroonahatwa hi mahaanubhaavaan
Sreyo bhoktum bhaikshyamapeeha loke;
Hatwaarthakaamaamstu guroon ihaiva
Bhunjeeya bhogaan rudhirapradigdhaan.

5. Far better for me to live on alms than slay my noble preceptors and thus enjoy the bloodstained pleasures of the world.

न चैतद्विद्मः कतरन्नो गरीयो
    यद्वा जयेम यदि वा नो जयेयुः।
यानेव हत्वा न जिजीविषाम—
    स्तेऽवस्थिताः प्रमुखे धार्तराष्ट्राः ।।६।।

Na chaitad vidmah kataran no gareeyo
Yadwaa jayema yadi vaa no jayeyuh.
Yaaneva hatwaa na jijeevishaamas
Te'vasthitaah pramukhe dhaartarashtraah.

6. We do not know which would be better for us— that they should overcome us or that we should conquer them? We do not even wish to live after killing the sons of Dritarashtra who are arrayed before us.

कार्पण्यदोषोपहतस्वभावः
    पृच्छामि त्वां धर्मसंमूढचेताः।
यच्छ्रेयः स्यान्निश्चितं ब्रूहि तन्मे
    शिष्यस्तेऽहं शाधि मां त्वां प्रपन्नम् ।।७।।

Kaarpanyadoshopahataswabhaavah
        Pricchaami twaam dharmasammoodha chetaah;
Yacchreyah syaan nischitam broohi tanme
        Sishyaste'ham saadhi maam twaamprapannam.

7. My true nature has been obscured by self pity
and my mind is totally confused about my duty. I
have taken refuge in You. I am Your disciple. I beg
You to tell me decisively what is best for me.

न हि प्रपश्यामि ममापनुद्याद्—
        यच्छोकमुच्छोषणमिन्द्रियाणाम् ।
अवाप्य भूमावसपत्नमृद्धं
        राज्यं सुराणामपि चाधिपत्यम् ।।८।।

Na hi prapasyaami mamaapanudyaad
        Yacchokam ucchoshanam indriyaanaam;
Avaapya bhoomaavasapatnam riddham
        Raajyam suraanaam api chaadhipatyam.

8. Even if I were to obtain undisputed suzerainty
of an affluent kingdom on this earth and sovereignty
over the gods, I do not think it would remove the
anguish which is scorching my senses.

संजय उवाच
एवमुक्त्वा हृषीकेशं गुडाकेशः परंतप ।
न योत्स्य इति गोविन्दमुक्त्वा तूष्णीं बभूव ह ।।९।।

Sanjaya uvaacha
Evam uktwaa hrisheekesam gudaakesah paramtapah;
Na yotsya iti govindam uktwaa tooshneem babhoova ha.

Thus spoke Sanjaya:

9.   Arjuna (Gudakesha, Paramtapa), having thus spoken to Krishna (Hrishikesha, Govinda), then said, "I will not fight," and became silent.

तमुवाच हृषीकेशः प्रहसन्निव भारत।
सेनयोरुभयोर्मध्ये विषीदन्तमिदं वचः ।।१०।।

Tam   uvaacha hrisheekesah prahasanniva bhaarata;
Senayor ubhayor madhye visheedantam idam vachah.

10. Then O Dritarashtra (Bharatha), Krishna (Hrishikesha) smilingly spoke the following words to him who was thus grieving in the middle of the battlefield, stationed between the two armies.

श्रीभगवानुवाच
अशोच्यानन्व शोचस्त्वं प्रज्ञावादांश्च भाषसे।
गतासूनगतासूंश्च नानुशोचन्ति पण्डिताः ।।११।।

Sree Bhagavaan uvaacha
Asochyaan anvasochastwam prajnavaadaamscha bhaashase;
Gataasoon agataasoomscha naanusochanti panditaah.

Thus spoke the Blessed Lord:

11. Though you seem to be speaking wisely, yet the fact is that you are grieving for those who do not merit your grief. The wise do not grieve over the living or the dead.

न त्वेवाहं जातु नासं न त्वं नेमे जनाधिपाः।
न चैव न भविष्यामः सर्वे वयमतः परम् ।।१२।।

Na twevaaham jaatu naasam na twam neme janaadhipaah;
Nachaiva na bhavishyaamah sarve vayam atah param.

12. Truly there was never a time when I or you or these kings did not exist. Nor will any of us cease to exist in the future.

देहिनोऽस्मिन्यथा देहे कौमारं यौवनं जरा।
तथा देहान्तरप्राप्तिर्धीरस्तत्र न मुह्यति ।।१३।।

Dehihno'smin yathaa dehe kaumaaram yauvanam jaraa;
Tathaa dehaantara praaptir dheeras tatra na muhyati.

13. The embodied Spirit appears to be experiencing the phases of childhood, youth and old age and then passing on to a new body. The sage is not deluded by this.

मात्रास्पर्शास्तु कौन्तेय शीतोष्णसुखदःखदाः।
आगमापायिनोऽनित्यास्तांस्तितिक्षस्व भारत ।।१४।।

Maatraasparsaastu kaunteya seetoshnasukhaduhkhadaah;
Aagamaapaayino'nityaas taamstitikshaswa bhaarata.

14. The contact of the senses with their objects gives
rise to the feelings of heat and cold, pleasure and
pain. They come and go, for they are transitory by
nature. Learn to endure them O Arjuna (Kaunteya,
Bharatha).

यं हि न व्यथयन्त्येते पुरुषं पुरुषर्षभ।
समदुःखसुखं धीरं सोऽमृतत्वाय कल्पते ।।१५।।

Yam hi na vyathayantyete purusham purusharshabhah;
Samaduhkha sukham dheeram somritatwaaya kalpate.

15. O Arjuna (Purusharshabha), the one who stands
unaffected in their midst, regarding with equanimity
both pleasure and pain becomes eligible for immortality.

नासतो विद्यते भावो नाभावो विद्यते सतः ।
उभयोरपि दृष्टोऽन्तस्त्वनयोस्तत्त्वदर्शिभिः ।१६।।

Naasato vidyate bhaavo naabhaavo vidyate satah;
Ubhayorapi drishtontastwanayos tattwadarshibhih.

16. The unreal can never come into existence and the
real can never cease to be. Both these verities have
been perceived by the seers of Truth.

ॐ

अविनाशि तु तद्विद्धि येन सर्वमिदं ततम्।
विनाशमव्ययस्यास्य न कश्चित्कर्तुमर्हति ।।१७।।

Avinaasi tu tad viddhi yena sarvam idam tatam;
Vinaasam avyayasyaasya na kaschit kartum arhati.

17. That by which all this is pervaded is indestructible, for none can bring about the destruction of the Immutable.

अन्तवन्त इमे देहा नित्यस्योक्ताः शरीरिणः।
अनाशिनोऽप्रमेयस्य तस्माद्युध्यस्व भारत ।।१८।।

Antavanta ime dehaa nityasyoktaah sareerinah;
Anaasino'prameyasya tasmad yudhyaswa bhaarata.

18. Only the bodies are perishable O Arjuna (Bharatha), which are inhabited by that unbounded, eternal and indestructible Spirit. Therefore prepare yourself to fight.

य एनं वेत्ति हन्तारं यश्चैनं मन्यते हतम्।
उभौ तौ न विजानीतो नायं हन्ति न हन्यते ।।१९।।

Ya enam vetti hantaaram yaschainam manyate hatam;
Ubhau tau na vijaaneeto naayam hanti na hanyate.

19. The one who considers the Spirit to be the slayer as well as the one who imagines It to be slain are both equally ignorant, for the Spirit can neither slay nor be slain.

न जायते म्रियते वा कदाचि–
   न्नायं भूत्वा भविता वा न भूयः।
अजो नित्यः शाश्वतोऽयं पुराणो
   न हन्यते हन्यमाने शरीरे ।।२०।।

Na jaayate mriyate vaa kadaachit
   Naayam bhootwaabhavitaa vaa na bhooyah;
Ajo nityah saaswato'yam puraano
   Na hanyate hanyamaane sareere.

20. It neither takes birth nor dies. It does not come into existence or cease to exist. It is unborn, eternal, changeless and primeval. It is not destroyed with the slaying of the body.

वेदाविनाशिनं नित्यं य एनमजमव्ययम्।
कथं स पुरुषः पार्थ कं घातयति हन्ति कम् ।।२१।।

Vedaavinaasinam nityam ya enam ajam avyayam;
Katham sa purushah paartha kam gaatayati hanti kam.

21. O Arjuna (Partha)! How can anyone who knows That (the Spirit) to be imperishable, eternal, birthless and immortal, slay anyone or be the cause of killing?

वासांसि जीर्णानि यथा विहाय
   नवानि गृह्णाति नरोऽपराणि।
तथा शरीराणि विहाय जीर्णा–
   न्यन्यानि संयाति नवानि देही ।।२२।।

Vaasaamsi jeernaani yathaa vihaaya
Navaani grihnaati naro'paraani;
Tathaa sareeraani vihaaya jeernaan
Yanyaani samyaati navaani dehi.

22. Just as a person casts off worn-out clothes in order to don new ones, so the embodied Spirit discards old bodies and enters new ones.

नैनं छिन्दन्ति शस्त्राणि नैनं दहति पावकः।
न चैनं क्लेदयन्त्यापो न शोषयति मारुतः ।।२३।।

Nainam chhindanti sastraani nainam dahati paavakah;
Na chainam kledayantyaapo na soshayati maarutah.

23. Weapons cannot cleave It, nor can fire burn It. Water cannot drench It, nor can wind dry It.

अच्छेद्योऽयमदाह्योऽयमक्लेद्योऽशोष्य एव च।
नित्यःसर्वगतः स्थाणुरचलोऽयं सनातनः ।।२४।।

Acchedyo'yam adaahyo'yam akledyo'soshya eva cha;
Nityah sarvagatah sthaanur achaloyam sanaatanah.

24. It (the Spirit) cannot be cut, burned, drenched or dried because It is eternal, changeless, all-pervading, stable and immovable.

अव्यक्तोऽयमचिन्त्योऽयमविकार्योऽयमुच्यते।
तस्मादेवं विदित्वैनंनानुशोचितुमर्हसि ।।२५।।

Avyakto'yam   achintyo'yamavikaaryo'yam uchyate;
Tasmaad evam viditwainam naanusochitum arhasi.

25. It is said to be unmanifest, immutable and beyond the range of thought. Knowing this you should stop grieving.

अथ चैनं नित्यजातं नित्यं वा मन्यसे मृॅतम्।
तथापि त्वं महाबाहो नैवं शोचितुमर्हसि ।।२६।।

Atha chainam nityajaatam nityam vaa manyase mritam;
Tathaapi twam mahaabaaho naivam sochitum arhasi.

26. O Arjuna (Mahabaho), even if you consider It to be constantly subject to birth and death, you should not grieve.

जातस्य हि ध्रुवो मृत्युर्ध्रुवं जन्म मृतस्य च।
तस्मादपरिहार्येऽर्थे न त्वं शोचितुमर्हसि ।।२७।।

Jatasya hi dhruvo mrityur dhruvam janma mritasya cha;
Tasmaad aparihaarye'rthe na twam sochitum arhasi.

27. For death is unavoidable for one who is born and rebirth is certain for one who dies. Therefore you should not grieve over the inevitable.

अव्यक्तादीनि भूतानि व्यक्तमध्यानि भारत।
अव्यक्तनिधनान्येव तत्र का परिदेवना ।।२८।।

Avyaktaadeeni bhootaani vyaktamadhyaani bhaarata;
Avyakta nidhanaanyeva tatra kaa paridevanaa.

28. O Arjuna (Bharatha), all beings were unmanifest
in the beginning and will become unmanifest in the
end. They are manifest only in the interim. What is
there in this to grieve?

आश्चर्यवत्पश्यति कश्चिदेन—
      माश्चर्यवद्वदति तथैव चान्यः ।
आश्चर्यवच्चैनमन्यःशृणोति
      श्रुत्वाप्येनं वेद न चैव कश्चित् ॥२६॥

Aascharyavatpasyati kaschid enam
      Aascharyavad vadati tathaiva chaanyah;
Aascharyavat chainam anyah srinoti
      Srutwaapyenam veda na chaiva kaschit.

29. Some perceive It (the Spirit) as a marvel, others
speak of it as a wonder and still others hear of it as
being mysterious, yet none can comprehend It.

देही नित्यमवध्योऽयं देहे सर्वस्य भारत।
तस्मात्सर्वाणि भूतानि न त्वं शोचितुमर्हसि ॥३०॥

Dehee nityam avadhyo'yam dehe sarvasya bhaarata;
Tasmaat sarvaani bhootaani na twam sochitum arhasi.

30. O Arjuna (Bharatha), this eternal Spirit, the

Indweller in all bodies is indestructible. Therefore there is no need for you to grieve over any creature.

स्वधर्ममपि चावेक्ष्य न विकम्पितुमर्हसि।
धर्म्याद्धि युद्धाच्छ्रेयोऽन्यत्क्षत्रियस्य न विद्यते ।।३१।।

Swadharmam api chaavekshya na vikampitum arhasi;
Dharmyaddhi yuddhaa cchreyo'nyat kshatriyasya na vidyate.

31. Even with regard to your own duty, you should not waver, for there is nothing more noble for a Kshatriya than participation in a righteous battle.

यदृच्छया चोपपन्नं स्वर्गद्वारमपावृतम्।
सुखिनः क्षत्रियाः पार्थ लभन्ते युद्धमीदृशम् ।।३२।।

Yadricchayaa chopapannam swargadwaaram apaavritam;
Sukhinah kshatriyaah paartha labhante yuddham eedrisam.

32. Fortunate indeed O Arjuna (Partha), are the Kshatriyas who are called upon to fight a battle like this which comes unsought, for it is an open gateway to Heaven.

अथ चेत्त्वमिमं धर्म्यं संग्रामं न करिष्यसि।
ततः स्वधर्मं कीर्तिं च हित्वा पापमवाप्स्यसि ।।३३।।

Atha chettwam imam dharmyam samgraamam na karishyasi;
Tatah swadharmam keertim cha hitwaa paapam avaapsyasi.

33. If however you abandon your duty and honour and refuse to engage in this righteous battle, you will surely incur sin.

अकीर्तिं चापि भूतानि कथयिष्यन्ति तेऽव्ययाम्
संभावितस्य चाकीर्तिर्मरणादतिरिच्यते ।।३४।।

Akeertim chaapi bhootaani kathayishyanti te'vyayaam;
Sambhaavitasya chaakeertir maranaad atirichyate.

34. People will keep speaking of your infamy and for the noble, dishonour is worse than death.

भयाद्रणादुपरतं मंस्यन्ते त्वां महारथाः।
येषां च त्वं बहुमतो भूत्वा यास्यसि लाघवम् ।।३५।।

Bhayaad ranaad uparatam mamsyante twaam mahaarathaah;
Yeshaam cha twam bahumato bhootwaa yaasyasi laaghavam.

35. The great chariot-warriors who hold you in such high esteem will speak disparagingly of you, believing that you have withdrawn from battle through fear.

अवाच्यवादांश्च बहून्वदिष्यन्ति तवाहिताः।
निन्दन्तस्तव सामर्थ्यं ततो दुःखतरं नु किम् ।।३६।।

Avaachyavaadamscha bahoon vadishyanti tavaahitaah;
Nindantastavasaamarthyam tato duhkhataram nu kim.

36. Your enemies will speak slightingly of your prowess and ridicule your valour. What can be more distressing than this?

हतो वा प्राप्स्यसि स्वर्गं जित्वा वा भोक्ष्यसे महीम्
तस्मादुत्तिष्ठ कौन्तेय युद्धाय कृतनिश्चयः ।।३७।।

Hato vaa praapsyasi swargam jitwaa vaa bhokshyase maheem;
Tasmaad uttishtha kaunteya yuddhaaya kritanischayah.

37. If you are slain you will attain Heaven, and if victorious you will enjoy the earth. Therefore resolve to fight and arise O Arjuna (Kaunteya)!

सुखदुःखे समे कृत्वा लाभालाभौ जयाजयौ।
ततो युद्धाय युज्यस्व नैवं पापमवाप्स्यसि ।।३८।।

Sukhaduhkhe same kritwaa laabhaalaabhau jayaajayau;
Tato yuddhaaya yujyaswa naivam paapamavaapsyasi.

38. Treating alike pleasure and pain, gain and loss, victory and defeat, engage yourself in battle. Thus, you shall incur no sin.

एषा तेऽभिहिता सांख्ये बुद्धियोंगे त्विमां शृणु।
बुद्धया युक्तो यया पार्थ कर्मबन्धं प्रहास्यसि ।।३६।।

Eshaa te'bhibhitaa saankhye buddhir yoge twimaam srinu;
Buddhya yukto yayaa paartha karma bandham prahaasyasi.

39. This wisdom has been presented to you from the
viewpoint of Sankhya *(Jnana yoga)*. Now hear of it
from the angle of *yoga (Karma Yoga)*, O Arjuna
(Partha), through which you will be able to break the
bonds of action *(karma)*.

नेहाभिक्रमनाशोऽस्ति प्रत्यवायो न विद्यते।
स्वल्पमप्यस्य धर्मस्य त्रायते महतो भयात् ।।४०।।

Nehaabhikramanaaso'sti pratyavaayo na vidyate;
Swalpam apyasya dharmasya traayate mahato bhayaat.

40. On this path no effort is in vain nor is there any
fear of contrary results. Even a little practice of this
discipline protects one from great fear.

व्यवसायात्मिका बुद्धिरेकेह कुरुनन्दन।
बहुशाखा ह्यनन्ताश्च बुद्धयोऽव्यवसायिनाम् ।।४१।।

Vyavasaayaatmikaa buddhirekehah kurunandana;
Bahusaakhaa hyanantaascha buddhayo'vyavasaayinaam.

41. O Arjuna (Kurunandana)! Here the intellect is

firm and resolute, while the intellect of the irresolute is scattered and diverse.

यामिमां पुष्पितां वाचं प्रवदन्त्यविपश्चितः ।
वेदवादरताः पार्थ नान्यदस्तीति वादिनः ।।४२।।

*Yaam imaam pushpitaam vaacham pravadantya-
vipaschitah;*
Vedavaadarataah paartha naanyad asteeti vaadinah

कामात्मानः स्वर्गपरा जन्मकर्मफलप्रदाम् ।
क्रियाविशेषबहुलां भोगैश्वर्यगतिं प्रति ।।४३।।

Kaamaatmaanah swargaparaa janmakarmaphalapradaam;
Kriyaavisesha bahulaam bhogaischarya gatim prati.

42&43. O Arjuna (Partha)! Those who cling to the letter of the *Vedas* and are obsessed by desires and look upon Heaven as the supreme goal and insist that there is nothing beyond this, are most unwise. The flowery speech of the *Vedas*, recommending various types of rituals for the attainment of pleasures and prosperity will lead to rebirth alone.

भोगैश्वर्यप्रसक्तानां तयापहृतचेतसाम् ।
व्यवसायात्मिका बुद्धिः समाधौ न विधीयते ।।४४।।

Bhogaischarya prasktaanaam tayaapahritachetasaam;
Vyavasaayaatmikaa buddhih samaadhau na vidheeyate.

44. Those whose discrimination has been carried away by their deep attachment to the path of pleasure, can never attain single-pointed concentration in meditation.

त्रैगुण्यविषया वेदा निस्त्रैगुण्यो भवार्जुन।
निर्द्वन्द्वो नित्यसत्त्वस्थो निर्योगक्षेम आत्मवान् ।।४५।।

Traigunyavishayaa vedaa nistraigunyo bhavaarjuna;
Nirdwandwo nityasatwastho niryogakshema aatmavaan.

45. O Arjuna! The *Vedas* deal with the three modes of Nature *(gunas)*. You should therefore transcend these modes and establish yourself in the Self. Be free from these and ever balanced between the pairs of opposites and totally unworried about procuring and hoarding.

यावानर्थ उदपाने सर्वतः संप्लुतोदके।
तावान्सर्वेषु वेदेषु ब्राह्मणस्य विजानतः ।।४६।।

Yaavaanartha udapaane sarvatah samplutodake;
Taavaan sarveshu vedeshu brahmanasya vijaanatah.

46. An enlightened Brahmin has as much use for the *Vedas* as one has for a reservoir in times of flood!

कर्मण्येवाधिकारस्ते मा फलेषु कदाचन।
मा कर्मफलहेतुर्भूर्मा ते सङ्गोऽस्त्वकर्मणि ।।४७।।

Karmanyevaadhikaraste ma phaleshu kadaachana;
Ma karmaphalahetur bhoor ma te sangostvakarmani

47. You have a right to perform action alone but never to the fruits thereof. Let not the results of the action be your objective nor allow yourself to be attached to inactivity.

योगस्थः कुरु कर्माणि सङ्गं त्यक्त्वा धनंजय।
सिद्धयसिद्धयोः समो भूत्वा समत्वं योग उच्यते।।४८।।

Yogasthah kuru karmaani sangam tyaktwaa dhananjaya;
Siddhyasiddhyoh samo bhootwaa samatwam yoga uchyate.

48. Established in *yoga* and abandoning attachments should you act, O Arjuna (Dhananjaya), unconcerned about success or failure. This equanimity of the mind is called *yoga*.

दूरेण ह्यवरं कर्म बुद्धियोगाद्धनंजय।
बुद्धौ शरणमन्विच्छ कृपणाः फलहेतवः ।।४९।।

Doorena hyavaram karma buddhiyogaad dhananyaja;
Buddhau sharanamanwiccha kripanaah phalahetavah.

49. Motivated action is far inferior to that done in conjunction with the intelligent will (unselfishly). Therefore O Arjuna (Dhananjaya), resort to this type of intellect. Wretched are they who work only for benefits.

बुद्धियुक्तो जहातीह उभे सुकृतदुष्कृते।
तस्माद्योगाय युज्यस्व योगः कर्मसु कौशलम् ।।५०।।

Buddhiyukto jahaateeha ubhe sukrita dushkrite;
Tasmaad yogaaya yujyaswa yogah karmasu kaushalam.

50. One who is established in this equanimity, becomes free from both virtue and vice in this very life.
Therefore unite yourself with this *yoga*, for *yoga* is
dexterity in action.

कर्मजं बुद्धियुक्ता हि फलंत्यक्त्वा मनीषिणः।
जन्मबन्धविनिर्मुक्ताः पदं गच्छन्त्यनामयम् ।।५१।।

Karmajam buddhiyuktaa hi phalam tyaktwaa maneeshinah;
Janmabandha vinirmuktaahpadam gacchantyanaamayam.

51. The wise, who practise equanimity of mind and
have renounced the fruit of action, are freed from the
shackles of birth and death and attain that state
which lies beyond misery.

यदा ते मोहकलिलं बुद्धिर्व्यतितरिष्यति।
तदा गन्तासि निर्वेदं श्रोतव्यस्य श्रुतस्य च ।।५२।।

Yadaa te mohakalilam buddhir vyatitarishyati;
Tadaa gantaasi nirvedam srotavyasya srutasya cha.

52. When your intellect goes beyond the mire of delusion, you will become indifferent to what has been heard and what is yet to be heard.

श्रुतिविप्रतिपन्ना ते यदा स्थास्यति निश्चला।
समाधावचला बुद्धिस्तदा योगमवाप्स्यसि ।।५३।।

Srutivipratipannaa te yadaa sthaasyati nischalaa;
Samaadhaavachalaa buddhistadaa yogam avaapsyasi.

53. When your intellect, which has been confused by listening to conflicting statements, becomes fixed in equanimity, you will be in a state of *yoga* (unity).

अर्जुन उवाच

स्थितप्रज्ञस्य का भाषा समाधिस्थस्य केशव।
स्थितधीः किं प्रभाषेत किमासीत व्रजेत किम् ।।५४।।

Arjuna uvaacha
Sthitaprajnyasya kaa bhashaa samaadhisthasya keshava;
Sthithadheeh kimprabhaasheta kimaaseeta vrajeta kim.

Thus spoke Arjuna:

54. O Krishna, what are the signs of the sage of steady wisdom (the enlightened one), who is established in divine consciousness? How does the sage of steady intellect speak, sit and walk?

श्रीभगवानुवाच
प्रजहाति यदा कामान्सर्वान्पार्थ मनोगतान्।
आत्मन्येवात्मना तुष्टः स्थितप्रज्ञस्तदोच्यते ।।५५।।

Sree Bhagavaan uvaacha
Prajahaati yadaa kaamaan sarvaan paartha manogataan;
Aatmanyevatmanaa tushtah stithaprajnasthadochyate.

Thus spoke the Blessed Lord:

55. O Arjuna (Partha), when a person completely casts away all desires from the mind and is content with the Self and by the Self alone, he can be said to be enlightened (of steady intellect).

ॐ

दुःखेष्वनुद्विग्नमनाः सुखेषु विगतस्पृहः।
वीतरागभयक्रोधः स्थितधीर्मुनिरुच्यते ।।५६।।

Dukheshwanudwignamanaah sukheshu vigatasprihah;
Veetaraagabhayakrodhah sthitadheer munir uchyate.

56. The sage whose mind is unperturbed in misfortune and not craving for pleasures, who is free from desire, fear and anger, can be considered enlightened (of steady intellect).

यः सर्वत्रानभिस्नेहस्तत्तत्प्राप्य शुभा शुभम्।
नाभिनन्दति न द्वेष्टि तस्य प्रज्ञा प्रतिष्ठिता ।।५७।

Yah sarvatraanabhisnehas tattat praapya subhaasubham;
Naabhinandati na dweshti tasya prajnaa pratitishthitaa.

57. The sage who is not attached to anything, who neither rejoices at good fortune nor grieves at bad, can be called enlightened.

यदा संहरते चायं कूर्मोऽङ्गानीव सर्वशः।
इन्द्रियाणीन्द्रियार्थेभ्यस्तस्य प्रज्ञा प्रतिष्ठिता ॥५८॥

Yadaa samharate chaayam koormo'ngaaneeva sarvasah;
Indriyaanindriyaarthebhyas tasya prajnaa pratishthitaa.

58. The one who can withdraw the senses from the sense objects like the tortoise withdrawing its limbs into its shell, can be called enlightened.

विषया विनिवर्तन्ते निराहारस्य देहिनः।
रसवर्जं रसोऽप्यस्य परं दृष्टवा निवर्तते ॥५९॥

Vishayaa vinivartante niraahaarasya dehinah;
Rasavarjam raso'pyasya param drishtwaa nivartate.

59. Sense objects may cease to attract the abstinent, but the taste for them will linger on. Even this will disappear with the vision of the Supreme.

यततो ह्यपि कौन्तेय पुरुषस्य विपश्चितः।
इन्द्रियाणि प्रमाथीनि हरन्ति प्रसभं मनः ॥६०॥

Yatato hyapi kaunteya purushasya vipaschitah;
Indriyaani pramaatheeni haranti prasabham manah.

60. O Arjuna (Kaunteya), the senses are so turbulent
that they will forcibly carry away the mind of even
a wise person striving for perfection.

तानि सर्वाणि संयम्य युक्त आसीत मत्परः।
वशे हि यस्येन्द्रियाणि तस्य प्रज्ञा प्रतिष्ठिता ।।६१।।

Taani sarvaani samyamya yukta aaseeta matparah;
Vase hi yasyendriyaani tasya prajnaa prathishthitaa.

61. Thus having controlled them (the senses), one
should sit with the mind totally immersed in Me.
Such a one whose senses are perfectly restrained can
be called enlightened.

ध्यायतो विषयान्पुंसः सङ्गस्तेषूपजायते।
सङ्गात्संजायते कामः कामात्क्रोधोऽभिजायते ।।६२।।

Dhyaayato vishayaan pumsah sangas teshoopajaayate;
Sangaat sanjaayate kaamah kaamaat krodhobhijaayate.

62. When the mind dwells on sense objects, it devel-
ops attachment towards them. From attachment
arises desire and from desire, anger.

क्रोधाद्भवति संमोहः संमोहात्स्मृतिविभ्रमः।
स्मृतिभ्रंशाद्बुद्धिनाशो बुद्धिनाशात्प्रणश्यति ।।६३।।

Krodhaad bhavati sammohah sammohaat smriti vibhramah;
smritibhramsaat budhinaaso buddhinaasaat pranasyati.

63. Anger leads to frustration and frustration to confusion of memory and inability to reason. When the reasoning power is lost the person perishes.

रागद्वेषवियुक्तैस्तु विषयानिन्द्रियैश्चरन् ।
आत्मवश्यैर्विधेयात्मा प्रसादमधिगच्छति ।।६४।।

Raagadwesha viyuktaistu vishayaanindryaischaran;
Aatmavasyair vidheyaatmaa prasaadamadhigacchati.

64. But the self-controlled sage who is free from attraction and repulsion, whose senses are under control, walks in peace even amongst the sense objects.

प्रसादे सर्वदुःखानां हानिरस्योपजायते ।
प्रसन्नचेतसो ह्याशु बुद्धिः पर्यवतिष्ठते ।।६५।।

Prasaade sarvaduhkhaanaam haanir asyopajaaayate;
Prasanna chetaso hyaasu buddhih paryavatishathate.

65. In this peace all sorrows perish. The intellect of such a serene person is fixed and firm.

नास्ति बुद्धिरयुक्तस्य न चायुक्तस्य भावना ।
न चाभावयतः शान्तिरशान्तस्य कुतः सुखम् ।।६६।।

Naasti buddhir ayuktasya na chaayuktasya bhaavanaa;
Na chaabhaavayatah saantir asaantasya kutah sukham.

66. The fickle-minded will not be able to concentrate. Without meditation how will one get peace and without peace how can one be happy?

इन्द्रियाणां हि चरतां यन्मनोऽनु विधीयते।
तदस्य हरति प्रज्ञां वायुर्नावमिवाम्भसि ।।६७।।

Indriyaanaam hi charataam yanmanonuvidheeyate;
Tadasya harati prajnyaam vaayur naavam ivaambhasi.

67. The mind which follows the wandering senses carries away the discrimination as the wind carries away a boat on the waters.

तस्माद्यस्य महाबाहो निगृहीतानि सर्वशः।
इन्द्रियाणीन्द्रियार्थेभ्यस्तस्य प्रज्ञा प्रतिष्ठिता ।।६८।।

Tasmaad yasya mahaabaaho nigriheetaani sarvasah;
Indriyaaneendriyaarthebhyas tasya prajnaa pratishthitaa.

68. Therefore O Arjuna (Mahabaho), the sage of steady intellect is one whose senses are completely restrained from their objects.

या निशा सर्वभूतानां तस्यां जागर्ति संयमी।
यस्यां जाग्रति भूतानि सा निशा पश्यतो मुनेः ।६९।

Yaa nisaa sarvabhootaanaam tasyaam jaagrati samyamee;
Yasyaam jaagrati bhoothaani saa nisaa pashyatho muneh.

69. In the dark night of all beings, the self-controlled sage is awake and when all beings are awake, it is night for the seer.

आपूर्यमाणमचलप्रतिष्ठं
    समुद्रमापः प्रविशन्ति यद्वत् ।
तद्वत्कामा यं प्रविशन्ति सर्वे
    स शान्तिमाप्नोति न कामकामी ।।७०।।

Aapooryamaanam achala pratistham
    Samudram aapah pravisanti yadvat;
Tadwat kaamaa yam pravisanti sarve
    Sa saantim aapnoti na kaama kamee.

70. As the ocean remains undisturbed though all waters flow into it, the sage in whom all desires are submerged remains at peace but not so the one who hankers after such enjoyments.

विहाय कामान्यः सर्वान्पुमांश्चरति निःस्पृहः ।
निर्ममो निरहंकारः स शान्तिमधिगच्छति ।।७१।।

Vihaaya kaamaan yah sarvaan pumaams charati nihsprihah;
Nirmamo nirahankaarah sa saanntim adhigacchati.

71. The person who moves about free from desire, egoism and craving for possessions, attains supreme peace.

एषा ब्राह्मी स्थितिः पार्थ नैनां प्राप्य विमुह्यति।
स्थित्वास्यामन्तकालेऽपि ब्रह्मनिर्वाणमृच्छति ।।७२।।

Eshaa brahmee sthithih paartha nainaam praapya vimuhyati.
Sthitwaa syaamanta kaalepi brahmanirvaanamricchati.

72. O Arjuna (Partha), such is the state of the self-realised soul. Having attained this, all delusions are overcome. The *yogi* who is established in this state at the hour of death is totally absorbed into the Brahman.

ॐ तत्सदिति श्रीमद्भगवद्गीतासूपनिषत्सु ब्रह्मविद्यायां
योगशास्त्रे श्रीकृष्णार्जुनसंवादे सांख्ययोगो
नाम द्वितीयोऽध्यायः ।।२।।

Aum tatsat iti Srimad bhagavad gitaasoopanishatsu Brahmavidyaayaam Yogashastre Sri Krishnaarjunasamvaade Sankhya yogo nama dwithiyodhyayah.

Aum Tat Sat:

Thus in the Upanishad of the Bhagavad Gita, the Knowledge of Supreme Brahman, the Scripture of *Yoga*, the dialogue between Sri Krishna and Arjuna, ends the second chapter entitled, "The *Yoga* of the the Wisdom of Sankhya."

अथ तृतीयोऽध्यायः
Atha Tritiyo'dhyayah

CHAPTER III
KARMA YOGA
The Yoga of Action

अर्जुन उवाच
ज्यायसी चेत्कर्मणस्ते मता बुद्धिर्जनार्दन।
तत्किं कर्मणि घोरे मां नियोजयसि केशव ।।१।।

Arjuna uvaacha
Jyaayasee chet karmanaste mataa buddhir janaardana;
Tat kim karmani ghore maam niyojayasi kesava.

Thus spoke Arjuna:

1. O Krishna (Janardana, Keshava)! If you think knowledge is superior to action, why do you urge me to do this terrible deed?

व्यामिश्रेणेव वाक्येन बुद्धिं मोहयसीव मे।
तदेकं वद निश्चित्य येन श्रेयोऽहमाप्नुयाम् ।।२।।

Vyaamisreneva vaakyena buddhim mohayaseeva mè;
Tad ekam vada nischitya yena sreyo'ham aapnuyaam.

2. You are confusing my intellect by these seemingly contradictory statements. Please tell me in truth by which path I may attain the Supreme.

श्रीभगवानुवाच
लोकेऽस्मिन्द्विविधा निष्ठा पुरा प्रोक्ता मयानघ।
ज्ञानयोगेन सांख्यानां कर्मयोगेन योगिनाम् ।।३।।

Sree Bhagavaan uvaacha
Loke'smin dwividhaa nishthaa puraa proktaa mayaanagha;
Jnaanayogena samkhyaanaam karmayogena yoginaam.

Thus spoke the Blessed Lord:

3.   O Arjuna (Anagha)! In this world there are two
paths to perfection—Jnana *Yoga* or the *yoga* of the
wisdom of the Sankhya for the intellectuals and
Karma *Yoga* or the *yoga* of action for the *karma yogis*,
taught by Me since ancient times.

न कर्मणामनारम्भात्रैष्कर्म्य पुरुषोऽश्नुते।
न च संन्यसनादेव सिद्धिं समधिगच्छति ।।४।।

Na karmanaam anaarambhaan naishkarmyam purus-
ho'snute;
Na cha sannyasanaad eva siddhim samadhigacchati.

4.   By abstaining from action a person cannot attain
the state of non-activity and by mere renunciation of
the world one cannot attain perfection.

न हि कश्चित्क्षणमपि जातु तिष्ठत्यकर्मकृत।
कार्यते ह्यवशः कर्म सर्वः प्रकृतिजैर्गुणैः ।।५।।

Na hi kaschit kshanamapi jaatu tishthatyakarmakrut;
Kaaryate hyavasah karma sarvah prakritijair gunaih.

5.   Indeed not even for a second can anyone remain

totally inactive. Everyone is helplessly driven to act by the modes *(gunas)* of Nature.

कर्मेन्द्रियाणि संयम्य य आस्ते मनसा स्मरन्।
इन्द्रियार्थान्विमूढात्मा मिथ्याचारः स उच्यते ।।६।।

Karmendriyaani samyamya ya aaste manasaa smaran;
Indriyaarthaan vimoodhaatmaa mithyaachaarah sa
uchyate.

6.   The one who restrains the organs of action and sits ruminating over the sense objects, is of deluded intellect and can be called a hypocrite.

यस्त्विन्द्रियाणि मनसा नियम्यारभतेऽर्जुन।
कर्मेन्द्रियैः कर्मयोगमसक्तः स विशिष्यते ।।७।।

Yastwindriyaani manasaa niyamyaarabhate'rjuna;
Karmendriyaih karmayogam asaktah sa visishyate.

7.   But one who controls the senses with the mind and engages the organs of action in the *yoga* of action, without attachment, excels, O Arjuna.

नियतं कुरु कर्म त्वं कर्म ज्यायो ह्यकर्मणः।
शरीरयात्रापि च ते न प्रसिद्धयेदकर्मणः ।।८।।

Niyatam kuru karma twam karma jyaayo hyakarmanah;
Sareera yaatraapi cha te na prasiddhyed akarmanah.

8.   Therefore you should perform your allotted duty, for action is superior to inaction. Even for the maintenance of the body, one needs to work.

यज्ञार्थात्कर्मणोन्यत्र लोकोऽयं कर्मबन्धनः।
तदर्थं कर्म कौन्तेय मुक्तसङ्गः समाचर ।।६।।

Yajnaarthaat karmano'nyatra loko'yam karmabandhanah;
Tadartham karma kaunteya muktasangah samaachara.

9.   The world is bound only by the performance of actions which are done selfishly (not as a *yajna*). Therefore O Arjuna (Kaunteya), do your work without attachment (to the fruits), as a *yajna*.

सहयज्ञाः प्रजाः सृष्ट्वा पुरोवाच प्रजापतिः।
अनेन प्रसविष्यध्वमेष वोऽस्त्विष्टकामधुक् ।।१०।।

Sahayajnaah prajaah srishtwaa purovaacha prajaapatih;
Anena prasavishyadhwam esha vo'stvishtakaamadhuk.

10. In the beginning, the creator, Prajapati fashioned human beings and instilled in them the spirit of self-sacrifice (*yajna*) and then declared, "By this shall you propagate. This shall be your wish-fulfilling cow."

देवान्भावयतानेन ते देवा भावयन्तु वः।
परस्परं भावयन्तः श्रेयः परमवाप्स्यथ ।।११।।

Devaan bhaavayataanena te devaa bhaavayantu vah;
Parasparam bhaavayantah sreyah parama vaapsyatha.

11. Honour the gods in this fashion and the gods in turn will cherish you. Thus fostering one another you will attain the supreme good.

इष्टान्भोगान्हि वो देवा दास्यन्ते यज्ञभाविताः ।
तैर्दत्तानप्रदायैभ्यो यो भुङ्क्ते स्तेन एव सः ।।१२।।

Ishtaan bhogaan hi vo devaadaasyante yajnabhaavitaah;
Tair dattaan apradaayaibhyo yo bhungte stena eva sah.

12. Pleased by this attitude of self-sacrifice, the gods will bestow upon you all that you desire. One who enjoys all this without giving something in return is verily a thief.

यज्ञशिष्टाशिनः सन्तो मुच्यन्ते सर्वकिल्बिषैः ।
भुञ्जते ते त्वघं पापा ये पचन्त्यात्मकारणात् ।।१३।।

Yajnashishtaasinah santo muchyante sarva kilbishaih;
Bhunjate te twagham paapaa ye pachantyaatma kaaranat.

13. The righteous who eat the remains of offerings are released from sin. But those evil ones who cook for themselves alone verily partake of sin.

अन्नाद्भवन्ति भूतानि पर्जन्यादन्नसंभवः ।
यज्ञाद्भवति पर्जन्यो यज्ञः कर्मसमुद्भवः ।।१४।।

Annaad bhavanti bhootaani parjanyaad anna sambhavah;
Yajnaad bhavati parjanyo yajnah karma samudbhavah.

कर्म ब्रह्मोद्भवं विद्धि ब्रह्माक्षरसमुद्भवम् ।
तस्मात्सर्वगतं ब्रह्म नित्यं यज्ञे प्रतिष्ठितम् ।।१५।।

Karma brahmodbhavam viddhi brahmaakshara
samudbhavam;
Tasmaat sarvagatam brahma nityam yajne pratishthitam.

14&15. All creatures come forth from food which in turn comes from rain. Rain falls due to the spirit of self-sacrifice (*yajna*) which again is born out of action. Action has its origin in the *Vedas* and the *Vedas* have emanated from the Imperishable. Therefore the all-pervading Brahman is ever centered in *yajna*.

एवं प्रवर्तितं चक्रं नानुवर्तयतीह यः ।
अघायुरिन्द्रियारामो मोघं पार्थ स जीवति ।।१६।।

Evam pravartitam chakram naanuvartayateeha yah;
Aghaayur indriyaaraamo mogham paartha sajeevati.

16. One who does not follow the wheel (of unselfish action) thus set in motion in the world, lives in sin and is a mere reveller in the senses. Vain indeed is such a life O Arjuna (Partha)!

यस्त्वात्मरतिरेव स्यादात्मतृप्तश्च मानवः ।
आत्मन्येव च संतुष्टस्तस्य कार्यं न विद्यते ।।१७।।

Yastwaatmaratir eva syaad aatmatriptascha maanavah;
Aatmanyeva cha santushtas tasya kaaryam na vidyate.

17. But for the one who revels in the Self and finds full satisfaction in the Self and is content with the Self, work is no longer obligatory.

नैव तस्य कृतेनार्थों नाकृतेनेह कश्चन।
न चास्य सर्वभूतेषु कश्चिदर्थव्यपाश्रयः ॥१८॥

Naiva tasya kritenaartho naakriteneha kaschana;
Na chaasya sarvabhooteshu kaschidartha vyapaasrayah.

18. Such a one has nothing to gain by working and nothing to lose by not working, nor any dependence on others for gaining an objective.

तस्मादसक्तः सततं कार्यं कर्म समाचर।
असक्तो ह्याचरन्कर्म परमाप्नोति पूरुषः ॥१९॥

Tasmaad asaktah satatam kaaryam karma samaachara;
Asakto hyaacharan karma param aapnoti poorushah.

19. Therefore you should constantly perform all obligatory duties without attachment (to the fruits). Indeed by performing action without attachment one can attain the Supreme.

कर्मणैव हि संसिद्धिमास्थिता जनकादयः।
लोकसंग्रहमेवापि संपश्यन्कर्तुमर्हसि ॥२०॥

Karmannaiva hi samsiddhim aasthitaa janakaadayah;
Lokasangraham evaapi sampasyan kartum arhasi.

20. King Janaka and others attained perfection only
through such action. So you should also act with a
view to the maintenance of the world order.

यद्यदाचरति श्रेष्ठस्तत्तदेवेतरो जनः।
स यत्प्रमाणं कुरुते लोकस्तदनुवर्त्तते ।।२१।।

Yadyad aacharati sreshthas tattadevetaro janah;
Sa yat pramaanam kurute lokastad anuvartate.

21. Whatever a great soul does, is emulated by
others. The example set by him is followed by the rest.

न मे पार्थास्ति कर्तव्यं त्रिषु लोकेषु किंचन।
नानवाप्तमवाप्तव्यं वर्त एव च कर्मणि ।।२२।।

Na me paarthaasti kartavyam trishu lokeshu kimchana;
Naanavaaptam avaaptavyam varta eva cha karmani.

22. O Arjuna (Partha), I have no duties to perform,
for I have nothing to gain which I have not yet
gained in all the three worlds, yet I keep Myself
engaged in action.

यदि ह्यहं न वर्तेयं जातु कर्मण्यतन्द्रितः।
मम वर्त्मानुवर्तन्ते मनुष्याः पार्थ सर्वशः ।।२३।।

Yadi hyaham na varteyam jaatu karmanyatandritah;
Mama vartmaanuvartante manushyaah paartha sarvasah.

उत्सीदेयुरिमे लोका न कुर्यां कर्म चेदहम् ।
संकरस्य च कर्ता स्यामुपहन्यामिमाः प्रजाः ।।२४।।

Utseedeyur ime lokaa na kuryaam karmached aham;
Sankarasya cha kartaa syaam upahanyaam imaah prajaah

23&24. If I did not engage Myself in constant action O Arjuna (Partha), others would follow my example and I would be the cause of creating confusion in the society which would lead to the destruction of all beings and these worlds would perish.

सक्ताः कर्मण्यविद्वांसो यथा कुर्वन्ति भारत
कुर्याद्विद्वांस्तथासक्तश्चिकीर्षुर्लोकसंग्रहम् ।।२५।।

Saktaah karmanyavidwaamso yathaa kurvanti bhaarata;
Kuryaad vidwaam sthathaa saktas chikeershur lokasamgraham.

25. O Arjuna (Bharatha), as the ignorant act with attachment, so the wise should act without attachment, for the welfare of the world.

न बुद्धिभेदं जनयेदज्ञानां कर्मसङ्गिनाम् ।
जोषयेत्सर्वकर्माणि विद्वान्युक्तः समाचरन् ।।२६।।

Na buddhibhedam janayed ajnaanaam karmasanginaam;
Joshayet sarva karmaani vidwaan yuktah samaacharan.

26. One should not confuse the minds of the ignorant who are attached to action (with desire for
fruits). One should encourage them to perform
disinterested action by persistently acting in that
manner.

प्रकृतेः क्रियमाणानि गुणैः कर्माणि सर्वशः।
अहंकारविमूढात्मा कर्ताहमिति मन्यते ।।२७।।

Prakriteh kriyamaanaani gunaih karmaani sarvasah;
Ahamkaara vimoodhaatmaa kartaaham iti manyate.

27. All actions are performed by the modes of
Nature but the deluded human being filled with
conceit thinks, "I am the doer."

तत्त्वविन्तु महाबाहो गुणकर्मविभागयोः।
गुणा गुणेषु वर्तन्त इति मत्वा न सज्जते ।।२८।।

Tathwavittu mahaabaaho gunakarma vibhaagayoh;
Gunaa guneshu vartanta iti matwaa na sajjate.

28. O Arjuna (Mahabaho), one who knows the secret
of the modes and of action, does not become entangled for such a one sees only the modes acting
and reacting with each other.

प्रकृतेर्गुणसंमूढाः सज्जन्ते गुणकर्मसु
तानकृत्स्नविदो मन्दान्कृत्स्नविन्न विचालयेत् ।।२६।।

Prakriter gunasammudhaah sajjante guna karmasu;
Taan akritsnavido mandaan kritsnavin na vichaalayet.

29. Deluded by the modes of Nature some people
get attached to their functions. Those with perfect
knowledge should not unsettle the minds of those
who know little.

मयि सर्वाणि कर्माणि संन्यस्याध्यात्मचेतसा।
निराशीर्निर्ममो भूत्वा युध्यस्व विगतज्वरः ।।३०।।

Mayi sarvaani karmaani samnyasyaadhyaatma chetasaa;
Niraaseer nirmamo bhootwa yudhyaswavigatajwarah.

30. With your mind illumined by the Self, defer all
actions to Me and fight without anxiety, free from
vain hopes and selfish desires.

ये मे मतमिदं नित्यमनुतिष्ठन्ति मानवाः।
श्रद्धावन्तोऽनसूयन्तो मुच्यन्ते तेऽपि कर्मभिः ।।३१।।

Ye me matam idam nityam anutisthanti maanavaah;
Sraddhaavanto'nasooyanto muchyante te'pi karmabhih.

31. Those who constantly practise this teaching of
Mine, uncritically and with full faith are released
from the bondage of action.

ॐ

ये त्वेतदभ्यसूयन्तो नानुतिष्ठन्ति मे मतम्।
सर्वज्ञानविमूढांस्तान्विद्धि नष्टानचेतसः ।।३२।।

Ye twetad abhyasooyanto naanutishthanti me matam;
Sarvajnaanavimoodhaam staan vidhdhi nashtaan
achetasah.

32. But know them to be lost, who decry this doctrine
of Mine and fail to practise it—who are deluded in
their knowledge and devoid of discrimination.

सदृशं चेष्टते स्वस्याः प्रकृतेर्ज्ञानवानपि।
प्रकृतिं यान्ति भूतानि निग्रहः किं करिष्यति ।।३३।।

Sadrisam cheshtate swasyaah prakriter jnaanavaan api;
Prakritim yaanti bhootaani nighrahah kim karishyati.

33. Even the wise follow the dictates of their own
nature. In fact all beings instinctively follow the
impulses of Nature. What can restraint do?

इन्द्रियस्येन्द्रियस्यार्थे रागद्वेषौ व्यवस्थितौ।
तयोर्न वशमागच्छेत्तौ ह्यस्य परिपन्थिनौ ।।३४।।

Indriyasyendriyasy aarthe raagadweshau vyavasthitau;
Tayor na vasam aagacchet tau hyasya paripanthinau.

34. Attraction and repulsion for objects abide in the
senses. Let none come under their sway for they are
like highway robbers.

श्रेयान्स्वधर्मो विगुणः परधर्मात्स्वनुष्ठितात् ।
स्वधर्मे निधनं श्रेयः परधर्मो भयावहः ।।३५।।

*Sreyaan swadharmo vigunah paradharmaat swanush-
thitaat;*
Swadharme nidhanam sreyah pardharmo bhayaavahah.

35. One's own path of duty *(swadharma)*, however
humble, is far better than that of another, however
well performed. Death in the discharge of one's own
duty is better; the duty of another is filled with fear.

अर्जुन उवाच
अथ केन प्रयुक्तोऽयं पापं चरति पूरुषः ।
अनिच्छन्नपि वार्ष्णेय बलादिव नियोजितः ।।३६।।

Arjuna uvaacha
Atha kena prayukto 'yam paapam charati poorushah;
Anicchann api vaarshneya balaad iva niyojitah.

Thus spoke Arjuna:

36. O Krishna (Varshneya), what is it that impels a
person to commit sin, unwillingly, as if by some
inner compulsion?

श्रीभगवानुवाच
काम एष क्रोध एष रजोगुणसमुद्भवः ।
महाशनो महापाप्मा विद्ध्येनमिह वैरिणम् ।।३७।।

Sree Bhagavaan uvaacha
Kaama esha krodha esha rajoguna samudbhavah;
Mahaasano mahaapaapmaa viddhyenam iha vairinam.

Thus spoke the Blessed Lord:

37. It is desire and wrath, begotten of the mode of passion (*rajas*), which is all-consuming and injurious. Know this to be your greatest enemy here.

धूमेनाग्रियते वहिर्यथादर्शो मलेन च।
यथोल्बेनावृतो गर्भस्तथा तेनेदमावृतम् ।।३८।।

Dhoomenaavriyate vahnir yathadarso malena cha;
Yatholbenaavrito garbhas tathaa tenedam aavritam.

38. As fire is clouded by smoke, as a mirror by dust and the embryo by the membrane, so "this" (knowledge) is veiled by "that" (desire).

आवृतं ज्ञानमेतेन ज्ञानिनो नित्यवैरिणा।
कामरूपेण कौन्तेय दुष्पूरेणानलेन च ।।३९।।

Aavritam jnaanam etena jnaanino nityavairinaa;
Kaamaroopena kaunteya dushpoorenaanalena cha.

39. O Arjuna (Kaunteya), knowledge is obscured by the insatiable fire of desire which is the constant enemy of even the wise.

इन्द्रियाणि मनो बुद्धिरस्याधिष्ठानमुच्यते।
एतैर्विमोहयत्येष ज्ञानमावृत्य देहिनम् ।।४०।।

Indriyaani mano buddhir asyaadhishthaanam uchyate;
Etair vimohayatyesha jnaanam aavritya dehinam.

40. The senses, mind and intellect are said to be its
abode. Veiling wisdom through these, it deludes the
embodied soul.

तस्मात्त्वमिन्द्रियाण्यादौ नियम्य भरतर्षभ।
पाप्मानं प्रजहि ह्येनं ज्ञानविज्ञाननाशनम् ।।४१।।

Tasmaat twam indriyaanyaadau niyamya bharatarshabha;
Paapmanam prajahi hyenam jnaana vijnaana naasanam.

41. Therefore O Arjuna (Bharatharshabha), first gain
control over the senses and then put an end to this
sinful destroyer of knowledge and realisation.

इन्द्रियाणि पराण्याहुरिन्द्रियेभ्यः परं मनः।
मनसस्तु परा बुद्धिर्यो बुद्धेः परतस्तु सः ।।४२।।

Indriyaani paraanyaahuh indriyebhyah param manah;
Manasas tu paraa buddhiryo buddheh paratastu sah.

42. It is said that the senses are superior (to the
objects), the mind is superior to the senses and the
intellect is superior to the mind. That which is
superior to the intellect is the Self (*atman*).

एवं बुद्धेः परं बुद्ध्वा संस्तभ्यात्मानमात्मना।
जहि शत्रुं महाबाहो कामरूपं दुरासदम् ।।४३।।

Evam buddheh param buddhwa samstabhyatmaanam
aatmanaa;
Jahi satrum mahaabaaho kaamaroopam duraasadam.

43. Thus O Arjuna (Mahabaho), knowing that which
is superior to the intellect and restraining the mind
by that Self, destroy this enemy in the form of desire
which is so hard to assail.

ॐ तत्सदिति श्रीमद्भगवद्गीतासूपनिषत्सु ब्रह्म—
विद्यायां योगशास्त्रे श्रीकृष्णार्जुनसंवादे
कर्मयोगो नाम तृतीयोऽध्यायः ।।३।।

Om tat sat iti srimad bhagavad gitaasoopanishatsu
Brahmavidyaayaam yogashaastre sri krishnaarjuna-
samvaade karmayogo naama tritiyo'dhyaayah.

Aum Tat Sat:

Thus in the Upanishad of the Bhagavad Gita, the
Knowledge of Supreme Brahman, the Scripture of
Yoga, the dialogue between Sri Krishna and Arjuna,
ends the third chapter entitled, "The *Yoga* of Action."

Aum Sri Krishnaya Paramatmane Namah!
Aum Sri Parthasarathaye Namah!

अथ चतुर्थोऽध्यायः
Atha Chaturdho'dhyayah

CHAPTER IV
JNANA KARMA SANNYASA YOGA
The Yoga of Renunciation of
Action through Knowledge

श्रीभगवानुवाच
इमं विवस्वते योगं प्रोक्तवानहमव्ययम् ।
विवस्वान्मनवे प्राह मनुरिक्ष्वाकवेऽब्रवीत् ।।१।।

Sree Bhagavaan uvaacha
Imam vivaswate yogam proktavaan aham avyayam;
Vivaswaan manave praaha manur ikswakave'braveet.

Thus spoke the Blessed Lord:

1. This imperishable knowledge was revealed by
Me to Vivasvan (the sun god). He in turn gave it to
Manu and Manu taught it to King Ikshvaku.

एवं परम्पराप्राप्तमिमं राजर्षयो विदुः ।
स कालेनेह महता योगो नष्टः परंतप ।।२।।

Evam paramparaa praaptam imam raajarshayo viduh;
Sa kaaleneha mahataayogo nashtah paramtapa.

2. Thus was it handed down in succession from
royal sage to royal sage but O Arjuna (Paramtapa),
due to the long passage of time, this knowledge has
been lost.

स एवायं मया तेऽद्य योगः प्रोक्तः पुरातनः ।
भक्तोऽसि मे सखा चेति रहस्यं ह्येतदुत्तमम् ।।३।।

Sa evaayam mayaa te'dya yogah proktah puraatanah;
Bhakto'si me sakhaa cheti rahasyam hyetad uttamam.

3.   Now I am revealing this ancient and esoteric knowledge to you for you are both My devotee and My friend.

अर्जुन उवाच

अपरं भवतो जन्म परं जन्म विवस्वतः।
कथमेतद्विजानीयां त्वमादौ प्रोक्तवानिति ।।४।।

Arjuna uvaacha
Aparam bhavato janma param janma vivaswatah;
Katham etadvijaaneeyaam twam aadau proktavaan iti.

Thus spoke Arjuna:

4.   Vivasvan's birth was prior to Yours. How then am I to understand that You told this to him in the beginning?

श्रीभगवानुवाच

बहूनि मे व्यतीतानि जन्मानि तव चार्जुन।
तान्यहं वेद सर्वाणि न त्वं वेत्थ परंतप ।।५।।

Sree Bhagavaan uvaacha
Bahooni me vyateetani janmaani tava chaarjuna;
Taanyaham veda sarvaani natwam vettha paramtapa.

Thus spoke the Blessed Lord:

5.   You and I have taken many births O Arjuna (Paramtapa). I know them all whereas you do not remember them.

अजोऽपि सन्नव्ययात्मा भूतानामीश्वरोऽपि सन्।
प्रकृतिं स्वामधिष्ठाय संभवाम्यात्ममायया ॥६॥

Ajo'pi sannavyayaatmaabhootaanaam esswaro'pi san;
Prakritim swaam'adhishthaaya sambhavaamyaatmam-
aayaya.

6. Though I am the unborn and immutable Lord of
all beings, I manifest Myself through My divine,
illusory power, with full control over My material
Nature.

यदा यदा हि धर्मस्य ग्लानिर्भवति भारत।
अभ्युत्थानमधर्मस्य तदात्मानं सृजाम्यहम् ॥७॥

Yadaa yadaa hi dharmasya glaanir bhavati bhaarata;
Abhyutthaanam adharmasya tadaatmaanam srijaamyaham.

7. Whenever there is a decline in righteousness and
an upsurge of unrighteousness (*dharma and adharma*),
O Arjuna (Bharatha), I embody Myself.

परित्राणाय साधूनां विनाशाय च दुष्कृताम्।
धर्मसंस्थापनार्थाय संभवामि युगे युगे ॥८॥

Paritraanaaya saaddhunaam vinaasaaya cha dushkritaam;
Dharma samsthaapanaarthaaya sambhavaami yuge yuge.

8. I manifest Myself from age to age, for the
protection of the virtuous and the destruction of the
wicked and the establishment of righteousness.

ॐ

जन्म कर्म च मे दिव्यमेवं यो वेत्ति तत्त्वतः।
त्यक्त्वा देहं पुनर्जन्म नैति मामेति सोऽर्जुन ।।६।।

Janmakarma cha me divyamevam yo vetti tatwatah;
Tyaktwa deham punarjanma naiti maameti so'rjuna.

9.   One who knows in truth the divine nature of My
birth and activities O Arjuna, is not born again. After
shedding the body he comes to Me.

वीतरागभयक्रोधा मन्मया मामुपाश्रिताः।
बहवो ज्ञानतपसा पूता मद्भावमागताः ।।१०।।

Veetaraagabhayakrodha manmayaa maam upaasritaah;
Bahavo jnaana tapasaa pootaa madbhaavam aagataah.

10. Purified by the fire of knowledge, free from
attachment, fear and anger, ever absorbed in Me and
taking refuge in Me, many have attained My Being.

ये यथा मां प्रपद्यन्ते तांस्तथैव भजाम्यहम्।
मम वर्त्मानुवर्तन्ते मनुष्याः पार्थ सर्वशः ।।११।।

Ye yathaa maam prapadyante taams tathaiva bhajaam-
yaham;
Mama vartmaanuvartante manushyaah paartha sarvasah.

11. Whatever be the method by which people solicit
Me, I bless them in the same manner. Many are the
ways O Arjuna (Partha), by which people approach Me.

काङ्क्षन्तः कर्मणां सिद्धिं यजन्त इह देवताः।
क्षिप्रं हि मानुषे लोके सिद्धिर्भवति कर्मजा ।।१२।।

Kaangshantah karmanaam siddhim yajanta iha devataah;
Kshipram hi maanushe loke siddhir bhavati karmajaa.

12. Desirous of success in action, people worship many gods, by which they quickly get successful results in the world.

चातुर्वर्ण्यं मया सृष्टं गुणकर्मविभागशः।
तस्य कर्तारमपि मां विद्ध्यकर्तारमव्ययम् ।।१३।।

Chaaturvarnyam mayaa srishtam gunakarma vibhagasah;
Tasya kartaaram api maam vidhyakartaaram avyayam.

13. The fourfold order of society was created by Me according to the divisions of the modes and their actions. Though I am its originator, know Me to be the unchanging non-actor.

न मां कर्माणि लिम्पन्ति न मे कर्मफले स्पृहा।
इति मां योऽभिजानाति कर्मभिर्न स बध्यते ।।१४।।

Na maam karmaani limpanti na me karmaphale sprihaa;
Iti maam yo'bhijaanaati karmabhir na sa badhyate.

14. Action does not taint Me, for I do not thirst for the result. Whoever knows Me thus is not bound by action.

ॐ

एवं ज्ञात्वा कृतं कर्म पूर्वैरपि मुमुक्षुभिः।
कुरु कर्मैव तस्मात्त्वं पूर्वैः पूर्वतरं कृतम् ।।१५।।

Evam jnatwaa kritam karma poorvair api mumukshubhih;
Kuru karmaiva tasmat twam poorvaih poorvataram kritam.

15. Knowing this, the seekers of liberation of a bygone age performed their work. Do you therefore discharge your duties as did the ancients of former times.

किं कर्म किमकर्मेति कवयोऽप्यत्र मोहिताः।
तत्ते कर्म प्रवक्ष्यामि यज्ज्ञात्वा मोक्ष्यसेऽशुभात् ।।१६।।

Kim karma kim akarmeti kavayo'pyatra mohitaah;
Tat te karma pravakshyaami yajjnaatwaa mokshyase's-ubhat.

16. Even the sages are at a loss to know the difference between action and inaction. I shall therefore explain the nature of action to you, by knowing which you will be freed from its evil consequences.

कर्मणो ह्यपि बोद्धव्यं बोद्धव्यं च विकर्मणः।
अकर्मणश्च बोद्धव्यं गहना कर्मणो गतिः ।।१७।।

Karmano hyapi boddhavyam boddhavyam cha vikarmanah;
Akarmanas cha boddhavyam gahanaa karmano gatih.

17. It is necessary to understand the nature of action, special action and inaction, for mysterious are the ways of action.

कर्मण्यकर्म यः पश्येदकर्मणि च कर्म यः।
स बुद्धिमान्मनुष्येषु स युक्तः कृत्स्नकर्मकृत् ।।१८।।

Karmanyakarma yah pasyed akarmani cha karma yah;
Sa buddhimaan manushyeshu sa yuktah kritsnakarmakrit.

18. One who is able to see action in inaction and inaction in the midst of activity is truly a *yogi* and a person of discernment who has accomplished all that needs to be done.

यस्य सर्वे समारम्भाः कामसंकल्पवर्जिताः।
ज्ञानाग्निदग्धकर्माणं तमाहुः पण्डितं बुधाः ।।१९।।

Yasya sarve samaarambhaah kaamasankalpa varjitaah;
.Jnaanaagni dagdhakarmaanam tamaahuh panditam budhaah.

19. The wise consider him to be a sage, whose undertakings are totally free from desire and whose actions have been consumed in the fire of knowledge.

त्यक्त्वा कर्मफलासङ्गं नित्यतृप्तो निराश्रयः।
कर्मण्यभिप्रवृत्तोऽपि नैव किञ्चत्करोति सः ।।२०।।

Tyaktwaa karmaphalaasangam nityatripto niraasrayah;
Karmanyabhipravritto'pi naiva kinchit karoti sah.

20. The one who has relinquished all attachment to

ॐ

the fruit of action, who has no dependence on anything and is ever content, in effect does nothing at all even though constantly engaged in action.

निराशीर्यतचित्तात्मा त्यक्तसर्वपरिग्रहः ।
शारीरं केवलं कर्म कुर्वन्नाप्नोति किल्बिषम् ।।२१।।

Niraaseer yatachittatma tyaktasarvaparigrahah;
Saareeram kevalam karma kurvannapnoti kilbisham.

21. One who is in control of the mind and is without any longing for, or attachment to, personal posses-sions, incurs no sin even though acting, for it is the body alone which acts.

ॐ

यदृच्छालाभसंतुष्टो द्वन्द्वातीतो विमत्सरः ।
समः सिद्धावसिद्धौ च कृत्वापि न निबध्यते ।।२२।।

Yadricchaalaabhasantushto dwandwaateeto vimatsarah;
Samah siddhaavasiddhau cha kritwaapi na nibadhyate.

22. One who is satisfied with whatever comes unsought, who is free from envy and the pairs of opposites, who is balanced in success and failure, is not bound even though continuing to act.

गतसङ्गस्य मुक्तस्य ज्ञानावस्थितचेतसः ।
यज्ञायाचरतः कर्म समग्रं प्रविलीयते ।।२३।।

Gatasangasya muktasya jnanaavasthitachetasah;
Yajnaayaacharatah karma samagram pravileeyate.

23. All actions dissolve for the liberated person who is free from attachment, fixed in Self-knowledge and does all work unselfishly, as a *yajna.*

ब्रह्मार्पणं ब्रह्म हविर्ब्रह्माग्नौ ब्रह्मणा हुतम् ।
ब्रह्मैव तेन गन्तव्यं ब्रह्मकर्मसमाधिना ।।२४।।

Brahmaarpanam brahma havir brahmagnau brahmanaa hutam;
Brahmaiva tena gantavyam brahma karma samaadhinaa.

24. The offering is Brahman, the oblation is Brahman. It is offered by Brahman into the fire of Brahman. One who thus perceives only Brahman in action, attains Brahman alone.

दैवमेवापरे यज्ञं योगिनः पर्युपासते ।
ब्रह्माग्नावपरे यज्ञं यज्ञेनैवोपजुह्वति ।।२५।।

Daivam evaapare yajnam yoginah paryupaasate;
Brahmaagnaavapare yajnam yajnenaivopajuhwati.

25. Some Yogis make sacrifices to the gods, while others offer their very selves into the fire of Brahman.

श्रोत्रादीनीन्द्रियाण्यन्ये संयमाग्निषु जुह्वति।
शब्दादीन्विषयानन्य इन्द्रियाग्निषु जुह्वति ।।२६।।

Srotraadeenindriyaanyanye samyamaagnishu juhwati;
Sabdaadeen vishayaananya indriyaagnishu juhwati.

26. Some offer their hearing and other senses into
the fire of self-control, while still others offer sound
and other sense objects into the fire of the senses.

सर्वाणीन्द्रियकर्माणि प्राणकर्माणि चापरे।
आत्मसंयमयोगाग्नौ जुह्वति ज्ञानदीपिते ।।२७।।

Sarvaanindriya karmaani pranakarmaani chaapare;
Aatmasamyamayogaagnau juhwati jnaanadeepite.

27. Some offer all the actions of their senses and
vital forces into the fire of self-control, kindled by
knowledge.

द्रव्ययज्ञास्तपोयज्ञा योगयज्ञास्तथापरे।
स्वाध्यायज्ञानयज्ञाश्च यतयः संशितव्रताः ।२८।

Dravyayajnaas tapoyajnaa yogayajnaastathaapare;
Swaadhyaayajnaan ayajnaascha yatayah samsitavrataah.

28. Others make an offering of their material wealth,
their austerity and their *yoga*, while still others
practising self-restraint and observing rigid vows
offer their knowledge and their study of the scriptures.

अपाने जुह्वति प्राणं प्राणेऽपानं तथापरे।
प्राणापानगती रुद्ध्वा प्राणायामपरायणाः ।।२९।।

Apaane juhwati praanam praane'paanam tathaapare;
Praanaapaana gatee ruddhwaa praanaayaamaparayanah.

29. Those who practise breath control regulate the flow of the incoming and outgoing breaths and offer the exhalations into the inhalations and the inhalations into the exhalations.

अपरे नियताहाराः प्राणान्प्राणेषु जुह्वति।
सर्वेऽप्येते यज्ञविदो यज्ञक्षपितकल्मषाः ।।३०।।

Apare niyataahaaraah praanaan praaneshu juhwati;
Sarve'pyete yajnavido yajnakshapita kalmashaah.

30. Others regulate their intake of food and offer their vital forces into their life breath. All these are well aware of the method of selfless offerings *(yajna)* and by this, their sins are wiped out.

यज्ञशिष्टामृतभुजो यान्ति ब्रह्म सनातनम्।
नायं लोकोऽस्त्ययज्ञस्य कुतोऽन्यः कुरुसत्तम ।।३१।।

Yajnasishtaamritabhujo yaanti brahma sanaatanam;
Naayam loko'styayajnasya kuto'nyah kurusattama.

31. Those who partake of the nectar of immortality left over from offerings attain the eternal Brahman.

O Arjuna (Kurusatthama), even this world is not for one who is not prepared for self-sacrifice, how much less any other world!

एवं बहुविधा यज्ञा वितता ब्रह्मणो मुखे।
कर्मजान्विद्धि तान्सर्वानेवं ज्ञात्वा विमोक्ष्यसे ।।३२।।

Evam bahuvidhaa yajnaa vitataa brahmano mukhe;
Karmajaan viddhi taan sarvaan evam jnaatwaa
vimokshyase.

32. Thus many types of selfless sacrifices (*yajna*) come from the Vedas. Know that all these are born of action and thus knowing, become liberated.

श्रेयान्द्रव्यमयाद्यज्ञाज्ज्ञानयज्ञः परंतप।
सर्वं कर्माखिलं पार्थ ज्ञाने परिसमाप्यते ।।३३।।

Sreyaan dravyamayaadyajnaaj jnaanayajnah paramtapa
Sarvam karmaakhilam paartha jnaane parisamaapyate.

33. The sacrifice of knowledge is superior to the offering of any material object O Arjuna (Paramtapa). All action without exception, culminates in knowledge, O Arjuna (Partha).

तद्विद्धि प्रणिपातेन परिप्रश्नेन सेवया।
उपदेक्ष्यन्ति ते ज्ञानं ज्ञानिनस्तत्त्वदर्शिनः ।।३४।।

Tadviddhi pranipaatena pariprasnena sevayaa;
Upadekshyanti te jnaanam jnaaninas tatwadarsinah.

34. Gain this knowledge by prostrating, questioning and serving the sages who have realised this truth for only they will be able to instruct you.

यज्ज्ञात्वा न पुनर्मोहमेवं यास्यसि पाण्डव।
येन भूतान्यशेषेण द्रक्ष्यस्यात्मन्यथो मयि ।।३५।।

Yajjnaatwa na punarmoham evam yaasyasi paandava;
Yena bhootaanyaseshena drakshyasyaatmanyatho mayi.

35. Having known this O Arjuna (Pandava), you will never again be deluded and you will be able to see that the whole of creation exists within you and you in Me!

अपि चेदसि पापेभ्यः सर्वेभ्यः पापकृत्तमः।
सर्वं ज्ञानप्लवेनैव वृजिनं संतरिष्यसि ।।३६।।

Api chedasi paapebhyah sarvebhyah paapakrittamah;
Sarvam jnaanaplavenaiva vrijinam samtarishyasi.

36. Even if you were the vilest of sinners you would be able to cross the sea of evil on the raft of wisdom.

यथैधांसि समिद्धोग्निर्भस्मसात्कुरुतेऽर्जुन।
ज्ञानाग्निः सर्वकर्माणि भस्मसात्कुरुते तथा।।३७।।

Yathaidhaamsi samiddho'gnir bhasmasaat kurute'rjuna;
Jnaanaagnih sarvakarmaani bhasmasaat kurute tathaa.

37. O Arjuna, as the blazing fire reduces all types of fuel to ashes, the fire of wisdom turns all action to cinders.

न हि ज्ञानेन सदृशं पवित्रमिह विद्यते।
तत्स्वयं योगसंसिद्धः कालेनात्मनि विन्दति ।।३८।।

Na hi jnaanena sadrisam pavitram iha vidyate;
Tat swayam yogasamsiddhah kaalenatmani vindati.

38. There is no greater purifying agent in this world than knowledge. One who has attained perfection in *yoga* will come to realise this in course of time in his own heart.

श्रद्धावाँल्लभते ज्ञानं तत्परः संयतेन्द्रियः।
ज्ञानं लब्ध्वा परां शान्तिमचिरेणाधिगच्छति ।।३९।।

Sraddhaavaan labhate jnaanam tatparah samyatendriyah;
Jnaanam labdhvaa param santimachirenaadhigacchati.

39. One who is endowed with faith, who is ever devoted and in full control of the mind and senses, gains this knowledge by which supreme peace will be attained swiftly.

अज्ञश्चाश्रद्दधानश्च संशयात्मा विनश्यति।
नायं लोकोऽस्ति न परो न सुखं संशयात्मनः ।।४०।

Ajnaschaasraddadhaanas cha samsayaatmaa vinasyati;
Naayam loko'sti na paro na sukham samsayaatmanah.

40. But the ignorant who have a doubting nature and no faith go to perdition. Neither this world, nor the next, nor joy can be had by the doubters.

योगसंन्यस्तकर्माणं ज्ञानसंछिन्नसंशयम्।
आत्मवन्तं न कर्माणि निबध्नन्ति धनंजय ।।४१।।

Yogasamnyasta karmaanam jnaanasamcchinnasamsayam;
Aatmavantam na karmaani nibadhnanti dhananjaya.

41. But one who is ever poised in the Self, who has renounced all action in *yoga*, whose doubts have been rent asunder by knowledge, is not bound by action O Arjuna (Dhananjaya).

तस्मादज्ञानसंभूतं हृत्स्थं ज्ञानासिनात्मनः।
छित्त्वैनं संशयं योगमातिष्ठोत्तिष्ठ भारत।।४२।।

Tasmaad ajnaanasambhootam hritstham jnaanaasinaa-tmanah;
Chhitwainam samsayam yogam aatishthottishtha bhaarata.

42. Therefore arise O Arjuna (Bharatha). Take refuge in *yoga* and destroy this doubt born of ignorance within your heart with the sword of knowledge.

ॐ

ॐ तत्सदिति श्रीमद्भगवद्गीतासूपनिषत्सु ब्रह्मविद्यायां योगशास्त्रे श्रीकृष्णार्जुनसंवादे ज्ञानकर्म संन्यास योगो नामचतुर्थो ऽध्यायः ॥४॥

Om tat sat iti srimad bhagavad gitaasoopanishatsu brahmavidyaayaam yogashaastre sri krishnaarjuna-samvaade jnanakarma sannyasayogo naama chatur-tho'dhyaayah.

Aum Tat Sat:

Thus in the Upanishad of the Bhagavad Gita, the Knowledge of Supreme Brahman, the Scripture of *Yoga*, the dialogue between Sri Krishna and Arjuna, ends the fourth chapter entitled, "The *Yoga* of Renunciation of Action through Knowledge."

ॐ

Aum Sri Krishnaya Paramatmane Namah!
Aum Sri Parthasarathaye Namah!

अथ पञ्चमोऽध्यायः
Atha Panchamo'dhyayah

CHAPTER V
KARMA SANNYASA YOGA
The Yoga of Renunciation and Action

अर्जुन उवाच

संन्यासं कर्मणां कृष्ण पुनर्योगं च शंससि।
यच्छ्रेय एतयोरेकं तन्मे ब्रूहि सुनिश्चितम् ।।१।।

Arjuna uvaacha
Sannyaasam karmanaam krishna punar yogam cha
samsasi;
Yachchreya etayorekam tanme broohi sunischitam.

Thus spoke Arjuna:

1. O Krishna! You have praised both renunciation of action as well as its unselfish performance. Tell me decisively which of the two is better.

श्रीभगवानुवाच

संन्यासः कर्मयोगश्च निःश्रेयसकरावुभौ।
तयोस्तु कर्मसंन्यासात्कर्मयोगो विशिष्यते ।।२।।

Sree Bhagavaan uvaacha
Sannyaasah karmayogascha nisreyasakaraa vubhau;
Tayostu karmasannyaasaat karmyogo visishyate.

Thus spoke the Blessed Lord:

2. Both renunciation of action as well as its unselfish performance lead to liberation but of the two, the unselfish carrying out of our duties (*karma yoga*) is superior to total renunciation of action (*karma sannyasa*).

ज्ञेयः स नित्यसंन्यासी यो न द्वेष्टि न काङ्क्षति।
निर्द्वन्द्वो हि महाबाहो सुखं बन्धात्प्रमुच्यते ।।३।।

Jneyah sa nityasannyaasi yo na dweshti na kaangshati;
Nirdwandwo hi mahaabaaho sukham bandhaat
pramuchyate.

3. O Arjuna (Mahabaho)! A person who is above
likes and dislikes must be considered a staunch
renunciate (sannyasin). Such a *yogi* who is free from
dualities will be easily released from bondage.

सांख्ययोगौ पृथग्बालाः प्रवदन्ति न पण्डिताः।
एकमप्यास्थितः सम्यगुभयोर्विन्दते फलम् ।।४।।

Saamkhya yogau prithagbaalaah pravadanti na panditaah;
Ekam apyaasthitah samyag ubhayor vindate phalam.

4. Only the childish speak of renunciation (Sankhya
or *sannyasa*) as being different from the unselfish
performance of action (*karma yoga*). One who is well-
established in either gets the same fruit for the fruit
of both is the same.

यत्सांख्यैः प्राप्यते स्थानं तद्योगैरपि गम्यते।
एकं सांख्यं च योगं च यः पश्यति स पश्यति ।।५।।

Yatsaankhyaihpraapyate sthaanam tad yogair api gamyate;
Ekam saamkhyam cha yogam cha yah pasyati sa pasyati.

5. The same state which is achieved through knowledge and renunciation (*Sankhya yoga*) is achieved by those who perform unselfish action (*karma yoga*). The true seer sees both *Sankhya* and *yoga* to be the same.

संन्यासस्तु महाबाहो दुःखमाप्तुमयोगतः ।
योगयुक्तो मुनिर्ब्रह्म नचिरेणाधिगच्छति ॥६॥

Sannyaasastu mahaabaaho dukham aaptum ayogatah;
Yogayukto munir brahma na chirenaadhigacchati.

6. O Arjuna (Mahabaho)! The state of total renunciation of action (*sannyasa*) is very difficult to attain without the practice of *karma yoga*. The sage who is continuously engaged in the performance of unselfish action (*karma yoga*), quickly attains Brahman.

योगयुक्तो विशुद्धात्मा विजितात्मा जितेन्द्रियः ।
सर्वभूतात्मभूतात्मा कुर्वन्नपि न लिप्यते ॥७॥

Yogayukto visuddhaatmaa vijitaatmaa jitendriyah;
Sarvabhootaatmaabhootaatmaa kurvannapi na lipyate.

7. That *yogi* whose mind has been purified by the constant performance of unselfish actions, who has controlled the senses and conquered his lower self and who sees his own Self as the Self in all beings, is not tainted even though continuing to act.

नैव किंचित्करोमीति युक्तो मन्येत तत्त्ववित्।
पश्यञ्शृण्वन्स्पृशञ्जिघ्रन्नश्नन्गच्छन्स्वपञ्श्वसन् ।।८।।

Naiva kinchit karomeeti yukto manyeta tatwavit;
Pasyan srinvan sprisan jighran nasnan gacchan swapan
swasan.

प्रलपन्विसृजन्गृह्णन्नुन्मिषन्निमिषन्नपि।
इन्द्रियाणीन्द्रियार्थेषु वर्तन्त इति धारयन् ।।९।।

Pralapan visrijan grihnnan unmishan nimishannapi;
Indriyaanindriyaartheshu vartanta iti dhaarayan.

8&9.   That knower of Truth, who is ever united
with the Supreme feels, "I am doing nothing at all,"
even while seeing, hearing, touching, smelling, eating, moving, sleeping, breathing, speaking, emitting,
grasping or blinking. He realises that all this is
merely the action of the senses moving amongst the
sense objects.

ब्रह्मण्याधाय कर्माणि सङ्गंत्यक्त्वा करोति यः।
लिप्यते न स पापेन पद्मपत्रमिवाम्भसा ।।१०।।

Brahmanyaadhaaya karmaani sangam tyaktwaa karoti
yah; Lipyate na sa paapena padmapatram ivaambhasaa.

10. As a lotus leaf in water, the one who dedicates
all actions to the Supreme and acts without attachment (to the fruits), is not tainted by sin.

कायेन मनसा बुद्ध्या केवलैरिन्द्रियैरपि।
योगिनः कर्म कुर्वन्ति सङ्गं त्यक्त्वात्मशुद्धये ।।११।

Kaayena manasaa budhyaa kevalair indriyair api;
Yoginah karma kurvanti sangam tyaktwatmasuddhaye.

11. Totally detached, the (*karma*) *yogi* performs action with the body, mind, intellect and senses alone, for self-purification.

युक्तःकर्मफलं त्यक्त्वा शान्तिमाप्नोति नैष्ठिकीम्
अयुक्तः कामकारेण फले सक्तो निबध्यते ।।१२।।

Yuktah karmaphalam tyaktwaa saantim aapnoti naishthikeem;
Ayuktah kaamakaarena phale sakto nibadhyate.

12. By giving up attachment to the fruit of action, the *yogi* attains peace, while the one who acts with a selfish motive for the sake of the benefits alone, is bound.

सर्वकर्माणि मनसा संन्यस्यास्ते सुखं वशी।
नवद्वारे पुरे देही नैव कुर्वन्न कारयन् ।।१३।।

Sarvakarmaani manasaa sannyasyaaste sukham vasee;
Navadwaare pure dehi naiva kurvan na kaarayan.

13. The embodied soul who has mentally renounced all action and is self-controlled, dwells happily in the

city of the nine gates (the body), neither acting nor causing others to act.

न कर्तृत्वं न कर्माणि लोकस्य सृजति प्रभुः।
न कर्मफलसंयोगं स्वभावस्तु प्रवर्तते ।।१४।।

Na kartritwam na karmaani lokasya srijati prabhuh;
Na karmaphala samyogam swabhaavas tu pravartate.

14. In this world, the Lord does not create the agency, the action or the connection between work and results. It is Nature alone that does all this.

नादत्ते कस्यचित्पापं न चैव सुकृतं विभुः।
अज्ञानेनावृतं ज्ञानं तेन मुह्यन्ति जन्तवः ।।१५।।

Naadatte kasyachitpaapam na chaiva sukritam vibhuh;
Ajnaanenaavritam jnaanam tena muhyanti jantavah..

15. The omnipresent Lord does not accept the sins and virtues of anyone. Knowledge is enveloped by ignorance and thus all beings are deluded.

ज्ञानेन तु तदज्ञानं येषां नाशितमात्मनः।
तेषामादित्यवज्ज्ञानं प्रकाशयति तत्परम् ।।१६।।

Jnaanena tu tad ajnaanam yesham naasitam aatmanah;
Teshaam aadityavat jnaanam prakaasayati tatparam.

16. Wisdom, shining like the sun will reveal the Supreme Self to those in whom ignorance has been destroyed by Self-realisation.

तद्बुद्धयस्तदात्मानस्तन्निष्ठास्तत्परायणाः ।
गच्छन्त्यपुनरावृत्तिं ज्ञाननिर्धूतकल्मषाः ॥१७॥

Tadbuddhayas tadaatmaanas tannishthaas tatparaayanaah;
Gacchantyapunaraavrittim jnaana nirdhoota kalmashaah.

17. They attain the state of no return, whose impurities have been cleansed by knowledge, whose intellect and mind are ever absorbed in That (the Supreme), who remain steadfast in That, and whose sole objective is That.

विद्याविनयसंपन्ने ब्राह्मणे गवि हस्तिनि।
शुनि चैव श्वपाके च पण्डिताः समदर्शिनः ॥१८॥

Vidyaavinaya sampanne braahmane gavi hastini;
Suni chaiva svapaake cha panditaah samadarsinah.

18. The sage regards everything as equal in value — whether it be a learned Brahmin filled with humility, a cow, an elephant, a dog or an outcaste.

इहैव तैर्जितः सर्गो येषां साम्ये स्थितं मनः।
निर्दोषं हि समं ब्रह्म तस्माद्ब्रह्मणि ते स्थिताः ॥१९।

Ihaiva tairjitah sargo yesham saamye sthitam manah;
Nirdosham hi samam brahma tasmaat brahmani te sthitah.

19. They who are established in equality can over-come this transmigratory existence even while living in this world. They are established in the flawless Brahman which is the same in all.

न प्रहृष्येत्प्रियं प्राप्य नोद्विजेत्प्राप्य चाप्रियम् ।
स्थिरबुद्धिरसंमूढो ब्रह्मविद्ब्रह्मणि स्थितः ।।२०।।

Na prahrishyet priyampraapya noddwijet praapya cha
apriyam;
Sthirabuddhir asammoodho brahmavit brahmani sthitah.

20. The knower of Brahman, who is established in Brahman, who is of undeluded and stable intellect, does not rejoice at getting what is pleasant or feel depressed on meeting with the unpleasant.

बाह्यस्पर्शेष्वसक्तात्मा विन्दत्यात्मनि यत्सुखम् ।
स ब्रह्मयोगयुक्तात्मा सुखमक्षयमश्नुते ।।२१।।

Baahyasparseshwasaktaatmaa vindatyaatmani yat sukham;
Sa brahma yoga yuktaatmaa sukham akshayam asnute.

21. The one who is ever united with the Supreme finds all happiness within and is detached from external objects and thus enjoys unending bliss.

ये हि संस्पर्शजा भोगा दुःखयोनय एव ते।
आद्यन्तवन्तः कौन्तेय न तेषु रमते बुधः ।।२२।।

Ye hi samsparsajaa bhogaa duhkhayonaya eva te;
Aadyantavantah kaunteya na teshu ramate budhah.

22. O Arjuna (Kaunteya), the joys arising from the
contact with the sense objects are veritable wombs
of sorrow. They have a beginning and an end. The
wise do not revel in them.

शक्नोतीहैव यः सोढुं प्राक्शरीरविमोक्षणात्।
कामक्रोधोद्भवं वेगं स युक्तः स सुखी नरः ।।२३।।

Saknoteehaiva yah sodhum praak sareera vimokshanaat;
Kaamakrodhodbhavam vegam sa yuktah sa sukhi narah.

23. The true *yogi* is one who is able to resist the
impulses of desire and anger even while dwelling in
this body and is thus a happy person.

योऽन्तःसुखोऽन्तरारामस्तथान्तर्ज्योतिरेव यः।
स योगी ब्रह्मनिर्वाणं ब्रह्मभूतोऽधिगच्छति ।।२४।।

Yo ntah sukho'ntaraaraamas tathaantarjyoti eva yah;
Sa yogee brahma nirvaanam brahmabhooto'dhigacchati.

24. That *yogi* whose happiness lies within himself, whose tranquillity stems from within and
who is illumined from within, attains the bliss of
Brahman—becomes Brahman.

ॐ

लभन्ते ब्रह्मनिर्वाणमृषयः क्षीणकल्मषाः।
छिन्नद्वैधा यतात्मानः सर्वभूतहिते रताः ।।२५।।

Labhante brahmanirvaanam rishayah khseenakalmashaah;
Chchinnadwaidhaa yataatmaanah sarvabhootahite rataah.

25. Those sages, whose sins have been wiped out,
whose doubts have been destroyed, who are self-
controlled and who delight in the welfare of others,
attain complete liberation in Brahman.

कामक्रोधवियुक्तानां यतीनां यतचेतसाम्।
अभितो ब्रह्मनिर्वाणं वर्तते विदितात्मनाम् ।।२६।।

Kaamakrodha viyuktaanaam yateenaam yatachetasaam;
Abhito brahma nirvaanam vartate viditatmanaam.

26. Those austere ones who are free from desire and
anger, whose minds are under control and who have
realised the Self, enjoy complete liberation all the
time, everywhere.

स्पर्शान्कृत्वा बहिर्बाह्यांश्चक्षुश्चैवान्तरे भ्रुवोः।
प्राणापानौ समौ कृत्वा नासाभ्यन्तरचारिणौ ।।२७।।

Sparsaan kritwaa bahir baahyaams chakshus chaivaantare
bhruvoh;
Praanaapaanau samau kritwaa naasaabhyantara
chaarinau.

यतेन्द्रियमनोबुद्धिर्मुनिर्मोक्षपरायणः ।
विगतेच्छाभयक्रोधो यः सदा मुक्त एव सः ।।२८।।

Yatendriya manobuddhir munir moksha paraayanah;
Vigatecchaabhaya krodho yah sadaa mukta eva sah.

27&28. Shutting out all external objects, fixing the inner gaze between the brows, equalising the inflow and outflow of breath and controlling the senses, mind and intellect, the sage who is intent on achieving liberation and who is free from desire, fear and anger, is verily liberated.

भोक्तारं यज्ञतपसां सर्वलोकमहेश्वरम् ।
सुहृदं सर्वभूतानां ज्ञात्वा मां शान्तिमृच्छति ।।२९।।

Bhoktaaram yajnatapasaam sarvaloka maheswaram;
Suhridam sarvabhootaanaam jnaatwaa maam saantim ricchati.

29. One who knows Me as the great Lord of all the worlds, the enjoyer of all offerings and austerities and the sole friend of all creatures, attains peace.

ॐ तत्सदिति श्रीमद्भगवद्गीतासूपनिषत्सु ब्रह्मविद्यायां
योगशास्त्रे श्रीकृष्णार्जुनसंवादे कर्मसंन्यासयोगो
नाम पञ्चमोऽध्यायः ।।५।।

Om tat sat iti srimad bhagavad gitaasoopanishatsu

brahmavidyaayaam yogashaastre sri krishnaarjuna-samvaade karmasanyasayogo naama panchamo'dhyaayah.

Aum Tat Sat:

Thus in the Upanishad of the Bhagavad Gita, the Knowledge of Supreme Brahman, the Scripture of *Yoga*, the dialogue between Sri Krishna and Arjuna, ends the fifth chapter entitled, "The *Yoga* of Renunciation and Action."

Aum Sri Krishnaya Paramatmane Namah!
Aum Sri Parthasarathaye Namah!

अथ षष्ठोऽध्यायः
Atha Shashto'dhyaayah

CHAPTER VI
ATMA SAMYAMA YOGA
The Yoga of Self-Discipline

श्रीभगवानुवाच

अनाश्रितः कर्मफलं कार्यं कर्म करोति यः।
स संन्यासी च योगी च न निरग्निर्न चाक्रियः ।।१।।

Sree Bhagavaan uvaacha
Anaashritah karmaphalam kaaryam karma karoti yah;
sa sannyaasi cha yogi cha na niragnirna chaakriyah.

Thus spoke the Blessed Lord:

1.   One who discharges all duties without expectation of reward is both a *sannyasin* and a *karma yogi*
but not so the one who has renounced the sacrificial
fire and other sacred rites. (These are the duties of
a householder.)

यं संन्यासमिति प्राहुर्योगं तं विद्धि पाण्डव।
न ह्यसंन्यस्तसंकल्पो योगी भवति कश्चन ।।२।।

Yam sannyasamiti praahuryogam tam viddhi paandava;
Na hyasannyastasankalpo yogee bhavati kaschana.

2.   Understand O Arjuna (Pandava), that that which
they term as *sannyasa* applies equally to *karma yoga,*
for none can become a *yogi* without giving up all
worldly speculations.

आरुरुक्षोर्मुनेर्योगं कर्म कारणमुच्यते।
योगारूढस्य तस्यैव शमः कारणमुच्यते ।।३।।

Aarurukshormuneryogam karma kaaranamuchyate;
Yogaarudhasya tasyaiva shamah kaaranamuchyate.

3. Karma *yoga* is said to be the path for the seeker
who wants to attain the heights of *yoga* but having
attained it, serenity is said to be the means.

यदा हि नेन्द्रियार्थेषु न कर्मस्वनुषज्जते।
सर्वसंकल्पसंन्यासी योगारूढस्तदोच्यते ।।४।।

Yadaa hi nendriyaartheshu na karmaswanushajjate;
Sarvasankalpasannyaasi yogaarudhas tadochyate.

4. One who is not attached to sense objects and has
given up all motivated action and worldly speculations, may be said to have attained *yoga*.

उद्धरेदात्मनात्मानं नात्मानमवसादयेत्।
आत्मैव ह्यात्मनो बन्धुरात्मैव रिपुरात्मनः ।।५।।

Uddharedaatmanaatmaanam naatmaanamavasaadayet;
Atmaiva hyaatmano bandhuratmaiva ripuraatmanah.

5. One should uplift oneself by the Self and not
degrade oneself for one's own self is both one's
friend and enemy.

बन्धुरात्मात्मनस्तस्य येनात्मैवात्मना जितः।
अनात्मनस्तु शत्रुत्वे वर्तेतात्मैव शत्रुवत् ।।६।।

Bandhuraatmaatmanastasya yenaatmaivaatmanaa jitah;
Anaatmanastu shatrutwe vartetaatmaiva shatruvat.

6. The Self of one who has conquered his (lower)
self can be considered a friend but the self of one
who has not been able to conquer himself is like an
enemy.

जितात्मनः प्रशान्तस्य परमात्मा समाहितः।
शीतोष्णसुखदुःखेषु तथा मानापमानयोः ।।७।।

Jitaatmanah prasaantasyaparamaatmaa samaahitah;
Sheetoshnasukhaduhkkheshu tathaa maanaapamaanayoh.

7. The highest Self of one who has conquered the
(lower) self is always at peace and is ever the same
in heat and cold, joy and sorrow, honour and
dishonour.

ज्ञानविज्ञानतृप्तात्मा कूटस्थो विजितेन्द्रियः।
युक्त इत्युच्यते योगी समलोष्टाश्मकाञ्चनः ।।८।।

Jnaanavijnaanatriptaatmaa kootastho vijitendriyah;
Yukta ityuchyate yogee samaloshtaashmakaanchanah.

8. A *yogi* is one, who finds full satisfaction in Self-
knowledge and discrimination and who remains
unshaken (in all circumstances) and is a master of
the senses. Such a one regards alike a clod, a stone
and a piece of gold.

सुहृन्मित्रार्युदासीनमध्यस्थद्वेष्यबन्धुषु ।
साधुष्वपि च पापेषु समबुद्धिर्विशिष्यते ।।६।।

Suhrinmitraaryudaaseenamadhyasthadweshyabandhushu;
Saadhushwapi cha paapeshu samabuddhirvishishyate.

9. The supreme *yogi* is one who is able to regard well-wishers, friends, foes, neutrals, arbiters, the despicable, relations, saints and sinners, without prejudice, as equals.

योगी युञ्जीत सततमात्मानं रहसि स्थितः ।
एकाकी यतचित्तात्मा निराशीरपरिग्रहः ।।१०।।

Yogee yunjeeta satatamaatmaanam rahasi sthitah;
Ekaaki yatachittaatmaa niraasheeraparigrahah.

10. The *yogi* should be constantly in union with the Self, living in solitude, with body and mind under control, with no desire and no craving for possessions.

शुचौ देशे प्रतिष्ठाप्य स्थिरमासनमात्मनः ।
नात्युच्छ्रितं नातिनीचं चैलाजिनकुशोत्तरम् ।।११।।

Suchau deshe pratishthaapya sthiramaasanamaatmanah;
Naatyucchritam naatineecham chailaajinakushottaram.

11. The seat for meditation should be in a clean spot which is neither too high nor too low. On this some

kusa grass, an antelope skin and a piece of cloth should be placed one above the other.

तत्रैकाग्रं मनः कृत्वा यतचित्तेन्द्रियक्रियः ।
उपविश्यासने युञ्ज्याद्योगमात्मविशुद्धये ।।१२।।

Tatraikaagram manah kritwaa yatachittendriyakriyah;
Upavishyaasane yunjyaadyogamaatmavishuddhaye.

12. Seated firmly on this, the *yogi* should keep the mind single-pointed and control the activity of the senses and imagination and thus practise *yoga* for self purification.

समं कायशिरोग्रीवं धारयन्नचलं स्थिरः ।
संप्रेक्ष्य नासिकाग्रं स्वं दिशश्चानवलोकयन् ।।१३।।

Samam kaayashirogreevam dhaarayannachalam sthirah;
Samprekshya naasikaagram swam dishaschaanavalokayan.

13. The head, neck and trunk should be kept erect, motionless and steady. The gaze should be fixed on the tip of the nose without shifting.

प्रशान्तात्मा विगतभीर्ब्रह्मचारिव्रते स्थितः ।
मनः संयम्य मच्चित्तो युक्त आसीत मत्परः ।।१४।।

Prashaantaatmaa vigatabheer brahmacharivrate sthitah;
Manah samyamya macchitto yukta aaseeta matparah.

ॐ

14. Serene and fearless, firm in the vow of continence, with mind subdued, the *yogi* should sit concentrated, devoted to Me and thoughts fixed on Me.

यञ्जयुन्नेवं सदात्मानं योगी नियतमानसः।
शान्तिं निर्वाणपरमां मत्संस्थामधिगच्छति ।।१५।।

Yunjannevam sadaatmaanam yogee niyatamaanasah;
Shaantim nirvaanaparamaam matsamsthaamadhigacchati.

15. The *yogi* who has been continuously disciplining himself attains the ultimate state of peace called *nirvana* which abides in Me.

नात्यश्नतस्तु योगोऽस्ति न चैकान्तमनश्नतः।
न चाति स्वप्नशीलस्य जाग्रतो नैव चार्जुन ।।१६।।

Naatyashnatastu yogosti nachaikaantamanashnatah;
Na chaatiswapnasheelasya jaagrato naiva chaarjuna.

16. O Arjuna, *yoga* is not for one who eats too much or does not eat at all, nor for one who sleeps too much or does not sleep at all.

युक्ताहारविहारस्य युक्तचेष्टस्य कर्मसु।
युक्तस्वप्नावबोधस्य योगो भवति दुःखहा ।।१७।।

Yuktaahaaravihaarasya yuktacheshtasya karmasu;
Yuktaswapnaavabodhasya yogo bhavati duhkkhahaa.

17. *Yoga* destroys all sorrow for one who is ever in union (with the Supreme), in both the waking and sleeping states, who is moderate in eating and regulated in work and recreation.

यदा विनियतं चित्तमात्मन्येवावतिष्ठते।
निःस्पृहः सर्वकामेभ्यो युक्त इत्युच्यते तदा ॥१८॥

Yadaa viniyatam chittamaatmanyevaavatishthate;
Nisprihah sarvakaamebhyo yukta ityuchyate tadaa.

18. When the mind is perfectly controlled and free from desire and rests in the Self alone, one can be called a *yogi*.

यथा दीपो निवातस्थो नेङ्गते सोपमा स्मृता।
योगिनो यतचित्तस्य युञ्जतो योगमात्मनः ॥१९॥

Yathaa deepo nivaatastho nengate sopamaa smritaa;
Yogino yatachittasya yunjato yogamaatmanah.

19. Motionless as the flame of a lamp in a windless spot is the disciplined mind of a *yogi* who is striving for union with the Supreme.

यत्रोपरमते चित्तं निरुद्धं योगसेवया।
यत्र चैवात्मनात्मानं पश्यन्नात्मनि तुष्यति ॥२०॥

Yatroparamate chittam niruddham yogasevayaa;
Yatra chaivaatmanaatmaanam pashyannaatmani tushyati.

20. When the mind becomes perfectly still through the practice of *yoga*, the Self is seen within the Self by the Self and rejoices in the Self.

सुखमात्यन्तिकं यत्तद्बुद्धिग्राह्यमतीन्द्रियम् ।
वेत्ति यत्र न चैवायं स्थितश्चलति तत्त्वतः ।।२१।।

Sukhamaatyantikam yattad buddhigraahyamateendriyam;
Vetti yatra na chaivaayam sthitashchalati tattwatah.

21. Then the *yogi* experiences exceeding bliss which transcends the senses and which can be grasped only by the intuitive intellect, wherein established he does not waver.

यं लब्ध्वा चापरं लाभं मन्यते नाधिकं ततः ।
यस्मिन्स्थितो न दुःखेन गुरुणापि विचाल्यते ।।२२।।

Yam labdhwaa chaaparam laabham manyate naadhikam tatah;
Yasmin sthito na duhkkhena gurunaapi vichaalyate.

22. No greater gain can be imagined than this. Established in this the greatest sorrow will fail to afflict.

तं विद्याद्दुःखसंयोगवियोगं योगसंज्ञितम् ।
स निश्चयेन योक्तव्यो योगोऽनिर्विण्णचेतसा ।।२३।।

Tam vidyaad duhkkhasamyogaviyogam yogasamjnitam;
Sa nishchayena yoktavyo yogonirvinnachetasaa.

23. *Yoga* is the state of total severance from pain and should be practised with determination and without depression.

संकल्पप्रभवान्कामांस्त्यक्त्वा   सर्वानशेषतः ।
मनसैवेन्द्रियग्रामं विनियम्य समन्ततः ।।२४।।

Sankalpaprabhavaan kaamaam styaktwaa sarvaan aseshatah;
Manasaivendriyagraamam viniyamya samantatah.

24. All worldly speculations should be completely abandoned and the roving senses should be restrained by the mind.

शनैः शनैरुपरमेद्बुद्ध्या   धृतिगृहीतया ।
आत्मसंस्थं मनः कृत्वा न किंचिदपि चिन्तयेत् ।।२५।

Shanaih shanairuparamet budhyaa dhritigriheetayaa;
Aaatmasamstham manah kritwaa na kinchidapi chintayet.

25. Gradually one should fix the mind and intellect firmly on the Self and then think of nothing else.

यतो यतो निश्चरति मनश्चञ्चलमस्थिरम् ।
ततस्ततो नियम्यैतदात्मन्येव वशं नयेत् ।।२६।।

Yato yato nishcharati manashchanchalamasthiram;
Tatastato niyamyaitat aatmanyeva vasham nayet.

26. Whenever the restless and fickle mind wanders, it should be curbed and brought back and fixed on the Self.

प्रशान्तमनसं ह्येनं योगिनं सुखमुत्तमम्।
उपैति शान्तरजसं ब्रह्मभूतमकल्मषम् ।।२७।।

Prashaantamanasam hyenam yoginam sukhamuttamam;
Upaiti shaantarajasam brahmabhootamakalmasham.

27. Supreme bliss is attained by the stainless, passionless *yogi* of tranquil mind who has become one with Brahman.

युरत्र्जन्नेवं सदात्मानं योगी विगतकल्मषः।
सुखेन ब्रह्मसंस्पर्शमत्यन्तं सुखमश्नुते ।।२८।।

Yunjannevam sadaatmaanam yogee vigatakalmashah;
Sukhena brahmasamsparsham atyantam sukham ashnute.

28. The sinless *yogi* who is constantly disciplining himself, easily experiences the exceeding bliss of contact with Brahman.

सर्वभूतस्थमात्मानं सर्वभूतानि चात्मनि।
ईक्षते योगयुक्तात्मा सर्वत्र समदर्शनः ।।२६।।

Sarvabhootasthamaatmaanam sarvabhootaani chaatmani;
Eekshate yogayuktaatmaa sarvatra samadarshanah.

29. One who is established in *yoga* regards everything as equal, beholding the same Self in all beings and all beings within himself. He sees the same in all.

यो मां पश्यति सर्वत्र सर्वं च मयि पश्यति।
तस्याहं न प्रणश्यामि स च मे न प्रणश्यति ।।३०।।

Yo maam pashyati sarvatra sarvam cha mayi pashyati;
Tasyaaham na pranashyaami sa cha me na pranashyati.

30. One who sees Me (the Universal Self), everywhere and all beings as existing in Me, is never parted from Me and I am never separated from him.

सर्वभूतस्थितं यो मां भजत्येकत्वमास्थितः।
सर्वथा वर्तमानोऽपि स योगी मयि वर्तते ।।३१।।

Sarvabhootasthitam yo maam bhajatyekatwamaasthitah;
Sarvathaa vartamaanopi sa yogee mayi vartate.

31. The *yogi* who is thus established in unity and worships Me as the indweller in all beings, always abides in Me, whatever be the life-style which is followed.

ॐ

आत्मौपम्येन सर्वत्र समं पश्यति योऽर्जुन।
सुखं वा यदि वा दुःखं स योगी परमो मतः ।।३२।।

Aaatmaupamyena sarvatra samam pashyati yo'rjuna;
Sukham vaa yadi vaa duhkkham sa yogee paramo matah.

32. O Arjuna, he is the supreme *yogi* who regards
all beings as equals and who considers the pains and
pleasures of others as being on par with his own.

अर्जुन उवाच
योऽयं योगस्त्वया प्रोक्तः साम्येन मधुसूदन।
एतस्याहं न पश्यामि चञ्चलत्वात्स्थितिं स्थिराम् ।।३३।।

Arjuna uvaacha
Yoyam yogastwayaa proktah saamyena madhusoodana;
Eetasyaaham na pashyaami chanchalatwaat sthitim
sthiraam.

Thus spoke Arjuna:

33. O Krishna (Madhusudana)! Due to the restless
state of the mind, I do not see how this *yoga* of
equanimity which you have just taught me, can be
stabilised.

चञ्चलं हि मनः कृष्ण प्रमाथि बलवद्दृढम्।
तस्याहं निग्रहं मन्ये वायोरिव सुदुष्करम् ।।३४।।

Chanchalam hi manah krishna pramaathi balavad dridham;
Tasyaaham nigraham manye vaayoriva sudushkaram.

34. O Krishna, I consider the mind to be restless, turbulent, strong and stubborn and as difficult to control as the wind.

श्रीभगवानुवाच

असंशयं महाबाहो मनो दुर्निग्रहं चलम्।
अभ्यासेन तु कौन्तेय वैराग्येण च गृह्यते ।।३५।।

Sree Bhagavaan uvaacha
Asamshayam mahaabaaho mano durnigraham chalam;
Abhyaasena tu kaunteya vairaagyena cha grihyate.

Thus spoke the Blessed Lord:

35. Undoubtedly O Arjuna (Mahabaho, Kaunteya), the mind is restless and difficult to control, but it can certainly be done with continuous practice and detachment.

असंयतात्मना योगो दुष्प्राप इति मे मतिः।
वश्यात्मना तु यतता शक्योऽवाप्तुमुपायतः ।।३६।।

Asamyataatmanaa yogo dushpraapa iti me matih;
Vashyaatmanaa tu yatataa shakyovaaptumupaayatah.

36. *Yoga* is certainly difficult for one whose mind is not controlled but I assure you that it can be done

by the self-controlled aspirant who uses the right method.

अर्जुन उवाच
अयतिः श्रद्धयोपेतो योगाच्चलितमानसः।
अप्राप्य योगसंसिद्धिं कां गतिं कृष्ण गच्छति ।।३७।

Arjuna uvaacha
Ayatis shraddhayopeto Yogaacchalitu-maanasah;
Apraapya yogasamsiddhim kaam gatim krishna gacchati.

Thus spoke Arjuna:

37. O Krishna, what is the fate of one who has full faith but is unable to subdue the mind and thus falls from *yoga* before attaining perfection?

कच्चिन्नोभयविभ्रष्टश्छिन्नभ्रमिव नश्यति।
अप्रतिष्ठो महाबाहो विमूढो ब्रह्मणः पथि ।।३८।।

Kacchinnobhayavibhrashtas cchinnabhramiva nashyati;
Apratishtho mahaabaaho vimoodho brahmanah pathi.

38. Deflected from the path to Brahman, and having lost his hold on both paths (that of *yoga* and of worldly enjoyments), totally without any support, will he not perish like a rent cloud, O Krishna (Mahabaho)?

एतन्मे संशयं कृष्ण छेत्तुमर्हस्यशेषतः।
त्वदन्यः संशयस्यास्य छेत्ता न ह्युपपद्यते ।।३६।।

Eetanme samshayam Krishna cchettumarhasyasheshatah;
Twadanyah samshayasyaasya cchettaa na hyupapadyate.

39. O Krishna! It behoves You to clear this doubt of
mine completely, for none but You can do so.

श्रीभगवानुवाच

पार्थ नैवेह नामुत्र विनाशस्तस्य विद्यते।
न हि कल्याणकृत्कश्चिद्दुर्गतिं तात गच्छति ।।४०।।

Sree Bhagavaan uvaacha
Paartha naiveha naamutra vinaashas tasya vidyate;
Nahi kalyaanakrit kaschit durgatim taata gacchati.

Thus spoke the Blessed Lord:

40. O Arjuna (Partha)! I assure you that there will
be no fall for such a person either here or in the
hereafter. My child, one who strives for self-perfec-
tion can never come to grief.

प्राप्य पुण्यकृतां लोकानुषित्वा शाश्वतीः समाः।
शुचीनां श्रीमतां गेहे योगभ्रष्टोऽभिजायते ।।४१।।

Praapya punyakritaam lokaanushitwaa shaashwateeh
samaah;
Shucheenaam shreemataam gehe yogabhrashtobhijaayate.

ॐ

41. Having attained the world of the righteous and lived there for countless years, one who has fallen from *yoga* will be born again in the home of the pure and the illustrious.

अथवा योगिनामेव कुले भवति धीमताम्।
एतद्धि दुर्लभतरं लोके जन्म यदीदृशम् ।।४२।।

Athavaa yoginaameva kule bhavati dheemataam;
Etaddhi durlabhataram loke janma yadeedrisham.

42. It is also possible that he may be born into a family of wise *yogis* even though this kind of birth is difficult to obtain in this world.

तत्र तं बुद्धिसंयोगं लभते पौर्वदेहिकम्।
यतते च ततो भूयः संसिद्धौ कुरुनन्दन ।।४३।।

Tattra tam buddhisamyogam labhate paurvadehikam;
Yatate cha tato bhooyahsamsiddhau kurunandana.

43. O Arjuna (Kurunandana)! In that birth he will regain the knowledge of his previous life and will be able to strive even harder for perfection.

पूर्वाभ्यासेन तेनैव ह्रियते ह्यवशोऽपि सः।
जिज्ञासुरपि योगस्य शब्दब्रह्मातिवर्तते ।।४४।।

Poorvaabhyaasena tenaiva hriyate hyavashopi sah;
Jijnaasurapi yogasya shabdabrahmaativartate.

44. He will be irresistibly carried forward by the impetus of all his previous practices. Even one who merely enquires about the path of *yoga* is deemed superior to the performer of Vedic rituals.

प्रयत्नाद्यतमानस्तु योगी संशुद्धकिल्बिषः।
अनेकजन्मसंसिद्धस्ततो याति परां गतिम् ।।४५।।

Prayatnaadyatamaanastu yogee samshuddhakilbishah;
Anekajanmasamsiddhas tato yaati paraam gatim.

45. The sinless *yogi* who strives ceaselessly with controlled mind, perfects himself gradually in the course of many lives and attains the Supreme state.

तपस्विभ्योऽधिको योगी ज्ञानिभ्योऽपि मतोऽधिकः।
कर्मिभ्यश्चाधिको योगी तस्माद्योगी भवार्जुन ।।४६।।

Tapaswibhyo'dhikoyogee jnaanibhyo'pi mato'dhikah;
Karmibhyaschaadhiko yogee tasmaad yogee bhavaarjuna.

46. A *yogi* is greater than an ascetic, superior to the intellectual and nobler than the ritualist. Therefore O Arjuna, become a *yogi*.

योगिनामपि सर्वेषां मद्गतेनान्तरात्मना।
श्रद्धावान्भजते यो मां स मे युक्ततमो मतः ।।४७।।

Yoginaamapi sarveshaam madgatenaantaraatmanaa;
Shraddhaavaan bhajate yo maam sa me yuktatamo matah.

47. In My opinion, even amongst *yogis*, the best are those who worship Me with full faith, with their inmost selves submerged in Me.

ॐ तत्सदिति श्रीमद्भगवद्गीतासूपनिषत्सु ब्रह्म—
विद्यायां योगशास्त्रे श्रीकृष्णार्जुनसंवादे आत्म—
संयमयोगो नाम षष्ठोऽध्यायः ॥६॥

Om tat sat iti srimad bhagavad gitaasoopanishatsu
brahmavidyaayaam yogashaastre sri krishnaarjuna-
samvaade aatmasamyamyogo naama shashtho'dhyaayah.

Aum Tat Sat:

Thus in the Upanishad of the Bhagavad Gita, the Knowledge of Supreme Brahman, the Scripture of *Yoga*, the dialogue between Sri Krishna and Arjuna, ends the sixth chapter entitled, "The *Yoga* of Self-Discipline."

Aum Sri Krishnaya Parmatmane Namah!
Aum Sri Parthasarathaye Namah!

अथ सप्तमोऽध्यायः
Atha Saptamo'dhyaayah

CHAPTER VII
JNANA VIJNANA YOGA
The Yoga of Wisdom and Realisation

मय्यासक्तमनाःपार्थ योगं युञ्जन्मदाश्रयः ।
असंशयं समग्रं मां यथा ज्ञास्यसि तच्छृणु ।।१।।

Sree Bhagavaan uvaacha:
Mayyaasaktasmanaah paartha yogam yunjanmadaa-
shrayah;
Asamshayam samagram maam yathaa jnaasyasi tatcc-
hrinu.

Thus spoke the Blessed Lord:

1.   Hear from Me O Arjuna (Partha), how you will be able to grasp My real nature in its totality, without misconceptions, by immersing your mind in Me and practising *yoga* with Me as your sole support.

ज्ञानं तेऽहं सविज्ञानमिदं वक्ष्याम्यशेषतः ।
यज्ज्ञात्वा नेह भूयोऽन्यज्ज्ञातव्यमवशिष्यते ।।२।।

Jnaanam te'ham savijnaanam idam vakshyaamyaseshatah;
Yajjnaatwaa neha bhooyonyat jnaatavyamavashishyate.

2. · I shall impart to you in full, this wisdom together with its realisation, knowing which nothing more will remain to be known.

मनुष्याणां सहस्रेषु कश्चिद्यतति सिद्धये ।
यततामपि सिद्धानां कश्चिन्मां वेति तत्त्वतः ।।३।।

Manushyaanaam sahasreshu kaschidyatati siddhaye;
Yatataamapi siddhaanaam kaschinmaam vetti tatwatah.

3.   Amongst thousands of people one rare soul may
strive for perfection and even amongst those who
strive and succeed, scarcely one comes to know My
essence.

भूमिरापोऽनलो वायुः खं मनो बुद्धिरेव च।
अहंकार इतीयं मे भिन्ना प्रकृतिरष्टधा ।।४।।

Bhhoomiraponalo vaayuh kham mano buddhireva cha;
Ahamkaara iteeyam me bhinnaa prakritirashtadhaa.

4.   Earth, water, fire, air, ether, mind, intellect and
ego—these constitute the eightfold division of My
Nature.

अपरेयमितस्त्वन्यां प्रकृतिं विद्धि मे पराम्।
जीवभूतां महाबाहो ययेदं धार्यते जगत् ।।५।।

Apareyamitastwanyaam prakritim viddhi me paraam;
Jeevabhootaam mahaabaaho yayedam dhaaryate jagat.

5.   Know this to be My lower (Nature). But O
Arjuna (Mahabaho)! My higher Nature—the spiritual Being which sustains the entire universe, is
quite different from this.

एतद्योनीनि भूतानि सर्वाणीत्युपधारय।
अहं कृत्स्नस्य जगतः प्रभवः प्रलयस्तथा ॥६॥

Eetadyoneeni bhootaani sarvaaneetyupadhaaraya;
Aham kritsnasya jagatah prabhavah pralayastathaa.

6. These two Natures form the womb of all beings.
I am thus the origin and the dissolution of the entire
universe.

मत्तः परतरं नान्यत्किंचिदस्ति धनंजय।
मयि सर्वमिदं प्रोतं सूत्रे मणिगणा इव ॥७॥

Mattah parataram naanyat kinchidasti dhananjaya;
Mayi sarvamidam protam sootre maniganaa iva.

7. O Arjuna (Dhananjaya)! There is nothing higher
than Me. All these are strung on Me like clusters of
pearls on a string.

रसोऽहमप्सु कौन्तेय प्रभास्मि शशिसूर्ययोः।
प्रणवः सर्ववेदेषु शब्दः खे पौरुषं नृषु ॥८॥

Rasohamapsu kaunteya prabhaasmi shashisooryayoh;
Pranavas sarvavedeshu shabdah khe paurusham nrishu.

8. O Arjuna (Kaunteya)! I am the sapidity in the
waters, the effulgence in the sun and moon, the
syllable *Aum* in all the *Vedas*, sound in ether and
manhood in men.

ॐ

पुण्यो गन्धः पृथिव्यां च तेजश्चास्मि विभावसौ।
जीवनं सर्वभूतेषु तपश्चास्मि तपस्विषु ।।९।।

Punyo gandhah prithivyaam cha tejashchasmi vibhaavasau;
Jeevanam sarvabhooteshu tapashchaasmi tapaswishu.

9.   I am the pure fragrance of earth and the radiance
of fire. I am the life-force in all existences and the
austerity of the ascetic.

बीजं मां सर्वभूतानां विद्धि पार्थ सनातनम्।
बुद्धिर्बुद्धिमतामस्मि तेजस्तेजस्विनामहम् ।।१०।।

Beejam maam sarvabhootaanaam viddhi paartha
sanaatanam;
Buddhir buddhimataamasmi tejastejaswinaamaham.

10. O Arjuna (Partha)! Know Me to be the eternal
seed of all existences—the intelligence of the intelligent and the spleandour of the splendid.

बलं बलवतां चाहं कामरागविवर्जितम्।
धर्माविरुद्धो भूतेषु कामोऽस्मि भरतर्षभ ।।११।।

Balam balavatuam chaaham kaamaraagavivarjitam;
Dharmaaviruddho bhooteshu kaamosmi bharatarshabha.

11. O Arjuna (Bharatarshabha)! I am the might of
the mighty, divorced from lust and passion and that
desire which is unopposed to righteousness.

ये चैव सात्त्विका भावा राजसास्तामसाश्च ये।
मत्त एवेति तान्विद्धि न त्वहं तेषु ते मयि ।।१२।।

Ye chaiva saattvikaa bhaaavaa raajasaastaamasaashcha ye;
Matta eveti taanviddhi natwaham teshu te mayi.

12. Know that all beings and objects whether *sattvic*,
rajasic or *tamasic* have emanated from Me alone, but
though they are in Me, I am not in them.

त्रिभिर्गुणमयैर्भावैरेभिः सर्वमिदं जगत्।
मोहितं नाभिजानाति मामेभ्यः परमव्ययम् ।।१३।।

Tribhirgunamayair bhaavairebhis sarvamidam jagat;
Mohitam naabhijaanaati maamebhyah paramavyayam.

13. Deluded by these three modes of Mine, this
world does not recognise Me for I am immutable
and far beyond these.

दैवी ह्येषा गुणमयी मम माया दुरत्यया।
मामेव ये प्रपद्यन्ते मायामेतां तरन्ति ते ।।१४।।

Daivee hyeshaa gunamayee mama maayaa duratyayaa;
Maameva ye prapadyante maayaametaam taranti te.

14. Verily, this divine illusion of Mine *(maya)*, made
up of the three modes *(sattva, rajas* and *tamas)* is
difficult to penetrate. They alone can transcend it
who have surrendered totally to Me.

ॐ

न मां दुष्कृतिनो मूढाः प्रपद्यन्ते नराधमाः।
माययापहृतज्ञाना आसुरं भावमाश्रिताः ॥१५॥

*Na maam dushkritino moodhaah prapadyante naraadh-
amaah;*
Maayayaapahritajnaanaa aasuram bhaavamaashritaah.

15. The evil-doers, the deluded and the degenerate
who have been deprived of their discrimination by
this illusion and have taken to an evil way of life, will
not think of taking refuge in Me.

चतुर्विधा भजन्ते मां जनाः सुकृतिनोऽर्जुन।
आर्तो जिज्ञासुरर्थार्थी ज्ञानी च भरतर्षम ॥१६॥

Chaturvidhaa bhajante maam janaah sukritinorjuna;
Aarto jijnaasurartharthee jnaanee cha bharatarshabha.

16. O Arjuna (Bharatharshabha)! There are four
types of noble souls who worship Me—the afflicted,
the seekers of knowledge, the seekers of enjoyment
and the wise.

तेषां ज्ञानी नित्ययुक्त एकभक्तिर्विशिष्यते।
प्रियो हि ज्ञानिनोऽत्यर्थमहं स च मम प्रियः ॥१७॥

Teshaam jnaanee nityayukta ekabhakttirvishishyate;
Priyo hi jnaaninotyartham aham sa cha mama priyah.

17. Of these the wise one who is in constant communion with and devoted to the One alone, is the best. Such a one is supremely dear to Me and and he (in turn) loves Me dearly.

उदाराः सर्व एवैते ज्ञानी त्वात्मैव मे मतम् ।
आस्थितः स हि युक्तात्मा मामेवानुत्तमां गतिम् ।।१८।

Udaaraah sarva evaite jnaanee twaatmaiva me matam;
Asthitah sa hi yuktaatmaa maamevaanuttamaam gatim.

18. All these types are undoubtedly noble but I consider the wise one to be My very self. His mind is steadfast and is ever established in Me, as the Supreme goal.

बहूनां जन्मनामन्ते ज्ञानवान्मां प्रपद्यते ।
वासुदेवः सर्वमिति स महात्मा सुदुर्लभः ।।१९।।

Bahoonaam janmanaamante jnaanavaanmaam prapadyate;
Vaasudevah sarvamiti sa mahaatmaa sudurlabhah.

19. It is only after passing through many lives that a person attains this type of wisdom which perceives everything as the Supreme Being (Vaasudeva). Rare indeed is such a noble soul!

कामैस्तैस्तैर्हृतज्ञानाः प्रपद्यन्तेऽन्यदेवताः ।
तं तं नियममास्थाय प्रकृत्या नियताः स्वया ।।२०।।

Kaamaistaistairhritajnaanah prapadyante anyadevatah;
Tam tam niyamamaasthaaya prakrityaa niyataah swayaa.

20. Those whose discrimination has been lost because of various desires worship other gods by numerous rites as demanded by their natures.

यो यो यां यां तनुं भक्तः श्रद्धयार्चितुमिच्छति।
तस्य तस्याचलां श्रद्धां तामेव विदधाम्यहम् ॥२१॥

Yo yo yaam yaam tanum bhaktah shraddhyaar-
chitumicchati;
Tasya tasyaachalaam shraddhaam taameva vidadhaam-
yaham.

21. Whatever form a devotee worships with faith, I see to it that his faith is made firm.

स तया श्रद्धया युक्तस्तस्याराधनमीहते।
लभते च ततः कामान्मयैव विहितान्हि तान् ॥२२॥

Sa tayaa shraddhayaa yuktastasyaaraadhanameehate;
Labhate cha tatah kaamaan mayaiva vihitaan hitaan.

22. Fortified with that faith the votary worships the form of that deity from which he gains all his desires as ordained by Me.

अन्तवत्तु फलं तेषां तद्भवत्यल्पमेधसाम्।
देवान्देवयजो यान्ति भद्भक्ता यान्ति मामपि ॥२३॥

Antavattu phalam teshaam tadbhavatyalpamedhasaam;
Devaan devayajo yaanti madbhaktaa yaanti maamapi.

23. But the fruits gained by these people of limited understanding are temporary. The worshippers of these gods go to the gods and My devotees come to Me.

अव्यक्तं व्यक्तिमापन्नं मन्यन्ते मामबुद्धयः।
परं भावमजानन्तो ममाव्ययमनुत्तमम् ।।२४।।

Avyaktam vyaktimaapannam manyante maamabuddhayah;
Param bhaavamajaananto mamaavyayamanuttamam.

24. Immature minds regard Me—the Unmanifest as being limited by manifestation. They know not My Supreme Nature which is immutable and unsurpassed.

नाहं प्रकाशः सर्वस्य योगमायासमावृतः।
मूढोऽयं नाभिजानाति लोको मामजमव्ययम् ।।२५।।

Naaham prakaashah sarvasya yogamaayaasamaavritah.
Moodhoyam naabhijaanaati loko maamajamavyayam.

25. Veiled as I am by My divine illusion (*yoga maya*), I am not apparent to all. This deluded world knows Me not as the Unborn and the Immutable.

ॐ

वेदाहं समतीतानि वर्तमानानि चार्जुन।
भविष्याणि च भूतानि मां तु वेद न कश्चन ।।२६।।

Vedaaham samateetaani vartamaanaani chaarjuna;
Bhavishyaani cha bhootani maam tu veda na kashchana.

26. O Arjuna! I have knowledge of all beings, past, present and future but no one knows Me.

इच्छाद्वेषसमुत्थेन द्वन्द्वमोहेन भारत।
सर्वभूतानि संमोहं सर्गे यान्ति परंतप ।।२७।।

Icchaadweshasamutthena dwandamohena bhaarata;
Sarvabhootaani sammoham sarge yaanti paramtapa.

27. O Arjuna (Bharatha, Paramtapa)! Right from the time of birth onwards all beings come under the sway of the pairs of opposites arising from desire and aversion.

येषां त्वन्तगतं पापं जनानां पुण्यकर्मणाम्।
ते द्वन्द्वमोहनिर्मुक्ता भजन्ते मां दृढव्रताः ।।२८।।

Yeshaam twantagatam paapam janaanaam punyakarm-
anaam;
Te dwandamohanirmuktaa bhajante maam dridha-vrataah.

28. However, those purified souls who have performed virtuous acts and are thus freed from the deluding power of the dualities, worship Me with firm resolve.

जरामरणमोक्षाय मामाश्रित्य यतन्ति ये।
ते ब्रह्म तद्विदुः कृत्स्नमध्यात्मं कर्म चाखिलम् ।।२९।।

Jaraamaranamokshaaya maamaashritya yatanti ye;
Te brahma tadviduh kritsnam adhyaatmam karma
chaakhilam.

29. Those who consider Me as their sole refuge for
deliverance from the coils of old age and death, will
come to know That Brahman, the individual Self
(*adhyatma*) as well as the whole field of cosmic action
(*karma*).

साधिभूताधिदैवं मां साधियज्ञं च ये विदुः।
प्रयाणकाले पि च मां ते विदुर्युक्तचेतसः ।।३०।।

Saadhibhootaadhidaivam maam saadhiyajnam cha ye
viduh;
Prayaanakaalepi cha maam te vidur yuktachetasah.

30. Those who know Me thus—as the totality of
creation (*adhibhuta*), as the divinity present in all
beings (*adidaiva*) and as the sole Master of all sacrifices (*adiyajna*), they will be in constant communion
with Me even at the hour of death.

ॐ तत्सदिति श्रीमद्भगवद्गीतासूपनिषत्सु ब्रह्म–
विद्यायां योगशास्त्रे श्रीकृष्णार्जुनसंवादे ज्ञान–
विज्ञानयोगो नाम सप्तमोऽध्यायः ।।७।।

Om tat sat iti srimad bhagavad gitaasoopanishatsu brahmavidyaayaam yogashaastre sri krishnaarjuna-samvaade jnaanavijnaanayogo naama saptamo'dhyaayah.

Aum Tat Sat:

Thus in the Upanishad of the Bhagavad Gita, the Knowledge of Supreme Brahman, the Scripture of *Yoga*, the dialogue between Sri Krishna and Arjuna, ends the seventh chapter entitled, "The *Yoga* of Wisdom and Realisation."

Aum Sri Krishnaya Paramatmane Namah!
Aum Sri Parthasarathaye Namah!

अथाष्टमोऽध्यायः
Atha Ashtamo'dhyayah

CHAPTER VIII
AKSHARA BRAHMA YOGA
The Yoga of the Imperishable Brahman

अर्जुन उवाच

किं तद्ब्रह्म किमध्यात्मं किं कर्म पुरुषोत्तम ।
अधिभूतं च किं प्रोक्तमधिदैवं किमुच्यते ॥१॥

Arjuna uvaacha
Kim tadbrahma kim adhyaatmam kim karma puru-
shottama;
Adhibhootam cha kim proktam adhidaivam kimuchyate.

Thus spoke Arjuna:

1.   O Krishna (Purushottama)! What do You mean
by Brahman? What is *adhyatma* and what is *karma*?
What is *adhibhuta* and what is *adhidaiva*?

अधियज्ञः कथं कोऽत्र देहेऽस्मिन्मधुसूदन ।
प्रयाणकाले च कथं ज्ञेयोऽसि नियतात्मभिः ॥२॥

Adhiyajnah katham kotra dehesmin madhusudana;
Prayaanakaale cha katham jneyosi niyataatmabhih.

2.   In this body what is it that is known as *adiyajna*
and O Krishna (Madhusudana), how are You to be
realised at the time of death by self-controlled persons?

श्रीभगवानुवाच

अक्षरं ब्रह्म परमं स्वभावोऽध्यात्ममुच्यते ।
भूतभावोद्भवकरो विसर्गः कर्मसंज्ञितः ॥३॥

Sree Bhagavaan uvaacha
Aksharam Brahma paramam swabhaavodhyaat-mamuchyate;
Bhootabhaavodbhavakaro visargah karmasamjnitah.

Thus spoke the Blessed Lord:

3.   The Supreme Imperishable is called Brahman and the very same within the individual is known as *adhyatma*. *Karma* is the creative movement which brings all beings into existence.

अधिभूतं क्षरो भावः पुरूषश्चाधिदैवतम् ।
अधियज्ञोऽहमेवात्र देहे देहभृतां वर ॥४॥

Adhibhootam ksharo bhaavah purushashchaadhidaivatam;
Adhiyajno'hamevaatra dehe dehabhritaam vara.

4.   The whole of this perishable creation is known as *adhibhuta* and the supreme divine agent (present in all things) is *adidaiva*. O Arjuna (Vara)! Know Me to be the *adiyajna*, the enjoyer of all experiences, in this body.

अन्तकाले च मामेव स्मरन्मुक्त्वा कलेवरम् ।
यः प्रयाति स मद्भावं याति नास्त्यत्र संशयः ॥५॥

Antakaale cha maameva smaran muktwaa kalevaram;
Yah prayaati sa madbhaavam yaati naastyatra samshayah.

5.   At the hour of death, whoever leaves this body

while remembering Me, attains Me. There is no
doubt about this.

यं यं वापि स्मरन्भावं त्यजत्यन्ते कलेवरम्।
तं तमेवैति कौन्तेय सदा तद्भावभावितः ।।६।।

Yamyam vaapi smaran bhaavam tyajatyante kalevaram;
Tam tamevaiti kaunteya sadaa tadbhaavabhaavitah.

6.   O Arjuna (Kaunteya), whatever be the state of
being that a person thinks of at the time of departing
from this body, that will be attained by him because
of his mind's constant absorption with it.

तस्मात्सर्वेषु कालेषु मामनुस्मर युध्य च।
मय्यर्पितमनोबुद्धिर्मामेवैष्यस्यसंशयम् ।।७।।

Tasmaat sarveshu kaaleshu maamanusmara yudhya cha;
Mayyarpitamanobuddhirmaamevaishyasyasamshayam.

7.   Therefore, let your mind be in constant communion with Me while fighting. If your mind and
intellect are ever absorbed in Me, you will surely
come to Me.

अभ्यासयोगयुक्तेन चेतसा नान्यगामिना।
परमं पुरुषं दिव्यं याति पार्थानुचिन्तयन् ।।८।।

Abhyaasayogayuktena chetasaa naanyagaamina;
Paramam purusham divyam yaati parthaanuchintayan.

ॐ

8.   O Arjuna (Partha)! If the mind thinks of nothing but that self-effulgent and Supreme Person all the time and practises the *yoga* of constant communion with Him, then it will surely attain Him.

कविं पुराणमनुशासितार–
मणोरणीयांसमनुस्मरेद्यः
सर्वस्य धातारमचिन्त्यरूप–
मादित्यवर्णं तमसः परस्तात् ॥६॥

Kavim puraanamanushaasitaaram
Anoraneeyaamsamanusmaredyah;
Sarvasya dhaataaramachintyaroopam
Aaadityavarnam tamasah parastaat.

प्रयाणकाले मनसाचलेन
भक्त्या युक्तो योगबलेन चैव।
भ्रुवोर्मध्ये प्राणमावेश्य सम्यक्।
स तं परं पुरुषमुपैति दिव्यम् ॥१०॥

Prayaanakaale manasaachalena
Bhakthya yukto yogabalena chaiva;
Bhruwormadhye praanamaaveshya samyak
Sa tam param purusham upaiti divyam.

9&10.   At the time of death, the one who concentrates on that Supreme Being, while holding the life-force between the eyebrows and meditating with a steadfast mind, filled with devotion on the Omniscient, the Ancient, the controller and sustainer of all, with form inconceivable, subtler than the subtlest, effulgent like the sun and beyond all darkness —such a one will surely reach that Supreme Divinity.

यदक्षरं वेदविदो वदन्ति
विशन्ति यद्यतयो वीतरागाः ।
यदिच्छन्तो ब्रह्मचर्यं चरन्ति
तत्ते पदं संग्रहेण प्रवक्ष्ये ।।११।।

Yadaksharam vedavido vadanti
    Vishanti yadyatayo veetaraagah;
Yadicchanto Brahmacharyam charanti
    Tatte padam samgrahena pravakshye.

11. Now I shall briefly tell you about That which the knowers of the *Veda* call the Imperishable, into which striving *yogis* who are free from attachment enter and desiring which they practise celibacy.

सर्वद्वाराणि संयम्य मनो हृदि निरुध्य च ।
मूर्ध्न्याधायात्मनः प्राणमास्थितो योगधारणाम् ।।१२।।

Sarvadwaaraani samyamya mano hridi nirudhya cha;
Moordhnyaadhaayaatmanah praanamaasthito yogadhaa-
ranaam.

ओमित्येकाक्षरं ब्रह्म व्याहरन्मामनुस्मरन् ।
यः प्रयाति त्यजन्देहं स याति परमां गतिम् ।।१३।।

Omityekaksharam Brahma vyaaharanmaamanusmaran;
Yah prayaati tyajan deham sa yaati paramaam gatim.

12&13. At the time of death, the *yogi* who leaves the
body and departs after having closed all the outlets
of perception and confined the mind within the
heart and the life-force between the brows and who
remains steadfast in *yogic* concentration while utter-
ing the one-syllabled *Aum* and constantly commun-
ing with Me, attains the Supreme goal.

अनन्यचेताः सततं यो मां स्मरति नित्यशः।
तस्याहं सुलभः पार्थ नित्ययुक्तस्य योगिनः ।।१४।।

Ananyachetaah satatam yo maam smarati nityashah;
Tasyaaham sulabhah paartha nityayuktasya yoginah.

14. O Arjuna (Partha)! I am easily attained by that
yogi who remembers Me constantly and thinks of
nothing else!

मामुपेत्य पुनर्जन्म दुःखालयमशाश्वतम्।
नाप्नुवन्ति महात्मानः संसिद्धिं परमां गताः ।।१५।।

Maamupetya punarjanma dukhaalayamashaashwatam;
Naapnuvanti mahaatmaanah samsiddhim paramaam
gataah.

15. Having attained their highest goal in Me, these
great souls are no longer subject to that transitory

state called rebirth which is the storehouse of pain.

आब्रह्मभुवनाल्लोकाः पुनरावर्तिनोऽर्जुन।
मामुपेत्य तु कौन्तेय पुनर्जन्म न विद्यते ।।१६।।

Aabrahmabhuvanaallokah punaraavartinorjuna;
Maamupetya tu kaunteya punarjanma na vidyate.

16. O Arjuna! All the worlds up to that of Brahma
(the creator) are bound to return (rebirth), but O
Arjuna (Kaunteya), for one who attains Me, there is
no rebirth.

सहस्रयुगपर्यन्तमहर्यद्ब्रह्मणो विदुः।
रात्रिं युगसहस्रान्तां तेऽहोरात्रविदो जनाः ।।१७।।

Sahasrayugaparyantam aharyad brahmano viduh;
Raatrim yugasahasraantaam tehoraatravido janaah.

17. They who know the day of Brahma as being a
thousand ages in duration and his night as another
thousand ages, are the knowers of night and day.

अव्यक्ताद्व्यक्तयः सर्वाः प्रभवन्त्यहरागमे।
रात्र्यागमे प्रलीयन्ते तत्रैवाव्यक्तसंज्ञके ।।१८।।

Avyaktaadvyaktayah sarvaah prabhavantyaharaagame;
Raatryaagame praleeyante tatraivaavyaktasamjnake.

18. At the dawn of the day (of Brahma), all mani-

festation comes into being out of the Unmanifest and
at the commencement of (Brahma's) night it dis-
solves back into it.

भूतग्रामः स एवायं भूत्वा भूत्वा प्रलीयते ।
रात्र्यागमेऽवशः   पार्थ   प्रभवत्यहरागमे   ॥१९॥

Bhootagraamah sa evaayam bhootwaa bhootwaa praleeyate;
Raatryagame'vashah paartha prabhavatyaharaagame.

19. These multitudes of beings O Arjuna (Partha),
are helplessly drawn into existence again and again
merging at the commencement of night into the
Unmanifest and emerging at the break of day.

परस्तस्मात्तु   भावोऽन्योऽव्यक्तो व्यक्तात्सनातनः ।
यः स सर्वेषु भूतेषु नश्यत्सु न विनश्यति ॥२०॥

Parastasmaat tu bhaavonyo avaktovyaktaatsanaatanah;
Yah sa sarveshu bhooteshu nashyatsu na vinashyati.

20. But beyond this Unmanifest (of Brahma) there is
an Unmanifest Eternal Existence which does not
perish with the perishing of all other existences.

अव्यक्तोऽक्षर इत्युक्तस्तमाहुः परमां गतिम् ।
यं प्राप्य न निवर्तन्ते तद्धाम परमं मम ॥२१॥

Avyaktokshara ityuktastamaahuh paramaam gatim;
Yam praapya na nivartante taddhaama paramam mama.

21. This imperishable Unmanifest is called the Supreme Goal. This is My supreme abode, having reached which there is no return (to the world process).

पुरुषः स परः पार्थ भक्त्या लभ्यस्त्वनन्यया ।
यस्यान्तःस्थानि भूतानि येन सर्वमिदं ततम् ।।२२।।

Purushahsaparah paartha bhaktyaa labhyastwananyayaa;
Yasyaantasthaani bhootaani yena sarvamidam tatam.

22. That Supreme Person O Arjuna (Partha), by whom all this is pervaded and within whom all beings dwell, is attainable only through exclusive devotion.

यत्र काले त्वनावृत्तिमावृत्तिं चैव योगिनः ।
प्रयाता यान्ति तं कालं वक्ष्यामि भरतर्षम ।।२३।।

Yatra kaale twanaavrittim aavrittim chaiva yoginah;
Prayaataa yaanti tam kaalam vakshyaami bharatarshabha.

23. O Arjuna (Bharatarshabha)! I shall now tell you of those times wherein departing a *yogi* does not have to return and those in which departing, he has perforce to return (to mortal existence).

ॐ

अग्निर्ज्योतिरहः शुक्लः षण्मासा उत्तरायणम्।
तत्र प्रयाता गच्छन्ति ब्रह्म ब्रह्मविदो जनाः ।।२४।।

Agnirjyotirahah suklah shanmaasaa uttaraayanam;
Tatra prayaata gacchanti Brahma brahmavido janaah.

24. The knowers of Brahman reach Brahman if they
go forth (leave the body), at the time of fire, light,
day, the bright fortnight (waxing phase of the moon),
and the six months of the northward course of the
sun (January to June).

धूमो रात्रिस्तथा कृष्णः षण्मासा दक्षिणायनम्।
तत्र चान्द्रमसं ज्योतिर्योगी प्राप्य निवर्तते ।।२५।।

Dhoomo ratristathaa krishnah shanmaasaa dakshinaa-
yanam;
Tatra chaandramasam jyotiryogee praapya nivartate.

25. The *yogi* who takes the path of smoke, night, the
dark fortnight (waning phase of moon), and the six
months of the southward course of the sun, reaches
the lunar regions and returns (to the world of birth
and death).

शुक्लकृष्णे गती ह्येते जगतः शाश्वते मते।
एकया यात्यनावृत्तिमन्ययावर्तते पुनः ।।२६।।

Shuklakrishne gatee hyete jagatah saashwate mate;
Ekayaa yaatyanaavrittim anyayaavartate punah.

26. These two paths, the bright and the dark are considered to be eternal. Proceeding by the first, one does not have to return and advancing by the second, one has to return.

नैते सृती पार्थ जानन्योगी मुह्यति कश्चन।
तस्मात्सर्वेषु कालेषु योगयुक्तो भवार्जुन ।।२७।।

Naite sritee paartha jaananyogi muhyati kashchana;
Tasmaat sarveshu kaaleshu yogayukto bhavaarjuna.

27. O Arjuna (Partha), the *yogi* who knows these two paths is never deluded. Therefore O Arjuna, be established in *yoga* at all times.

वेदेषु यज्ञेषु तपःसु चैव
दानेषु यत्पुण्यफलं प्रदिष्टम्।
अत्येति तत्सर्वमिदं विदित्वा
योगी परं स्थानमुपैति चाद्यम् ।।२८।।

Vedeshu yajneshu tapahssu chaiva
Daaneshu yatpunyaphalam pradishtam;
Atyeti tatsarvamidam viditwaa
Yogi param sthaanamupaiti chaadyam.

28. The *yogi* who knows all this transcends the fruits of all meritorious deeds like the study of the *Vedas*, the performance of sacrifices, practice of austerities and the giving of alms and attains the Supreme status, the ancient source of the entire creation.

ॐ

ॐ तत्सदिति श्रीम द्भद्गीतासूपनिषत्सु ब्रह्म—
विद्यायां योगशास्त्रे श्रीकृष्णार्जुनसंवादे अक्षर—
ब्रह्मयोगो नामाष्टमोऽध्यायः ।।८।।

Om tat sat iti srimad bhagavad gita..soopanishatsu brahmavidyaayaam yogashaastre sri krishnaarjuna-samvaade aksharabrahmayogo naama ashtamo'dhyaayah.

Aum Tat Sat:

Thus in the Upanishad of the Bhagavad Gita, the Knowledge of Supreme Brahman, the Scripture of *Yoga*, the dialogue between Sri Krishna and Arjuna, ends the eighth chapter entitled, "The *Yoga* of the Imperishable Brahman."

ॐ

Aum Sri Krishnaya Paramatmane Namah!
Aum Sri Parthasarathaye Namah!

अथ नवमोऽध्यायः

Atha Navamo'dhyaayah

CHAPTER IX

RAJA VIDYA RAJA GUHYA YOGA
The Yoga of the Sovereign Knowledge and
Sovereign Mystery

श्रीभगवानुवाच

इदं तु ते गुह्यतमं प्रवक्ष्याम्यनसूयवे ।
ज्ञानं विज्ञानसहितं यज्ज्ञात्वा मोक्ष्यसेऽशुभात् ।।१।।

Sree Bhagavaan uvaacha
Idam tu te guhyatamam pravakshyaamyanasooyave;
Jnaanam vijnaanasahitam yajjnaatwa mokshyasesubhat.

Thus spoke the Blessed Lord:

1.   I shall now impart to you that profound knowledge and its realisation by which you will be released from all evil, for your nature is free from envy.

राजविद्या राजगुह्यं पवित्रमिदमुत्तमम् ।
प्रत्यक्षावगमं धर्म्यं सुसुखं कर्तुमव्ययम् ।।२।।

Raajavidyaa raajaguhyam pavitramidamuttamam;
Pratyakshaavagamam dharmyam susukham kartuma-
vyayam.

2.   This is a most profound knowledge and mystery. It is pure, full of virtue, supreme and imperishable, yet easy to practise and verifiable through direct spiritual experience.

अश्रद्दधानाः पुरुषा धर्मस्यास्य परंतप ।
अप्राप्य मां निवर्तन्ते मृत्युसंसारवर्त्मनि ।।३।।

Ashradhadhaanaah purushaa dharmasyaasya paramtapa;
Apraapya maam nivartante mrityusamsaaravartmani.

3.   O Arjuna (Paramtapa)! Those who have no faith in this law of righteousness, fail to reach Me and continue to wander in the world of birth and death.

मया ततमिदं सर्व जगदव्यक्तमूर्तिना।
मत्स्थानि सर्वभूतानि न चाहं तेष्ववस्थितः ।।४।।

Mayaa tatamidam sarvam jagadavyaktamoortinaa;
Matsthaani sarvabhootaani na chaaham teshvavasthitah.

4.   In My unmanifest form I pervade this entire creation. All beings abide in Me but I do not dwell in them.

न च मत्स्थानि भूतानि पश्य मे योगमैश्वरम्।
भूतभृन्न च भूतस्थो ममात्मा भूतभावनः ।।५।।

Na cha matsthaani bhootaani pashya me yogamaishwaram;
Bootabhrinna cha bhootastho mamaatmaa bhootabhaa-
vanah.

5.   And in truth they do not exist in Me. Such is the mysterious power of My *yoga*. Though I am the source and support of all beings, I do not dwell in them.

यथाकाशस्थितो नित्यं वायुः सर्वत्रगो महान्।
तथा सर्वाणि भूतानि मत्स्थानीत्युपधारय ।।६।।

Yathaakaashasthito nityam vaayus sarvatrago mahaan;
Tathaa sarvaani bhootani matsthaaneetyupadhaaraya.

6. As the mighty wind, though blowing everywhere, is contained within the etheric sphere, so all
existences are contained within Me.

सर्वभूतानि कौन्तेय प्रकृतिं यान्ति मामिकाम्।
कल्पक्षये पुनस्तानि कल्पादौ विसृजाम्यहम् ।।७।।

Sarvabhootaani kaunteya prakritim yaanti maamikaam;
Kalpakshaye punastaani kalpaadau visrijaamyaham.

7. O Arjuna (Kaunteya)! All beings merge into My
material Nature (*Prakriti*) at the end of a cycle of
creation (*kalpa* or day of Brahma). At the beginning
of another cycle, I send them forth again.

प्रकृतिं स्वामवष्टभ्य विसृजामि पुनः पुनः।
भूतग्राममिमं कृत्स्नमवशं प्रकृतेर्वशात् ।।८।।

Prakritim swaamavashtabhya visrijaami punah punah;
Bhootagraamamimam kritsnamavasham prakritervashaat.

8. Utilising My own material nature (*Prakriti*), I
eject all these multitudes of existences again and
again, all helpless under the sway of Nature!

न च मां तानि कर्माणि निबध्नन्ति धनंजय।
उदासीनवदासीनमसक्तं तेषु कर्मसु ।।६।।

Na cha maam taani karmaani nibadhnanti dhananjaya;
Udaasseenavadaaseenamasaktam teshu karmasu.

9. O Arjuna (Dhananjaya)! These actions do not
bind Me for I am quite unattached to them and
totally impartial.

मयाध्यक्षेण प्रकृतिः सूयते सचराचरम्।
हेतुनानेन कौन्तेय जगद्विपरिवर्तते ।।१०।।

Mayaa'dhyakshena prakritih sooyate sacharaacharam;
Hetunaanena kaunteya jagadwiparivartate.

10. O Arjuna (Kaunteya)! I am the presiding witness
under whose gaze Nature produces all this creation
of moving and unmoving objects, thus causing this
creation to revolve.

अवजानन्ति मां मूढा मानुषीं तनुमाश्रितम्।
परं भावमजानन्तो मम भूतमहेश्वरम् ।।११।।

Avajaananti maam moodhaah maanusheem tanumaa-
shritam;
Param bhaavamajaananto mama bhootamaheshwaram.

11. Unaware of My supreme state as the Lord of all
creation, deluded persons disregard Me who am
lodged within the human frame.

मोघाशा मोघकर्माणो मोघज्ञाना विचेतसः।
राक्षसीमासुरीं चैव प्रकृतिं मोहिनी श्रिताः ।।१२।।

Moghaashaa moghakarmaano moghajnaanaa vichetasah;
Raakshaseemaasureem chaiva prakritim mohineem
shritaah.

12. Totally lacking in discrimination and deluded by
the highly egoistic natures of evil beings, their hopes,
actions and learning are all in vain.

महात्मानस्तु मां पार्थ दैवीं प्रकृतिमाश्रिताः।
भजन्त्यनन्यमनसो ज्ञात्वा भूतादिमव्ययम् ।।१३।।

Mahaatmaanastu maam paartha daiveem prakritimaa-
shritaah;
Bhajantyananyamanaso jnaatwaa bhootaadimavyayam.

13. But those great souls who have a divine nature,
O Arjuna (Partha), know Me to be the immutable
cause of all beings and worship Me with a single-
pointed and undivided love.

सततं कीर्तयन्तो मां यतन्तश्च दृढव्रताः।
नमस्यन्तश्च मां भक्त्या नित्ययुक्ता उपासते ।।१४।।

Satatam keertayanto maam yatantashcha dhridhavrataah;
Namasyantashcha maam bhaktyaa nityayuktaa upaasate.

14. They worship Me constantly, true to their spiritual vows and are ever engaged in glorifying Me and prostrating before Me with devotion.

ज्ञानयज्ञेन चाप्यन्ये यजन्तो मामुपासते।
एकत्वेन पृथक्त्वेन बहुधा विश्वतोमुखम् ।।१५।।

Jnaanayajnena chaapyanye yajanto maamupaasate;
Ekatwena prithaktwena bahudhaa vishwatomukham.

15. Some worship Me through the path of Knowledge (*jnana yajna*) as the One, as the manifold and as the Omnifaced.

अहं क्रतुरहं यज्ञः स्वधाहमहमौषधम्।
मन्त्रोऽहमहमेवाज्यमहमग्निरहं हुतम् ।।१६।।

Aham kraturaham yajnah swadhaahamahamaushadham;
Mantrohamahamevaajyam ahamagniraham hutam.

16. For I am the ritual and the sacrifice, the oblation and the medicinal herb, the sacred formula as also the clarified butter, the fire into which it is offered and the very act of offering!

पिताहमस्य जगतो माता धाता पितामहः।
वेद्यं पवित्रमोंकार ऋक्साम यजुरेव च ।।१७।।

Pitaahamasya jagato maataa dhaataa pitaamahah;
Vedyam pavritramomkaara riksaama yajureva cha.

17. Know Me to be the father and the mother, the
ordainer and the grandsire of this entire universe. I
am the sole purifier, the object of knowledge, the
sacred syllable *Aum* as well as the *Rig, Sama and
Yajur Vedas.*

गतिर्भर्ता प्रभुः साक्षी निवासः शरणं सुह्रत् ।
प्रभवः प्रलयः स्थानं निधानं बीजमव्ययम् ॥१८॥

Gatirbhartaa prabhuh saakshee nivaasah sharanam suhrit;
Prabhavah pralayah sthaanam nidhaanam beejamavyayam.

18. I am the origin and the dissolution as well as the
substratum for all things—the immutable seed and
storehouse. I alone am the goal, the support, the
Lord, the witness, the abode, the sole friend and
refuge.

तपाम्यहमहं वर्ष निगृह्णाम्युत्सृजामि च ।
अमृतं चैव मृत्युश्च सदसच्चाहमर्जुन ॥१९॥

Tapaamyahamaham varsham nigrihnaamyutsrijaami cha;
Amritam chaiva mrityushcha sadasacchaahamarjuna.

19. O Arjuna! I radiate heat. I withhold and send
forth rain. I am both death and immortality—existence and non-existence.

त्रैविद्या मां सोमपाः पूतपापा
        यज्ञैरिष्ट्वा स्वर्गतिं प्रार्थयन्ते।
ते पुण्यमासाद्य सुरेन्द्रलोक—
        मश्नन्ति दिव्यान्दिवि देवभोगान् ।।२०।।

Traividyaa maam somapaah pootapaapaa
        Yajnairishtwaa swargatim praarthayante;
Te punyamaasaadya surendraloka-
        Mashnanti divyaan divi devabhogaan.

20. The knowers of the triple *Vedas* who purify
themselves by drinking the *soma* juice, worship Me
with sacrifices and pray for access to the Heavens.
They ascend to the immaculate world of the Lord of
gods and enjoy the celestial pleasures of the gods.

ते तं भुक्त्वा स्वर्गलोकं विशालं
        क्षीणे पुण्ये मर्त्यलोकं विशन्ति।
एवं त्रयीधर्ममनुप्रपन्ना
        गतागतं कामकामा लभन्ते ।।२१।।

Te tam bhuktwaa swargalokam vishaalam
        Ksheene punye martyalokam vishanti;
Evam trayeedharmamanuprapannaa
        Gataagatam kaamakaamaa labhante.

21. After exhausting their merits by enjoying the
extensive pleasures of the heavenly worlds, they

return to the world of mortals. These seekers of worldly enjoyments who resort to motivated action as enjoined in the three *Vedas* keep going up and down (to heaven and back).

अनन्याश्चिन्तयन्तो मां ये जनाः पर्युपासते।
तेषां नित्याभियुक्तानां योगक्षेमं वहाम्यहम् ।।२२।।

Ananyaasshchintayanto maam ye janaah paryupaasate;
Teshaam nityaabhiyuktaanaam yogakshemam vahaam-
yaham.

22. However for those who think of Me alone, making Me the sole object of their worship, who are in constant communion with Me, I Myself will provide for their every need and safeguard their possessions.

येऽप्यन्यदेवता भक्ता यजन्ते श्रद्धयान्विताः।
तेऽपि मामेव कौन्तेय यजन्त्यविधिपूर्वकम् ।।२३।।

Ye pyanyadevataa bhaktaa yajante shraddhayaanvitaah;
Te'pi maameva kaunteya yajantyavidhipoorvakam.

23. O Arjuna (Kaunteya)! Even the devotees of other gods who worship them with faith, actually worship Me alone, though not with the right understanding.

अहं हि सर्वयज्ञानां भोक्ता च प्रभुरेव च।
न तु मामभिजानन्ति तत्त्वेनातश्च्यवन्ति ते ।।२४।।

Aham hi sarvayajnaanaam bhoktaa cha prabhureva cha;
Na tu maamabhijaananti tatwenaatashchyavanti te.

24. For verily I alone am the sole enjoyer and Lord of all worship, but since they fail to grasp My essential nature, they fall (they return to mortal existence).

यान्ति देवव्रता देवान्पितॄन्यान्ति पितृव्रताः।
भूतानि यान्ति भूतेज्या यान्ति मद्याजिनोऽपि माम् ।।२५।।

Yaanti devavrataa devaan pitreenyaanti pitrivrataah;
Bhootaani yaanti bhootejyaa yaanti madyaajinopi maam.

25. Those who worship the gods attain the gods, those who adore the elementals reach the spirit world, those who practise ancestor worship go to the manes and those who worship Me come to Me.

पत्रं पुष्पं फलं तोयं यो मे भक्त्या प्रयच्छति।
तदहं भक्त्युपहृतमश्नामि प्रयतात्मनः ।।२६।।

Patram pushpam phalam toyam yo me bhaktyaa
prayacchati;
Tadaham bhaktyupahritamashnaami prayataatmanah.

26. I am happy to accept the loving gift of a pure soul offered with devotion—be it a leaf, a flower, a fruit or even a few drops of water.

यत्करोषि यदश्नासि यज्जुहोषि ददासि यत्।
यत्तपस्यसि कौन्तेय तत्कुरुष्व मदर्पणम् ।।२७।।

Yatkaroshi yadashnaasi yajjuhoshi dadaasi yat;
Yattapasyasi kaunteya tatkurushva madarpanam.

27. Therefore O Arjuna (Kaunteya), whatever you
do, whatever you eat, whatever you offer in sacrifice, whatever you give in charity and whatever
austerities you might practise, offer it all unto Me.

शुभाशुमफलैरेवं मोक्ष्यसे कर्मबन्धनैः।
संन्यासयोगयुक्तात्मा विमुक्तो मामुपैष्यसि ।।२८।।

Shubhaashubhaphalairevam mokshyase karmabandhanaih;
Sannyasayogayuktaatmaa vimukto maamupaishyasi.

28. In this way you will be freed from the bondage
of the good and evil fruits of actions. Fixed in the
yoga of renunciation, you will be liberated and will
attain Me.

समोऽहं सर्वभूतेषु न मे द्वेष्योऽस्ति न प्रियः।
ये भजन्ति तु मां भक्त्या मयि ते तेषु चाप्यहम् ।।२९।।

Samoham sarvabhooteshu na me dveshyosti na priyah;
Ye bhajanti tu maam bhaktyaa mayi te teshu chaapyaham.

29. I am the same to all beings. There is none hateful
or dear to Me. However, those who worship Me

ॐ

with undeviating devotion, always abide in Me and so I am always present in them.

अपि चेत्सुदुराचारो भजते मामनन्यभाक् ।
साधुरेव स मन्तव्यः सम्यग्व्यवसितो हि सः ।।३०।।

Api chetsuduraachaaro bhajate maamananyabhaak;
Saadhureva sa mantavyah samyagvyavasito hi sah.

30. Even a most degenerate person who worships Me with exclusive devotion should be thought of as righteous, for he has made the right choice.

ॐ क्षिप्रं भवति धर्मात्मा शश्वच्छान्तिं निगच्छति ।
कौन्तेय प्रति जानीहि न मे भक्तः प्रणश्यति ।।३१।।

Kshipram bhavati dharmaatmaa shashwacchaantim
nigacchati;
Kaunteya pratijaaneehi na me bhaktah pranashyati.

31. Such a person will soon turn into a soul of righteousness and attain everlasting peace. O Arjuna (Kaunteya)! I give you My solemn pledge that My devotee will never perish.

मां हि पार्थ व्यपाश्रित्य येऽपि स्युः पापयोनयः ।
स्त्रियो वैश्यास्तथा शूद्रास्तेऽपि यान्ति परां गतिम् ।।३२।।

Maam hi paartha vyapaashritya yepi syuh paapayonayah;
Striyo vaisyaastathaa soodraaste'pi yaanti paraam gatim.

32. Those who take refuge in Me O Arjuna (Partha),
will attain the supreme goal, even though they be
outcastes, women, merchants or menials.

किं पुनर्ब्राह्मणाः पुण्या भक्ता राजर्षयस्तथा।
अनित्यमसुखं लोकमिमं प्राप्य भजस्व माम् ।।३३।।

Kim punarbraahmanaah punyaa bhaktaa raajars-
hayastatha;
Anityamasukhamlokam imam praapya bhajaswa maam.

33. What need then to speak of holy Brahmins and
royal sages? Thus having come to this joyless and
transient world, worship Me always.

मन्मना भव मद्भक्तो मद्याजी मां नमस्कुरु।
मामेवैष्यसि युक्त्वैवमात्मानं मत्परायणः ।।३४।।

Manmanaa bhava madbhakto madyaajee maam
namaskuru;
Maamevaishyasi yuktwaivamaatmaanam matparaayanah.

34. Be My devotee, fill your mind with Me, worship
Me and make obeisance to Me. Consider Me as the
Supreme goal and be in constant union with Me and
thus you will undoubtedly come to Me.

ॐ तत्सदिति श्रीमद्भगवद्गीतासूपनिषत्सु ब्रह्मविद्यायां
योगशास्त्रे श्रीकृष्णार्जुनसंवादे राजविद्याराजगुह्य—
योगो नाम नवमोऽध्यायः ।।६।।

Om tat sat iti srimad bhagavad gitaasoopanishatsu brabmavidyaayaam yogashaastre sri krishnaarjuna-samvaade raajavidyaaraajaguhyayogo naama navamo'dh-yaayah.

Aum Tat Sat:

Thus in the Upanishad of the Bhagavad Gita, the Knowledge of Supreme Brahman, the Scripture of *Yoga*, the dialogue between Sri Krishna and Arjuna, ends the ninth chapter entitled, "The *Yoga* of the Sovereign Knowledge and Sovereign Mystery."

Aum Sri Krishnaya Paramatmane Namah!
Aum Sri Parthasarathaye Namah!

अथ दशमोऽध्यायः
Atha Dashamo'dhyaayah

CHAPTER X
VIBHUTI YOGA
The Yoga of the Divine Manifestations

भूय एव माहबाहो शृणु मे परमं वचः।
यत्तेऽहं प्रीयमाणाय वक्ष्यामि हितकाम्यया ।।१।।

Sree Bhagavaan uvaacha
Bhooya eva mahaabaaho srinu me paramam vaachah;
Yathe'ham preeyamaanaaya vakshyaami hitakaamyayaa.

Thus spoke the Blessed Lord:

1.   Since you seem to delight in My words O Arjuna
(Mahabaho), listen to My supreme instruction which
I shall repeat for your benefit.

न मे विदुः सुरगणाः प्रभवं न महर्षयः।
अहमादिर्हि देवानां महर्षीणां च सर्वशः ।।२।।

Na me viduh suraganaah prabhavam na maharshayah;
Ahamaadirhi devaanaam maharsheenaam cha sarvashah.

2.   Neither the heavenly hosts nor the sages know
My origin for in truth I am the source of everything
— the gods and the sages.

यो मामजमनादिं च वेत्ति लोकमहेश्वरम्।
असंमूढः स मर्त्येषु सर्वपापैः प्रमुच्यते ।।३।।

Yo maamajamanaadim cha vetti lokamaheshwaram;
Asammoodhah sa martyeshu sarvapaapaih pramuchyate.

3. Whoever knows Me as the mighty Lord of all the worlds, without birth and without beginning, is undeluded amongst mortals and is freed from all sin.

बुद्धिर्ज्ञानमसंमोहः क्षमा सत्यं दमः शमः।
सुखं दुःखं भवोऽभावो भयं चाभयमेव च ।।४।।

Buddhirjnaanamasammohah kshamaa satyam damah shamah;
Sukham dukham bhavo'bhaavo bhayam chaabhayameva cha.

अहिंसा समता तुष्टिस्तपो दानं यशोऽयशः।
भवन्ति भावा भूतानां मत्त एव पृथग्विधाः ।।५।।

Ahimsaa samataa tushtistapo daanam yasho'yashah;
Bhavanti bhaavaa bhootaanaam matha eva prithagvidhaah.

4&5. Intelligence, wisdom, freedom from delusion, forbearance, truthfulness, restraint of the senses, tranquillity, happiness and unhappiness, creation and destruction, fear and fearlessness, non-violence, equanimity, contentment, austerity, charity, fame and infamy—these various types of qualities found in all beings proceed from Me alone.

महर्षयः सप्त पूर्वे चत्वारो मनवस्तथा।
मद्भावा मानसा जाता येषां लोक इमाः प्रजाः ।।६।।

Maharshayah sapta poorve chatwaaro manavastathaa;
Madbhaava maanasaa jaata yeshaam loka imaah prajaah.

6. The seven ancient sages as well as the four law-givers, originated from Me—born of My mind. All the other creatures of the world have sprung from them.

एतां विभूतिं योगं च मम यो वेत्ति तत्त्वतः ।
सोऽविकम्पेन योगेन युज्यते नात्र संशयः ।।७।।

Etaam vibhootim yogam cha mama yo vetti tattwatah;
So'vikampena yogena yujjate naatra samshayah.

7. One who knows My manifold manifestations and My *yogic* power in full, becomes established in an unfaltering *yoga*. There is no doubt about it.

अहं सर्वस्य प्रभवो मत्तः सर्वं प्रवर्तते ।
इति मत्वा भजन्ते मां बुधा भावसमन्विताः ।।८।।

Aham sarvasya prabhavo matha sarvam pravartate;
Iti matwaa bhajante maam budhaa bhaavasamanvitaah.

8. I am the origin of all creation. From Me everything proceeds. Knowing this, the wise, filled with devotion, worship Me.

मच्चित्ता मद्गतप्राणा बोधयन्तः परस्परम् ।
कथयन्तश्च मां नित्यं तुष्यन्ति च रमन्ति च ।।९।।

Macchithaa madgatapraanaa bodhayantah parasparam;
Kathayantashcha maam nityam tushyanti cha ramanti
cha.

9.   With their consciousness submerged in Me, their entire life dedicated to Me, they enlighten one another by constantly conversing about Me and thus remain ever content and joyful.

तेषां सततयुक्तानां भजतां प्रीतिपूर्वकम् ।
ददामि बुद्धियोंगं तं येन मामुपयान्ति ते ।।१०।।

Teshaam satatayuktaanaam bhajataam preetipoorvakam;
Dadaami buddhiyogam tam yena maamupayaanti te.

10. On them who are thus in constant communion with Me and who worship Me with intense love, I bestow the *yoga* of wisdom by which they can attain Me.

तेषामेवानुकम्पार्थमहमज्ञानजं तमः ।
नाशयाम्यात्मभावस्थो ज्ञानदीपेन भास्वता ।।११।।

Teshaamevaanukampaarthamahamajnaanajam tamah;
Naashayaamyaatmabhaavastho jnaanadeepena bhaaswataa.

11. Out of compassion for them I, who abide in their hearts, destroy their darkness born of ignorance with the blazing lamp of knowledge.

अर्जुन उवाच

परं ब्रह्म परं धाम पवित्रं परमं भवान्।
पुरुषं शाश्वतं दिव्यमादिदेवमजं विभुम् ।।१२।।

Arjuna uvaacha
Param Brahma param dhaama pavitram paramam
bhavaan;
Purusham saashvatam divyamaadidevamajam vibhum.

Thus spoke Arjuna:

12. Thou art the Supreme Brahman, the Supreme
abode, the Supreme purifier, the eternal and effulgent
Person, the original Godhead, unborn and all-pervading.

ॐ

आहुस्त्वामृषयः सर्वे देवर्षिर्नारदस्तथा।
असितो देवलो व्यासः स्वयं चैव ब्रवीषि मे ।।१३।।

Aahustwaam rishayah sarve devarshirnaaradastathaa;
Asito devalo vyaasah swayam chaiva braveeshi me.

13. All the sages like Asita, Devala, Vyasa and the
divine sage Narada have declared this of Thee. Thou
hast stated this Thyself.

सर्वमेतदृतं मन्ये यन्मां वदसि केशव।
न हि ते भगवन्व्यक्तिं विदुर्देवा न दानवाः ।।१४।।

Sarvametadritam manye yanmaam vadasi keshava;
Nahi te bhagavan vyaktim vidurdevaa na daanavaah.

14. I am convinced of the truth of all that Thou hast declared O Krishna (Keshava)! O Blessed One, neither the gods nor the Titans, know Thy manifestations.

स्वयमेवात्मनात्मानं वेत्थ त्वं पुरुषोत्तम।
भूतभावन भूतेश देवदेव जगत्पते ।।१५।।

Swayamevaatmanaatmaanam vettha twam purushottama;
Bhootabhaavana bhootesha devadeva jagatpate.

15. O Krishna (Purushottama)! Thou art the source of all beings and the Lord of all beings. Thou art God of gods and Lord of the universe. Thou alone canst know Thyself by Thyself.

वक्तुमर्हस्यशेषेण दिव्या ह्यात्मविभूतयः।
याभिर्विभूतिमिर्लोकानिमांस्त्वं व्याप्य तिष्ठसि ।।१६।।

Vaktumarhasyasheshena divyaa hyaatmavibhootayah;
Yaabhir vibhootibhirlokaanimaamstwam vyaapya tishthasi.

16. Thou alone can describe in full Thy divine glories by which Thou dost remain pervading the three worlds.

कथं विद्यामहं योगिंस्त्वां सदा परिचिन्तयन्।
केषु केषु च भावेषु चिन्त्योऽसि भगवन्मया ।।१७।।

Katham vidyaamaham yogimstwaam sadaa parichintayan;
Keshu keshu cha bhaaveshu chintyosi bhagavanmayaa.

17. O Master Yogi! How shall I come to know Thee
through constant meditation! O Blessed One! What
are Thy various aspects on which I should meditate
upon?

विस्तरेणात्मनो योगं विभूतिं च जनार्दन।
भूयः कथय तृप्तिर्हि शृण्वतो नास्ति मेऽमृतम् ।।१८।

Vistarenaatmano yogam vibootim cha janaardana;
Bhooyah kathaya triptirhi srunvato naasti me'mritam.

18. O Krishna (Janardana)! Tell me once again the
details of Thy divine manifestations and Thy *yogic*
powers, for I am never satiated with hearing Thy
ambrosial words.

श्रीभगवानुवाच
हन्त ते कथयिष्यामि दिव्या ह्यात्मविभूतयः।
प्राधान्यतः कुरुश्रेष्ठ नास्त्यन्तो विस्तरस्य मे ।।१९।।

Sree bhagavaan uvaacha
Hanta te kathayishyaami divyaa hyaatmavibhootayah;
Praadhaanyatah kurushreshta naastyanto vistarasya me.

Thus spoke the Blessed Lord:

19. O Arjuna (Kurushreshta)! My divine manifestations are endless, so I shall enumerate only some of the principal ones for you.

अहमात्मा गुडाकेश सर्वभूताशयस्थितः।
अहमादिश्च मध्यं च भूतानामन्त एव च ।।२०।।

Ahamaatmaa gudaakesha sarvabhootaashayasthitah;
Ahamaadishcha madhyam cha bhootaanaamanta eva cha.

20. Know that I am the Self abiding in the hearts of all beings O Arjuna (Gudakesha). I am their beginning, middle and end.

आदित्यानामहं विष्णुर्ज्योतिषां रविरंशुमान्।
मरीचिर्मरुतामस्मि नक्षत्राणामहं शशी ।।२१।।

Aadityaanaamaham vishnur jyotishaam raviramshumaan;
Mareechirmarutaamasmi nakshatraanaamaham shashee.

21. Among the Adityas, I am Vishnu. Among luminaries I am the radiant sun. Among the Maruts, I am Marichi. Among stellar objects I am the moon.

वेदानां सामवेदोऽस्मि देवानामस्मि वासवः।
इन्द्रियाणां मनश्चास्मि भूतानामस्मि चेतना ।।२२।।

Vedaanaam saamavedosmi devaanaam asmi vaasavah;
Indriyaanaam manashchaasmi bhootaanaamasmi chetanaa.

22. Of the Vedas, I am Sama and Indra among the gods. Of the senses I am the mind and consciousness in all living beings.

रुद्राणां शंकरश्चास्मि वित्तेशो यक्षरक्षसाम् ।
वसूनां पावकश्चास्मि मेरुः शिखरिणामहम् ।।२३।।

Rudraanaam shankarashchaasmi vittesho yaksharak-shasaam;
Vasoonaam paavakashchaasmi merus shikharinaamaham.

23. Among the Rudras, I am Shiva and among Yakshas and Rakshasas I am Kubera. Among the Vasus, I am the god of Fire and of peaks, I am Meru.

पुरोधसां च मुख्यं मां विद्धि पार्थ बृहस्पतिम् ।
सेनानीनामहं स्कन्दः सरसामस्मि सागरः ।।२४।।

Purodhasaam cha mukhyam maam viddhi paartha brihaspatim;
Senaaneenaamaham skandah sarasaamasmi saagarah.

24. Among priests O Arjuna (Partha), I am their chief—Brihaspathi. Among generals I am Skanda and of bodies of water I am the ocean.

महर्षीणां भृगुरहं गिरामस्म्येकमक्षरम् ।
यज्ञानां जपयज्ञोऽस्मि स्थावराणां हिमालयः ।।२५।।

*Maharsheenaam bhriguraham giraamasmyekamaksharam;
yajnaanaam japayajnosmi sthaavaraanaam himaalayah.*

25. Among sages I am Bhrigu. Among letters I am the monosyllable Aum. Among rituals I am *japa* and among immovables I am the Himalaya.

अश्वत्थः सर्ववृक्षाणां देवर्षीणां च नारदः ।
गन्धर्वाणां चित्ररथः सिद्धानां कपिलो मुनिः ।।२६।।

*Aswatthah sarvavrikshaanaam devarsheenaam cha naaradah;
Gandharvaanaam chitrarathah siddhaanaam kapilo munih.*

26. Among trees I am the peepul tree. Among the divine sages I am Narada. Among the celestial singers, I am Chitraratha. Among perfected beings I am the sage Kapila.

उच्चैःश्रवसमश्वानां विद्धि माममृतोद्भवम् ।
ऐरावतं गजेन्द्राणां नराणां च नराधिपम् ।।२७।।

*Ucchaishravasamashwaanaam viddhi maamamritod-bhavam;
Airaavatam gajendraanaam naraanaam cha naraadhipam.*

27. Among horses I am Ucchaisravas, born out of

the ocean of nectar. Of lordly elephants I am Airavatha. Among humans I am the sovereign.

आयुधानामहं वज्रं धेनूनामस्मि कामधुक् ।
प्रजनश्चास्मि कन्दर्पः सर्पाणामस्मि वासुकिः ॥२८॥

Aayudhaanaamaham vajram dhenoonaamasmi kaamadhuk;
Prajanashchaasmi kandarpah sarpaanaamasmi vaasukih.

28. Of weapons I am the thunderbolt and among cows I am Kamadhenu. Among progenitors, I am the god of love and among serpents I am Vasuki.

अनन्तश्चास्मि नागानां वरुणो यादसामहम् ।
पितॄणामर्यमा चास्मि यमः संयमतामहम् ॥२९॥

Anantashchaasmi naagaanaam varuno yaadasaamaham;
Pitreenaamaryamaa chaasmi yamah samyamataamaham.

29. Among water-snakes I am Ananta. Among the denizens of the waters, I am Varuna. Among the manes, I am Aaryaman and among controllers I am the God of Death.

प्रहलादश्चास्मि दैत्यानां कालः कलयतामहम् ।
मृगाणां च मृगेन्द्रोऽहं वैनतेयश्च पक्षिणाम् ॥३०॥

Prahlaadashchaasmi daityaanaam kaalah kalayataamaham;
Mrigaanaam cha mrigendro'ham vainateyashcha pakshinaam.

30. Among the Titans I am Prahlada. Among reckoners I am Time. Among beasts, I am the lion. Among birds I am the eagle.

पवनः पवतामस्मि रामः शस्त्रभृतामहम् ।
झषाणां मकरश्चास्मि स्रोतसामस्मि जा ह्नवी ।।३१।।

Pavanah pavataamasmi raamah shastrabhritaamaham;
Jhashaanaam makarashchaasmi srotasaamasmi jaahnavee.

31. Among purifiers I am the wind and among those who wield weapons I am Rama. I am the alligator among aquatic creatures and of rivers I am Ganga.

सर्गाणामादिरन्तश्च मध्यं चैवाहमर्जुन।
अध्यात्मविद्या विद्यानां वादः प्रवदतामहम् ।।३२।।

Sargaanaamaadirantashcha madhyam chaivaahamarjuna;
Adhyaatmavidyaa vidyaanaam vaadah pravadataamaham.

32. O Arjuna! Know Me to be the beginning, end and middle of all creation. I am the science of the Self among sciences and logic among debaters.

अक्षराणामकारोऽस्मि द्वन्द्वः सामासिकस्य च।
अहमेवाक्षयः कालो धाताहं विश्वतोमुखः ।।३३।।

Aksharaanaamakaaro'smi dwandwah saamaasikasya cha;
Ahamevaakshayah kaalo dhaataaham vishwatomukhah.

33. Among letters I am A and among compound words I am the copulative. Endless Time am I, as well as the sustainer of all, facing every direction.

मृत्युः सर्वहरश्चाहमुद्भवश्च भविष्यताम् ।
कीर्तिः श्रीर्वाक्च नारीणां स्मृतिर्मेधा धृतिः क्षमाः ।।३४।।

Mrityuh sarvaharashchaahamudbhavashcha bhavishyataam;
Keertih shreevaakcha naareenaam smritirmedha dritih kshamaah.

34. I am all devouring death as well as the source of all future beings. Among feminine qualities I am fame, auspiciousness, speech, memory, intelligence, steadfastness and forbearance.

बृहत्साम तथा साम्नां गायत्री छन्दसामहम् ।
मासानां मार्गशीर्षोऽहमृतूनां कुसुमाकरः ।।३५।।

Brihatsaama tathaa saamnaam gaayatree cchandasaamaham;
Maasaanaam maargasheershohamritoonaam kusumaakarah.

35. Of the *Saman* hymns, I am Brihatasaman and of metres I am the gayatri. Of months I am Margashirsha and of seasons I am the flowery spring.

ॐ

द्यूतं छलयतामस्मि तेजस्तेजस्विनामहम्।
जयोऽस्मि व्यवसायोऽस्मि सत्त्वं सत्त्ववतामहम् ।।३६।।

*Dyootam cchalayataamasmi tejastejaswinaamaham;
Jayosmi vyavasaayosmi sattvam sattvavataamaham.*

36. Among the fraudulent, I am gambling. I am the
glory of the glorious. I am victory and perseverance
and the quality of *sattva* in the noble.

वृष्णीनां वासुदेवोऽस्मि पाण्डवानां धनंजयः।
मुनीनामप्यहं व्यासः कवीनामुशना कविः ।।३७।।

*Vrishneenaam   vaasudevosmi   paandavaanaam
dhananjayah;
Muneenaamapyaham vyaasah kaveenaamushanaa kavih.*

37. Among the Vrishnis I am Vaasudeva. Among
the Pandavas I am Arjuna. Among seers I am Vyasa
and among poets I am Shukra.

दण्डो दमयतामस्मि नीतिरस्मि जिगीषताम्।
मौनं चैवास्मि गुह्यानां ज्ञानं ज्ञानवतामहम् ।।३८।।

*Dando damayataamasmi neetirasmi jigeeshataam;
Mounam chaivaasmi guhyaanaam jnaanam jnaanavataa-
maham.*

38. I am the sceptre of those who need to punish and
policy in those who seek to conquer. Among secrets
I am silence. I am the wisdom of the wise.

यच्चापि सर्वभूतानां बीजं तदहमर्जुन।
न तदस्ति विना यत्स्यान्मया भूतं चराचरम् ।।३६।।

Yachchaapi sarvabhootaanaam beejam tadahamarjuna;
Na tadasti vinaa yatsyaanmayaa bhootam charaacharam.

39. O Arjuna! Know Me to be the seed of all things.
There is nothing either moving or unmoving which
can exist without Me.

नान्तोऽस्ति मम दिव्यानां विभूतीनां परंतप।
एष तूद्देशतः प्रोक्तो विभूतेर्विस्तरो मया ।।४०।।

Naantosti mama divyaanaam vibhooteenaam paramtapa;
Esha tooddeshatah prokto vibhootervistaro mayaa.

40. There is no limit to My divine glories O Arjuna
(Paramtapa)! I have given you only a brief description of the extent of My manifestations.

यद्यद्विभूतिमत्सत्त्वं श्रीमदूर्जितमेव वा।
तत्तदेवावगच्छ त्वं मम तेजोंऽशसंभवम् ।।४१।।

Yadyadvibhootimatsattwam shreemadoorjitameva vaa;
Tattadevaavagaccha twam mama tejomshasambhavam.

41. Whenever a being is endowed with glory, brilliance or power, know it to be only a spark of My
splendour!

अथवा बहुनैतेन किं ज्ञातेन तवार्जुन।
विष्टभ्याहमिदं कृत्स्नमेकांशेन स्थितो जगत् ।।४२।।

Athavaa bahunaitena kim jnaatena tavaarjuna
Vishtabhyaahamidam kritsnamekaamshena sthito jagat.

42. But what need is there for you to know all these details O Arjuna! Take it from Me that I support this entire universe with an infinitesimal portion of Myself.

ॐ तत्सदिति श्रीमद्भगवद्गीतासूपनिषत्सु ब्रह्म—
विद्यायां योगशास्त्रे श्रीकृष्णार्जुनसंवादे विभूति—
योगो नाम दशमोऽध्यायः ।।१०।।

Om tat sat iti srimad bhagavad gitaasoopanishatsu
brahmavidyaayaam yogashaastre sri krishnaarjunasamvade
vibhootiyogo naama dashamo'dhyaayah.

Aum Tat Sat:

Thus in the Upanishad of the Bhagavad Gita, the Knowledge of Supreme Brahman, the Scripture of Yoga, the dialogue between Sri Krishna and Arjuna, ends the tenth chapter entitled, "The Yoga of the Divine Manifestations."

Aum Sri Krishnaya Paramatmane Namah!
Aum Sri Parthasarathaye Namah!

अथैकादशोऽध्यायः
Atha Ekaadasho'dhyaayah

CHAPTER XI
VISHVAROOPA DARSHANA YOGA
The Yoga of the Vision of the Cosmic Form

अर्जुन उवाच

मदनुग्रहाय परमं गुह्यमध्यात्मसंज्ञितम् ।
यत्त्वयोक्तं वचस्तेन मोहोऽयं विगतो मम ।।१।।

Arjuna uvaacha
Madanugrahaaya paramam guhyamadhyaatmasamjnitam;
Yattwayoktam vachastena mohoyam vigato mama.

Thus spoke Arjuna:

1. My delusion has been dispelled by this most
profound discourse concerning the deepest mystery
of the supreme Self, which Thou hast told me out
of love.

भवाप्ययौ हि भूतानां श्रुतौ विस्तरशो मया ।
त्वत्तः कमलपत्राक्ष माहात्म्यमपि चाव्ययम् ।।२।।

Bhavaapyayau hi bhootaanaam srutau vistarasho mayaa;
Twattah kamalapatraaksha maahaatmyamapi chaavyayam.

2. O Krishna (Kamalapatraksha)! I have heard in
detail from Thee about the origin and dissolution of
all existences as well as of Thy unchanging glory.

एवमेतद्यथात्थ त्वमात्मानं परमेश्वर ।
द्रष्टुमिच्छामि ते रूपमैश्वरं पुरुषोत्तम ।।३।।

Evametadyathaattha twamaatmaanam parameshwara;
Drashtumicchaami te roopamaishwaram purushottama.

ॐ

3. O Krishna (Parameshwara)! Thou art precisely what Thou hast declared Thyself to be but I still have a desire to see Thy divine form O Thou Supreme Person!

मन्यसे यदि तच्छक्यं मया द्रष्टुमिति प्रभो ।
योगेश्वर ततो मे त्वं दर्शयात्मानमव्ययम् ॥४॥

Manyase yadi tacchakyam mayaa drashtumiti prabho.
Yogeshwara tato me twam darshayaatmaanamavyayam.

4. O Lord! If Thou thinkest me to be capable of perceiving Thy immutable form, please reveal it to me O Thou Master Yogi!

श्रीभगवानुवाच
पश्य मे पार्थ रूपाणि शतशोऽथ सहस्रशः ।
नानाविधानि दिव्यानि नानावर्णाकृतीनि च ॥५॥

Sree Bhagavan uvaacha
Pashya me paartha roopaani shatashotha sahasrashah;
Naanaavidhaani divyaani naanaavarnaakriteeni cha.

Thus spoke the Blessed Lord:

5. Behold O Arjuna (Partha), My different celestial forms by the hundreds and thousands, in many shapes and colours.

पश्यादित्यान्वसून्रुद्रानश्विनौ मरुतस्तथा ।
बहून्यदृष्टपूर्वाणि पश्याश्चर्याणि भारत ।।६।।

Pashyaadityaan vasoonrudraan ashwinau marutastathaa;
Bahoonyadrishtapoorvaani pashyaashcharyaani Bhaarata.

6.   Behold in Me O Arjuna (Bharatha), the Adityas,
Vasus, Rudras, Asvins and Maruts and many mar-
vels which have never been seen before.

इहैकस्थं जगत्कृत्स्नं पश्याद्य सचराचरम् ।
मम देहे गुडाकेश यच्चान्यद्द्रष्टुमिच्छसि ।।७।।

Ihaikastham jagatkritsnam pashyaadya sacharaacharam;
Mama dehe gudaakesha yacchaanyad drashtumicchasi.

7.   Behold O Arjuna (Gudakesha), the whole universe of movables and immovables, unified within
My body and whatever else you might wish to see.

न तु मां शक्यसे द्रष्टुमनेनैव स्वचक्षुषा ।
दिव्यं ददामि ते चक्षुः पश्च मे योगमैश्वरम् ।।८।।

Na tu maam shakyase drashtumanenaiva swachakshushaa;
Divyam dadaami te chakshuh pashya me yogamaishwaram.

8.   But you will not be able to see this with your
human eyes so I shall grant you divine sight in order
to behold the glory of My unique *yoga*.

संजय उवाच

एवमुक्त्वा ततो राजन्महायोगेश्वरो हरिः।
दर्शयामास पार्थाय परमं रूपमैश्वरम् ।।६।।

Sanjaya uvaacha
Evamuktwaa tato raajan mahaayogeshwaro harih;
Darshayaamaasa paarthaaya paramam roopamaishwaram.

Thus spoke Sanjaya:

9. O King, having spoken thus, Krishna (Hari)—
that Supreme Lord of Yoga, revealed His divine
form to Arjuna (Partha).

अनेकवक्त्रनयनमनेकाद्भुतदर्शनम्
अनेकदिव्याभरणं दिव्यानेकोद्यतायुधम् ।१०।

Anekavaktranayanam anekaadbhutadarshanam;
Anekadivyaabharanam divyaanekodyataayudham.

दिव्यमाल्याम्बरधरं दिव्यगन्धानुलेपनम्।
सर्वाश्चर्यमयं देवमनन्तं विश्वतोमुखम् ।११।

Divyamaalyaambaradharam divagandhaanulepanam;
Sarvaashcharyamayam devamanantam vishwatomukham.

10&11. That endless, awe-inspiring form, with faces
on all sides, possessing many mouths and eyes,
presented an astounding spectacle, decked with
many divine ornaments and celestial garlands and
garments, anointed with heavenly unguents and
brandishing many uplifted weapons.

दिवि सूर्यसहस्रस्य भवेद्युगपदुत्थिता।
यदि भाः सदृशी सा स्याद्भासस्तस्य महात्मनः ।।१२।।

Divi sooryashasrasya bhavedyugapadutthitaa;
Yadi bhaah sadrishee saa syaadbhaasastasya mahaatmanah.

12. The splendour of that mighty Being was like the
brilliance of a thousand suns blazing forth simultaneously in the sky.

तत्रैकस्थं जगत्कृत्स्नं प्रविभक्तमनेकधा।
अपश्यद्देवदेवस्य शरीरे पाण्डवस्तदा ।।१३।।

Tatraikastham jagatkritsnam pravibhaktamanekadha;
Apashyaddevadevasya shareere paandavastadaa.

13. There within the body of that God of gods,
Arjuna (Pandava) saw the whole universe with its
manifold divisions unified into one whole.

ततः स विस्मयाविष्टो हृष्टरोमा धनंजयः।
प्रणम्य शिरसा देवं कृताञ्जलिरभाषत ।।१४।।

Tatah sa vismayaavishto hrishtaromaa dhananjayah;
Pranamya shirasaa devam kritaanjalirabhaashata.

14. Then the awe-struck Arjuna (Dhananjaya), with
hair standing on end addressed that divine Being
with bowed head and folded palms.

ॐ

अर्जुन उवाच
पश्यामि देवांस्तव देव देहे
    सर्वांस्तथा भूतविशेषसङ्घान्।
ब्रह्माणमीशं कमलासनस्थ—
    मृषींश्च सर्वानुरगांश्च दिव्यान् ।।१५।।

Arjuna uvaacha
Pashyaami devaamstava deva dehe
        Sarvamstathaa bhootavisheshasanghaan;
Brahmaanameesham kamalaasanastham
        Risheemshcha sarvaanuragaamshcha divyaan.

Thus spoke Arjuna:

15. O God! I behold in Thee all the gods and hosts
of different beings—Brahma seated on His lotus, all
the sages and many celestial serpents.

अनेकबाहूदरवक्त्रनेत्रं
        पश्यामि त्वां सर्वतोऽनन्तरूपम्।
नान्तं न मध्यं न पुनस्तवादिं
        पश्यामि विश्वेश्वर विश्वरूप ।।१६।।

Anekabaahoodaravaktranetram
        Pashyaami twaam sarvato'nantaroopam;
Naantam na madhyam na punastavaadim
        Pashyaami vishweshwara vishwaroopa.

16. O Lord of the Universe! O Form Universal! I see

Thy infinite form on all sides, with countless arms
and bellies, eyes and faces but I am unable to see Thy
beginning, middle or end.

किरीटिनं गदिनं चक्रिणं च
		तेजोराशिं सर्वतो दीप्तिमन्तम्।
पश्यामि त्वां दुर्निरीक्ष्यं समन्ता—
		दीप्तानलार्कद्युतिमप्रमेयम् ।।१७।।

*Kireetinam gadinam chakrinam cha
		Tejoraashim sarvato deeptimantam;
Pashyaami twaam durnireekshyam samantaat
		Deeptaanalaarkadyutimaprameyam.*

17. I see Thee with diadem, mace and discus but I
find it impossible to look at Thee for Thou art a
luminous mass of energy, blazing immeasurably on
all sides like the dazzling sun or a flaming conflagration.

त्वमक्षरं परमं वेदितव्यं
		त्वमस्य विश्वस्य परं निधानम्।
त्वमव्ययः शाश्वतधर्मगोप्ता
		सनातनस्त्वं पुरुषो मतो मे ।।१८।।

*Twamaksharam paramam veditavyam
		Twamasya vishwasya param nidhaanam;
Twamavyayah shaashwatadharmagoptaa
		Sanaatanastwam purusho mato me.*

18. Thou art the unchanging and Supreme Being, the Supreme object of knowledge. Thou art the ultimate resort of this universe. I deem Thee to be that ancient and immutable Being, the custodian of the eternal law of righteousness.

अनादिमध्यान्तमनन्तवीर्य—
　　मनन्तबाहुं शशिसूर्यनेत्रम् ।
पश्यामि त्वां दीप्तहुताशवक्त्रं
　　स्वतेजसा विश्वमिदं तपन्तम् ।।१९।।

Anaadimadhyaantamanantaveeryam
　　Anantabaahum shashisooryanetram;
Pashyaami twaam deeptahutaashavaktram
　　Swatejasaa vishwamidam tapantam.

19. I see Thee to be without beginning, middle or end, with numberless arms wielding infinite power. The sun and moon are Thy eyes. Thy mouth is a blazing conflagration, scorching the entire universe with Thy energy.

द्यावापृथिव्योरिदमन्तरं हि
　　व्याप्तं त्वयैकेन दिशश्च सर्वाः ।
दृष्ट्वादभुतं रूपमुग्रं तवेदं
　　लोकत्रयं प्रव्यथितं महात्मन् ।।२०।।

Dyaavaaprithivyoridamantaram hi
    Vyaaptam twayaikena dishashcha sarvaah;
Drishtwaadbhutam roopamugram tavedam.
    Lokatrayam pravyathitam mahaatman.

20. The space between the heavens and the earth
and all the quarters are filled by Thee alone. Beholding Thy marvellous and awe-inspiring form, O Thou
mighty Spirit, the three worlds are trembling.

अमी हि त्वां सुरसङ्घा विशन्ति
    केचिद्भीताः प्राञ्जलयो गृणन्ति।
स्वस्तीत्युक्त्वा महर्षि सिद्धसङ्घाः।
    स्तुवन्ति त्वां स्तुतिभिः पुष्कलाभिः ।।२१।।

Amee hi twaam surasanghaah vishanti
    Kechit bheetaah praanjalayo grinanti;
Swasteetyuktwaa maharshisiddhasanghaah.
    Stuvanti twaam stutibhih pushkalaabhih.

21. Hosts of deities are entering into Thee, some in
fear and others extolling Thee with folded palms.
The sages and perfected beings praise Thee with
sublime hymns and pronounce, "May all be well!"

रुद्रादित्या वसवो ये च साध्या
    विश्वेऽश्विनौ मरुतश्चोष्मपाश्च।
गन्धर्वयक्षासुरसिद्धसङ्घा
    वीक्षन्ते त्वां विस्मिताश्चैव सर्वे ।।२२।।

Rudraadityaa vasavo ye cha saddhyaa
      Vishwe'shvinau marutashchoshmapaashcha;
Gandharvayakshaasurasiddhasanghaa
      Veekshante twaam vismitaashchaiva sarve.

22. The Rudras, Adityas, Vasus, Sadhyas, Vishvadevas, Asvins, Maruts, Ushmapas, Gandharvas, Yakshas, Asuras and Siddhas are gazing at Thee in wonder.

रूपं महत्ते बहुवक्त्रनेत्रं
      महाबाहो बहुबाहूरुपादम् ।
बहूदरं बहुदंष्ट्राकरालं
      दृष्टवा लोकाः प्रव्यथितास्तथाहम् ।।२३।।

Roopam mahat te bahuvaktranetram
      Mahaabaaho bahubaahoorupaadam;
Bahoodaram bahudamshtraakaraalam
      Drishtwaa lokaah pravyathitaastathaaham.

23. O Mighty Armed! Seeing Thy immeasurable form with innumerable mouths, eyes, arms, thighs, feet, bellies and fangs, all the worlds are terrified and so am I.

नभःस्पृशं दीप्तमनेकवर्णं
      व्यात्ताननं दीप्तविशालनेत्रम् ।
दृष्टवा हि त्वां प्रव्यथितान्तरात्मा
      धृतिं न विन्दामि शमं च विष्णो ।।२४।।

Nabhasprisham deeptamanekavarnam
  Vyaattaananam deeptavishaalanetram;
Drishtwaa hi twaam pravyathitaantaraatmaa
  Dhritim na vindaami shamam cha vishno.

24. O Vishno! When I see Thy form, stretching up
to the heavens, blazing with many colours, gaping
mouths and cavernous, burning eyes, my heart
quakes with fear and I am fast losing all peace and
courage.

दंष्ट्राकरालानि च ते मुखानि
  दृष्टैव कालानलसन्निभानि।
दिशो न जाने न लभे च शर्म
  प्रसीद देवेश जगन्निवास ।।२५।।

Damshtraakaraalaani cha te mukhaani
  Drishtwaiva kaalaanalasannibhaani;
Disho na jaane na labhe cha sharma
  Praseeda devesha jagannivaasa.

25. When I behold Thy mouths filled with terrifying
fangs, resembling the conflagration at the time of
universal destruction, I seem to lose all sense of
direction and know no peace. Be merciful unto me,
O Thou God of gods! Abode of the Universe!

अमी च त्वां धृतराष्ट्रस्य पुत्राः
  सर्वे सहैवावनिपालसंघैः।

भीष्मो द्रोणः सूतपुत्रस्तथासौ
सहास्मदीयैरपि योधमुख्यैः ।।२६।।

Amee cha twaam dhritaraashtrasya putraah
Sarve sahaivaavanipaalasanghaih;
Bhismo dronah sootaputrastathaasau
Sahaasmadeeyairapi yodhamukhyaih.

वक्त्राणि ते त्वरमाणा विशन्ति
दंष्ट्राकरालानि भयानकानि।
केचिद्विलग्ना दशनान्तरेषु
संदृश्यन्ते चूर्णितैरुत्तमाङ्गैः ।।२७।।

Vaktraani te twaramaanaa vishanti
Damshtraakaraalaani bhayaanakaani;
Kechidwilagnaa dashanaantareshu
Samdrishyante choornitairuttamaangaih.

26&27. The sons of Dritarashtra along with multitudes of kings, including Bhishma, Drona, Karna
and the principal warriors on our side are seen to be
rushing headlong into Thy gruesome, tusked jaws,
fearful to behold. Some, with crushed heads are
seen to be stuck in the gaps between Thy teeth.

यथा नदीनां बहवोऽम्बुवेगाः
समुद्रमेवाभिमुखा द्रवन्ति।
तथा तवामी नरलोकावीरा
विशन्ति वक्त्रण्यभिविज्वलन्ति ।।२८।।

Yathaa nadeenaam bahavombuvegaah
Samudramevaabhimukhaah dravanti;
Tathah tavaamee naralokaveerah
Vishanti vaktraanyabhivijwalanti.

28. As the torrential waters of flooded rivers, surge towards the ocean, the heroes of this mortal world are seen to be racing into Thy blazing jaws.

यथा प्रदीप्तं ज्वलनं पतङ्गा
    विशन्ति नाशाय समृद्धवेगाः।
तथैव नाशाय विशन्ति लोका–
    स्तवापि वक्त्राणि समृद्धवेगाः ।।२९।।

Yathaa pradeeptam jwalanam patangaa
Vishanti naashaaya samriddhavegaah;
Tathaiva naashaaya vishanti lokaa-
stavaapi vaktraani samriddhavegaah.

29. As moths zoom into a flaming fire only to be destroyed, these heroes are speeding into Thy jaws only to perish.

ॐ

लेलिह्यसे ग्रसमानः समन्ता–
    ल्लोकान्समग्रान्वदनैर्ज्वलद्भिः।
तेजोभिरापूर्य जगत्समग्रं
    भासस्तवोग्राःप्रतपन्ति विष्णो ।।३०।।

Lelihyase grasamaanah samantaa
Lokaan samagraan vadanair jwaladbhih
Tejobhiraapoorya jagatsamagram
Bhaasastavograah pratapanti vishno

30. O Vishno! Thou art licking the regions all around and devouring the worlds with Thy flaming tongues. The brilliant energy of Thy fiery rays has engulfed the world and is scorching it.

आख्याहि मे को भवानुग्ररूपो
नमोऽस्तु ते देववर प्रसीद।
विज्ञातुमिच्छामि भवन्तमाद्यं
न हि प्रजानामि तव प्रवृत्तिम् ।।३१।।

Aaakhyaahi me ko bhavaanugraroopo
Namostu te devavara praseeda;
Vijnaatumicchaami bhavantamaadyam
Nahi prajaanaami tava pravrittim.

31. Salutations unto Thee O Supreme Godhead! Have mercy! Pray declare unto me who Thou art, with form so fierce. I wish to know Thee O primeval One, for I am unable to gauge Thy will.

श्रीभगवानुवाच
कालोऽस्मि लोकक्षयकृत्प्रवृद्धो
लोकान्समाहर्तुमिह प्रवृत्तः।

ऋतेऽपि त्वां न भविष्यन्ति सर्वे
        येऽवस्थिताः प्रत्यनीकेषु योधाः ।।३२।।

Sree Bhagavaan uvaacha
Kaalosmi lokakshayakrit pravriddho
        Lokaansamaahartumiha pravrittah;
Rite'pi twaam na bhavishyanti sarve
        Ye'awasthitaah pratyaneekeshu yodhah.

Thus spoke the Blessed Lord:

32. Know Me to be the Time Spirit—the destroyer
of all the worlds, now engaged in the destruction of
these nations. Even if you were not here, these
warriors arrayed on the opposite side will not live.

तस्मात्त्वमुत्तिष्ठ यशो लभस्व
        जित्वा शत्रून् भुङ्क्ष्व राज्यं समृद्धम्।
मयैवैते निहताः पूर्वमेव
        निमित्तमात्रं भव सव्यसाचिन् ।।३३।।

Tasmaat twam uttishtha yasho labhaswa
        Jitwaa shatroon bhunkshwa raajyam samriddham;
Mayaivaite nihataah poorvameva
        Nimittamaatram bhava savyasaachin.

33. Therefore arise O Arjuna (Savyasachin)! Win
fame and enjoy an affluent kingdom by conquering
your foes who have already been slain by Me.
Regard yourself as an instrument alone.

ॐ

द्रोणं च भीष्मं च जयद्रथं च
    कर्णं तथान्यानपि योधवीरान्।
मया हतांस्त्वं जहि मा व्यथिष्ठा
    युध्यस्व जेतासि रणे सपत्नान् ।।३४।।

Dronam cha bheeshmam cha jayadratham cha
    Karnam tathaanyaanapi yodhaveeraan;
Mayaa hataamstwam jahi maa vyathishthaa
    Yudhyaswa jetaasi rane sapatnaan.

34. Slay Drona, Bhishma, Jayadratha, Karna and the
other brave warriors who have already been slain by
Me. Be not frightened or distressed. Fight and you
will surely conquer your enemies in battle.

संजय उवाच

एतच्छुत्वा वचनं केशवस्य
    कृताञ्जलिर्वेपमानः किरीटी।
नमस्कृत्वा भूय एवाह कृष्णं
    सगद्गदं भीतभीतः प्रणम्य ।।३५।।

Sanjaya uvaacha
Etacchrutwaa vachanam keshavasya
    Kritaanjalirvepamaanah kireetee;
Namaskritwaa bhooya evaaha krishnam
    Sagadgadam bheetahbheetah pranamya.

Thus spoke Sanjaya:

35. Arjuna (Kireeti), who was quaking with fear, heard these words of Krishna (Keshava) and folding his palms, he bowed and prostrated before Krishna and addressed Him in a tremulous voice.

अर्जुन उवाच
स्थाने हृषीकेश तव प्रकीर्त्या
    जगत्प्रहृष्यत्यनुरज्यते च।
रक्षांसि भीतानि दिशो द्रवन्ति
    सर्वे नमस्यन्ति च सिद्धसङ्घाः ।।३६।।

Arjuna uvaacha
Sthaane hrisheekesha tava prakeertyaa
        Jagatprahrishyatyanurajyate cha;
Rakshaamsi bheetaani disho dravanti
        Sarve namasyanti cha siddhasanghaah.

36. It is only right and fitting O Krishna (Hrishikesha), that the universe exults and rejoices in chanting Thy names. The terrified demons are fleeing in all directions and the hosts of perfected souls are bowing to Thee in adoration.

कस्माच्च ते न नमेरन्महात्मन्
    गरीयसे ब्रह्मणोऽप्यादिकर्त्रे।
अनन्त देवेश जगन्निवास
    त्वमक्षरं सदसत्तत्परं यत् ।।३७।।

Kasmaat cha te na nameran mahaatman
    Gareeyase Brahmanopyaadikartre;
Ananta devesha jagannivaasa
    Twamaksharam sadasattatparam yat.

37. Indeed why should they not pay homage to Thee O Thou Great Soul! Art Thou not greater than the greatest of them—the primeval cause of even Brahma (the creator)? O Infinite Being! O God of gods! Abode of the Universe! Thou art the Imperishable! Thou art both being and non-being as also that which is beyond both.

ॐ

त्वमादिदेवः पुरुषः पुराण—
    स्त्वमस्य विश्वस्य परं निधानम्।
वेत्तासि वेद्यं च परं च धाम
    त्वया ततं विश्वमनन्तरूप ।।३८।।

Twamaadidevah purushah puraana —
    Stwamasya vishwasya param niddhaanam;
Vettaasi vedyam cha param cha dhaama
    Twayaa tatam vishwamanantaroopa.

38. Thou art the Ancient One, the primeval deity, the ultimate resort of the universe. Thou art both the Knower and that which is to be known, as well as the Supreme goal. O Thou of infinite forms! By Thee alone this entire universe is pervaded.

वायुर्यमो ग्निर्वरुणः शशाङ्कः
प्रजापतिस्त्वं प्रपितामहश्च ।
नमो नमस्तेऽस्तु सहस्रकृत्वः
पुनश्च भूयोऽपि नमो नमस्ते ।।३६।।

Vaayuryamognirvarunah shasaankah
Prajaapatistwam prapitaamahashcha;
Namo namastestu sahasrakritwah
Punashcha bhooyopi namo namaste.

नमः पुरस्तादथ पृष्टतस्ते
नमोऽस्तु ते सर्वत एव सर्व ।
अनन्तवीर्यामितविक्रमस्त्वं
सर्वं समाप्नोषि ततोऽसि सर्वः ।।४०।।

Namah purastaadatha prishtataste
Namostu te sarvata eva sarva;
Anantaveeryaamitavikramastwam
Sarvam samaapnoshi tatosi sarvah.

39&40. Thou art Vayu, Yama, Agni, Varuna, Soma
as well as the father and great grandsire of all beings.
Salutations to Thee a hundred, thousand times, from
the front, from the back and from every side. Thou
art infinite in power and immeasurable in prowess.
Thou art each and all. Thou pervadest all. Therefore
Thou art all!

सखेति मत्वा प्रसभं यदुक्तं
    हे कृष्ण हे यादव हे सखेति
अजानता महिमानं तवेदं
    मया प्रमादात्प्रणयेन वापि ।।४१।।

Sakheti matwaa prasabham yaduktam
        He krishna he yaadava he sakheti;
Ajaanataa mahimaanam tavedam
        Mayaa pramaadaatpranayena vaapi.

यच्चावहासार्थमसत्कृ तोऽसि
    विहारशच्यासनभोजनेषु
एकोऽथवाप्यच्युत तत्समक्षं
    तत्क्षामये त्वामहमप्रमेयम् ।।४२।।

Yacchaavahaasaarthamasatkritosi
        Vihaarashayaasanabhojaneshu;
Ekothavaapyachyuta tatsamaksham
        Tatkshaamaye twaamaham aprameyam.

41&42. O Krishna (Achyutha)! O Thou Immeasurable One! Pray forgive me for whatever I might have presumptuously said to Thee through carelessness or familiarity born out of love, either alone or in the company of others, in whatever way I might have slighted Thee either jocularly in play or while reposing, sitting or eating, addressing Thee familiarly as "Hey Krishna! Hey Yadava! Hey friend!" regarding Thee as a mere friend and quite unaware of Thy greatness.

पितासि लोकस्य चराचरस्य
    त्वमस्य पूज्यश्च गुरुर्गरीयान्।
न त्वत्समोऽस्त्यभ्यधिकः कुतोऽन्यो
    लोकत्रयेऽप्यप्रतिमप्रभाव   ।।४३।।

Pitaasi lokasya charaacharasya
    Twamasya poojyashcha gururgareeyaan;
Na twatsamostyabhyadhikah kuto'nyo
    Lokatraye'pyapratimaprabhaava.

43. Thou art the father of the world of animate and
inanimate things. Thou art the most venerable Guru,
most worthy of adoration. O Thou of incomparable
might! There is none equal to Thee in all the three
worlds, let alone any who can excel Thee.

तस्मात्प्रणम्य प्रणिधाय कायं
    प्रसादये त्वामहमीशमीड्यम्।
पितेव पुत्रस्य सखेव सख्युः
    प्रियः प्रियायार्हसि देव सोढुम्   ।।४४।।

Tasmatpranamya pranidhaaya kaayam
    Prasaadaye twaamahameeshameedyam;
Piteva putrasya sakheva sakhyuh
    Priyah priyaayaarhasi deva sodhum.

44. Therefore I salute Thee and prostrate myself
before Thee. O adorable Lord! Pray bear with me
and forgive me as a father would his son, a friend
his friend and a lover his beloved.

अदृष्टपूर्वं हृषितोऽस्मि दृष्टवा
    भयेन च प्रव्यथितं मनो मे।
तदेव मे दर्शय देव रूपं
    प्रसीद देवेश जगन्निवास ।।४५।।

Adrishtapoorvam hrishito'smi drishtwaa
    Bhayena cha pravyathitam mano me;
Tadeva me darshaya deva roopam
    Praseeda devesha jagannivaasa.

45. O God of gods! Abode of the Universe! Having beheld that which has never been seen before, I rejoice, yet my mind is still agitated and frightened. Be gracious unto me O Lord and reveal Thy other form to me.

किरीटिनं गदिनं चक्रहस्त–
    मिच्छामि त्वां द्रष्टुमहं तथैव।
तेनैव रूपेण चतुर्भुजेन
    सहस्रबाहो भव विश्वमूर्ते ।।४६।।

Kireetinam gadinam chakrahastam
    Icchaami twaam drashtumaham tathaiva;
Tenaiva roopena chaturbhujena
    Sahasrabaaho bhava vishwamoorte.

46. O Form Universal! I wish to see Thy original form with diadem, mace and discus. O Thousand armed One! Pray assume Thy four-armed form.

श्रीभगवानुवाच

मया प्रसन्नेन तवार्जुनेदं
	रूपं परं दर्शितमात्मयोगात् ।
तेजोमयं विश्वमनन्तमाद्यं
	यन्मे त्वदन्येन न दृष्टपूर्वम् ॥४७॥

*Sree Bhagavaan uvaacha
Mayaa prasannena tavaarjunedam
	Roopam param darshitamaatmayogaat;
Tejomayam vishwamanantamaadyam
	Yanme twadanyena na drishtapoorvam.*

Thus spoke the blessed Lord:

47. Being pleased with you O Arjuna, I have displayed by the power of My *yoga*, My cosmic form, resplendent, ancient and infinite, which has never been seen by anyone other than you.

न वेदयज्ञाध्ययनैर्न दानै—
	र्न च क्रियाभिर्न तपोभिरुग्रैः ।
एवंरूपः शक्य अहं नृलोके
	द्रष्टुं त्वदन्येन कुरुप्रवीर ॥४८॥

*Na vedayajnaadhyayanairna daanair
	Na cha kriyaabhirna tapobhirugraih;
Evam roopah shakya aham nriloke
	Drashtum twadanyena kurupraveera.*

48. O Arjuna (Kurupraveera)! In this mortal world none but you has seen this form, for it cannot be seen by the mere study of the Vedas or through sacrifices, charities, rituals or even through the practice of severe austerities.

मा ते व्यथा मा च विमूढभावो
दृष्ट्वा रूपं घोरमीदृङ्ममेदम् ।
व्यपेतभीः प्रीतमनाः पुनस्त्वं
तदेव मे रूपमिदं प्रपश्य ॥४६॥

Maa te vyathaa maa cha vimoodhabhaavo
Drishtwaa roopam ghorameedringmamedam;
Vyapetabheeh preetamanaah punastwam
Tadeva me roopamidam prapashya.

49. Be not frightened or bewildered at seeing this terrible form of Mine. Dispel your fears and with a joyous heart, behold once again My original form.

संजय उवाच
इत्यर्जुनं ·वासुदेवस्तथोक्त्वा
स्वकं रूपं दर्शयामास भूयः ।
आश्वासयामास च भीतमेनं
भूत्वा पुनः सौम्यवपुर्महात्मा ॥५०॥

Sanjaya uvaacha
Ityarjunam vaasudevastathoktwaa

Swakam roopam darshayaamaasa bhooyah;
Aaashwaasayaamaasa cha bheetamenam
    Bhootwaa punah saumyavapurmahaatmaa.

Thus spoke Sanjaya:

50. Having spoken thus, Krishna (Vaasudeva), once again assumed His original form. Having resumed His gentle appearance, that great Souled One, pacified the terrified Arjuna.

अर्जुन उवाच

दृष्ट्वेदं मानुषं रूपं तव सौम्यं जनार्दन।
इदानीमस्मि संवृत्तः सचेताः प्रकृतिं गतः ।।५१।।

Arjuna uvaacha
Drishtwedam maanusham roopam tava saumyam janaardana;
Idaaneemasmi samvrittah sachetaah prakritim gatah.

Thus spoke Arjuna:

51. Seeing Thee assume Thy gentle human physiognomy once again O Krishna (Janardana), my mind is at peace and my mental poise has been restored.

श्रीभगवानुवाच

सुदुर्दर्शमिदं रूपं दृष्टवानसि यन्मम।
देवा अप्यस्य रूपस्य नित्यं दर्शनकाङ्क्षिणः ।।५२।।

Sree Bhagavaan uvaacha
Sudurdarshamidam roopam drishtavaanasi yanmama;
Devaa apyasya roopasya nityam darshanakaankshinah.

Thus spoke the Blessed Lord:

52. Even the gods long to behold this form which you have just perceived, for it is rarely seen.

नाहं वेदैर्न तपसा न दानेन न चेज्यया।
शक्य एवंविधो द्रष्टुं दृष्टवानसि मां यथा ।।५३।।

Naaham vedairna tapasaa na daanena na chejyayaa;
Shakya evamvidho drashtum drishtavaanasi maam yathaa.

53. Not by the study of the Vedas, or by austerities or by giving charity and practising rituals can I be seen in that form which you have just seen.

भक्त्या त्वनन्यया शक्य अहमेवंविधोऽर्जुन।
ज्ञातुं द्रष्टुं च तत्त्वेन प्रवेष्टुं च परंतप ।।५४।।

Bhaktyaa twananyayaa shakyam ahamevamvidhooarjuna;
Jnaatum drashtum cha tattwena praveshtum cha paramtapa.

54. O Arjuna (Paramtapa)! Only through unswerving devotion to Me can I be seen in that form and understood in depth and entered into.

मत्कर्मकृन्मत्परमो मद्भक्तः सङ्गवर्जितः।
निर्वैरः सर्वभूतेषु यः स मामेति पाण्डव ।।५५।।

Matkarmakrinmatparamo madbhaktah sangavarjitah;
Nirvairah sarvabhooteshu yah sa maameti paandava.

55. O Arjuna (Pandava)! One who performs all
action for My sake, who accepts Me as the supreme
goal, who is devoted to Me and who is free from all
other attachments, who bears malice to none—such
a person comes to Me!

ॐ तत्सदिति श्रीमद्भगवद्गीतासूपनिषत्सु ब्रह्मविद्यायां
योगशास्त्रे श्रीकृष्णार्जुनसंवादे विश्वरूपदर्शनयोगो
नामैकादशोऽध्यायः ।।११।।

Om tat sat iti srimad bhagavad gitaasoopanishatsu
brahmavidyaayaam yogashaastre sri krishnaarjuna-
samvaade vishwaroopdarshanayogo naama ekadasho'dhy-
aayah.

Aum Tat Sat:

Thus in the Upanishad of the Bhagavad Gita, the
Knowledge of Supreme Brahman, the Scripture of
Yoga, the dialogue between Sri Krishna and Arjuna,
ends the eleventh chapter, entitled, "The Yoga of the
Vision of the Cosmic Form."

ॐ

Aum Sri Krishnaya Paramatmane Namah!
Aum Sri Parthasarathaye Namah!

अथ द्वादशोऽध्यायः
Atha Dwadasho'dhyaayah

CHAPTER XII
BHAKTHI YOGA
The Yoga of Devotion

अर्जुन उवाच

एवं सततयुक्ता ये भक्तास्त्वां पर्युपासते ।
ये चाप्यक्षरमव्यक्तं तेषां के योगवित्तमाः ।।१।।

Arjuna uvaacha
Evam satatayuktaa ye bhaktaastwaam paryupaasate;
Ye chaapyaksharamavyaktam tesham ke yogavittamaah.

Thus spoke Arjuna:

1. Which of the following has the most perfect understanding of *yoga*—those who worship You with a constant and undeviating devotion or those who worship You as the Imperishable and the Unmanifest?

श्रीभगवानुवाच

मय्यावेश्य मनो ये मां नित्ययुक्ता उपासते ।
श्रद्धया परयोपेतास्ते मे युक्ततमा मताः ।।२।।

Sree Bhagavaan uvaacha
Mayyaveshya mano ye maam nityayuktaa upaasate;
Shraddhayaa parayopetaaste me yuktatamaa mataah.

Thus spoke the Blessed Lord:

2. In My opinion, the most perfect in *yoga* are those who invest their minds in Me and worship Me with supreme faith, being in constant communion with Me.

ये त्वक्षरमनिर्देश्यमव्यक्तं पर्युपासते।
सर्वत्रगमचिन्त्यं च कूटस्थमचलं ध्रुवम् ।।३।।

Ye twaksharamanirdeshyamavyaktam paryupaasate;
Sarvatragamachintyam cha kootasthamachalam dhruvam.

संनियम्येन्द्रियग्रामं सर्वत्र समबुद्धयः।
ते प्राप्नुवन्ति मामेव सर्वभूतहिते रताः ।।४।।

Samniyamyendriyagraamam sarvatra samabuddhayah;
Te praapnuvanti maameva sarvabhootahite rataah.

3&4.   But even they who worship that which is
beyond thought—the Unmanifest, the Imperishable,
the Undefinable, the Omnipresent, the Immovable
and the ever constant, come to Me, so long as they
keep a firm control over their senses and regard
everything impartially and are ever concerned over
the welfare of all creatures.

क्लेशोऽधिकतरस्तेषामव्यक्तासक्तचेतसाम्।
अव्यक्ता हि गतिर्दुःखं देहवद्भिरवाप्यते ।।५।।

Kleshodhikatarasteshaamavyaktaasaktachetasaam;
Avyaktaa hi gatirduhkham dehavadbhiravaapyate.

5.   However the difficulties are greater for those
who have set their hearts on the Unmanifest for the
Unmanifest is hard to attain for embodied souls.

ये तु सर्वाणि कर्माणि मयि संन्यस्य मत्पराः।
अनन्येनैव योगेन मां ध्यायन्त उपासते ।।६।।

Ye tu sarvaani karmaani mayi sannyasya matparaah;
Anannyenaiva yogena maam dhyaayanta upaasate.

तेषामहं समुद्धर्ता मृत्युसंसारसागरात्।
भवामि नचिरात्पार्थ मय्यावेशितचेतसाम् ।।७।।

Teshaamaham samuddhartaa mrityusamsaarasaagaraat;
Bhavaami nachiraat paartha mayyaaveshitachetasaam.

6&7. O Arjuna (Partha)! I speedily rescue from
the ocean of transmigratory existence all those who
regard Me as their supreme goal, who offer all their
actions to Me, who invest their minds in Me and
worship Me with the undeviating *yoga* of constant
communion.

मय्येव मन आधत्स्व मयि बुद्धिं निवेशय।
निवसिष्यसि मय्येव अत ऊर्ध्वं न संशयः ।।८।।

Mayyeva mana aadhatswa mayi buddhim niveshaya;
Nivasishyasi mayyeva ata aordhwam na samshayah.

8. Therefore fix your mind on Me, let your intellect
be lodged in Me and thereafter you will undoubtedly dwell in Me.

अथ चित्तं समाधातुं न शक्नोषि मयि स्थिरम्।
अभ्यासयोगेन ततो मामिच्छाप्तुं धनंजय ।।६।।

Atha chittam samaadhaatum na shaknoshi mayi sthiram;
Abhyaasayogena tato maamicchaaptum dhanananjaya.

9.   O Arjuna (Dhananjaya)! If you are unable to fix
your mind steadily on Me, you should keep trying
and you will eventually reach Me.

अभ्यासेऽप्यसमर्थोऽसि मत्कर्मपरमो भव।
मदर्थमपि कर्माणि कुर्वन्सिद्धिमवाप्स्यसि ।।१०।।

Abhyaasepyasamarthosi matkarmaparamo bhava;
Madarthamapi karmaani kurvansiddhimavaapsyasi.

10. If you are unable to keep up this practice, then
perform all action for My sake. By doing all action
for Me alone, you will certainly attain perfection.

अथैतदप्यशक्तोऽसि कर्तुं मद्योगमाश्रितः।
सर्वकर्मफलत्यागं ततः कुरु यतात्मवान् ।।११।।

Athaitadapyashaktosi kartum madyogamaashritah;
Sarvakarmaphalatyaagam tatah kuru yataatmavaan.

11. If you are unable to do even this much, then
practise self-control, take complete refuge in Me and
abandon the fruit of all action to Me.

श्रेयो हि ज्ञानमभ्यासाज्ज्ञानाद्ध्यानं विशिष्यते।
ध्यानात्कर्मफलत्यागस्त्यागाच्छान्तिरनन्तरम् ।।१२।।

Shreyo hi jnaanamabhyaasaat jnaanaddhyaanam vishishyate;
Dhyaanaat karmaphalatyaagastyaagaatcchaantiranant-aram.

12. Knowledge (scriptural) is better than (blind) practice. Meditation is better than knowledge but renunciation of the fruits of action is even better, for peace immediately follows in the wake of renunciation.

अद्वेष्टा सर्वभूतानां मैत्रः करुण एव च।
निर्ममो निरहंकारः समदुःखसुखः क्षमी ।।१३।।

Adweshtaa sarvabhootaanaam maitrah karuna eva cha;
Nirmamo nirahankaarah samaduhkhasukah kshamee.

संतुष्टः सततं योगी यतात्मा दृढनिश्चयः।
मय्यर्पितमनोबुद्धिर्यो मद्भक्तः स मे प्रियः ।।१४।।

Santushtah satatam yogee yataatmaa dridhanishchayah;
Mayaarpitamanobuddhiryo madbhaktah sa me priyah.

13&14. My devotee is one, who has no aversion to any living creature, who is friendly and compassionate to all, who is unselfish and unegoistic, balanced in pleasure and pain, forbearing, always contented and self-controlled, who has firm convictions and has surrendered mind and intellect to Me. Such a one is dear to Me.

यस्मान्नोद्विजते लोको लोकान्नोद्विजते च यः।
हर्षामर्षभयोद्वेगैर्मुक्तो यः स च मे प्रियः ॥१५॥

Yasmaanodwijate loko lokaannodwijate cha yah;
Harshamarshabhayodwegairmukto yah sa cha me priyah.

15. One who does not trouble the world and who is not troubled by it, who is free from elation, envy, fear and anxiety, is dear to Me.

अनपेक्षः शुचिर्दक्ष उदासीनो गतव्यथः।
सर्वारम्भपरित्यागी यो मद्भक्तः स मे प्रियः ॥१६॥

Anapekshah shuchirdaksha udaaseeno gatavyathah;
Sarvaarambhaparityaagee yo madbhaktah sa me priyah.

16. My devotee is one, who is free from all worldly expectations, who is pure, skilful in action yet unconcerned and unworried (about results) and who does not initiate any undertaking. Such a one is dear to Me.

यो न हृष्यति न द्वेष्टि न शोचति न काङ्क्षति।
शुभाशुभपरित्यागी भक्तिमान्यः स मे प्रियः ॥१७॥

Yo na hrishyati na dweshti na shochati na kaankshati;
Shubhaashubhaparityaagi bhaktimaan yah sa me priyah.

17. One who does not easily get excited or disgusted, who neither desires nor grieves, who no longer discriminates between auspicious and inauspicious happenings and who is totally devoted to Me, is dear to Me.

समः शत्रौ च मित्रे च तथा मानापमानयोः।
शीतोष्णसुखदुःखेषु समः सङ्गविवर्जितः ।।१८।।

Samah shatrau cha mitre cha tathaa maanaapamaanayoh;
Sheetoshnasukhaduhkheshu samah sangavivarjitah.

तुल्यनिन्दास्तुतिर्मौनी संतुष्टो येन केनचित्।
अनिकेतः स्थिरमतिर्भक्तिमान्मे प्रियो नरः ।।१९।।

Tulyanindaastutirmaunee santushto yena kenachit;
Aniketah sthiramatir bhaktimaanme priyo narah.

18&19. That person, who is full of devotion, who is impartial to friend and foe, indifferent to honour and dishonour, free from attachment and unaffected by heat and cold, pleasure and pain, censure and praise, who is quiet, content and satisfied with whatever comes unsought, who has no fixed abode and whose mind is steady, is dear to Me.

ॐ

ये तु धर्म्यामृतमिदं यथोक्तं पर्युपासते।
श्रद्दधाना मत्परमा भक्तास्तेऽतीव मे प्रियाः ।।२०।।

Ye tu dharmyaamritamidam yathoktam paryupaasate;
Shraddadhaanaah matparamaa bhaktaasteteeva me priyaah.

20. My devotees, who consider Me as their supreme goal, who are full of faith and who follow this immortal doctrine as set forth above, are extremely dear to Me.

ॐ तत्सदिति श्रीमद्भगवद्गीतासूपनिषत्सु ब्रह्म—
विद्यायां योगशास्त्रे श्रीकृष्णार्जुनसंवादे भक्ति—
योगो नाम द्वादशोऽध्यायः ।।१२।।

Om tat sat iti srimad bhagavad gitaasoopanishatsu
brahmavidyaayaam yogashaastre sri krishnaarjunas-
amvaade bhaktiyogo naama dwaadasho'dhyaayah.

Aum Tat Sat:

Thus in the Upanishad of the Bhagavad Gita, the Knowledge of Supreme Brahman, the Scripture of *Yoga*, the dialogue between Sri Krishna and Arjuna, ends the twelfth chapter entitled, "The *Yoga* of Devotion."

Aum Sri Krishnaya Paramatmane Namah!
Aum Sri Parthasarathaye Namah!

अथ त्रयोदशोऽध्यायः
Atha Trayodasho'dhyayah.

CHAPTER XIII
KSHETRA KSHETRAJNA VIBHAGA YOGA
The Yoga of the Distinction between the Field
and the Knower of the Field

अर्जुन उवाच

प्रकृतिं पुरुषं चैव क्षेत्रं क्षेत्रज्ञमेव च।
एतद्वेदितुमिच्छामि ज्ञानं ज्ञेयं च केशव ॥

Arjuna uvaacha
Prakritim purusham chaiva kshetram khsetrajnameva
cha;
Etadveditumicchaami jnaanam jneyam cha kesava.

Thus spoke Arjuna:

O Krishna (Keshava)! I would like to know more about Nature and Spirit, the Field and the Knower of the Field, Knowledge and the object of Knowledge.

श्रीभगवानुवाच

इदं शरीरं कौन्तेय क्षेत्रमित्यभिधीयते।
एतद्यो वेत्ति तं प्राहुः क्षेत्रज्ञ इति तद्विदः ॥१॥

Sree Bhagavaan uvaacha
Idam shareeram kaunteya kshetramityabhidheeyate;
Etadyo vetti tam praahuh kshetrana iti tadvidah.

Thus spoke the Blessed Lord:

1.   This body O Arjuna (Kaunteya), is known as the Field. The sages call the cogniser of this Field as the Knower.

ॐ

क्षेत्रज्ञं चापि मां विद्धि सर्वक्षेत्रेषु भारत।
क्षेत्रक्षेत्रज्ञयोर्ज्ञानं यत्तज्ज्ञानं मतं मम ।।२।।

Kshetrajnam chaapi maam viddhi sarvakshetreshu
bhaarata;
Kshetrakshetrajnayorjnaanam yattatjnaanam matam
mama.

2. O Arjuna (Bharatha)! Know Me to be the sole
cogniser of all Fields. I consider true knowledge to
be the knowledge of the Field and its Knower.

तत्क्षेत्रं यच्च यादृक्च यद्विकारि यतश्च यत्।
स च यो यत्प्रभावश्च तत्समासेन मे शृणु ।।३।।

Tat kshetram yatcha yaadrik cha yadvikaari yatashcha
yat;
Sa cha yo yatprabhaavashcha tatsamaasena me shrinu.

3.   Now hear from Me in brief about the character,
nature, source and modifications of the Field and
also about Him—the Knower of the Field—who and
what His powers are.

ऋषिभिर्बहुधा गीतं छन्दोभिर्विविधैः पृथक्।
ब्रह्मसूत्रपदैश्चैव हेतुमद्भिर्विनिश्चितैः ।।४।।

Rishibhirbahudhaa geetam cchandobhirvividhaih prithak;
Brahmasootrapadaishchaiva hetumadbhirvinishchitaih.

4.   These truths have been hymned by the sages in various inspired verses in the Vedas and also delineated rationally and convincingly in passages concerning Brahman.

महाभूतान्यहंकारो बुद्धिरव्यक्तमेव च।
इन्द्रियाणि दशैकं च पञ्च चेन्द्रियगोचराः ।।५।।

Mahaabhootaanyahamkaaro buddhiravyaktameva cha;
Indriyaani dasaikam cha pancha chendriyagocharaah.

इच्छा द्वेषः सुखं दुःखं संघातश्चेतना धृतिः।
एतत्क्षेत्रं समासेन सविकारमुदाहृतम् ।।६।।

Ichcha dweshah sukham duhkham sanghaatashchetanaa dhritih;
Etat kshetram samaasena savikaaramudaahritam.

5&6.   The five elementary states of primordial matter, the ten senses and their five objective counterparts, the mind, intelligence, ego, body, firmness and the dualities of attraction and repulsion, pleasure and pain, constitute the Field and its modifications.

अमानित्वमदम्भित्वमहिंसा क्षान्तिरार्जवम्।
आचार्योपासनं शौचं स्थैर्यमात्मविनिग्रहः ।।७।।

Amaanitwam adambhitwam ahimsaa kshaantiraarjavam;
Aacharyopaasanam shaucham sthairyamaatmavinigrahah.

7. Absence of pride and arrogance, non-violence, forbearance, straightforwardness, devotion to the preceptor, purity, steadfastness and self control...

इन्द्रियार्थेषु वैराग्यमनहंकार एव च।
जन्ममृत्युजराव्याधिदुःखदोषानुदर्शनम् ।।८।।

Indriyaartheshu vairaagyamanahamkaara eva cha;
Janmamrityujaraavyaadhiduhkhadoshaanudarshanam.

8. Dispassion towards the objects of the senses, total absence of ego, constant reflection upon the evils of birth, death, old age, disease and sorrow...

ॐ

असक्तिरनभिष्वङ्गः पुत्रदारगृहादिषु।
नित्यं च समचित्तत्वमिष्टानिष्टोपपत्तिषु ।।९।।

Asaktiranabhishwangah putradaaragrihaadishu;
Nityam cha samachittatwam ishtaanishtopapatishu.

9. Non-attachment and non-identification with things like son, wife and home, equanimity of mind in the face of desirable and undesirable happenings...

मयि चानन्ययोगेन भक्तिरव्यभिचारिणी।
विविक्तदेशसेवित्वमरतिर्जनसंसदि ।।१०।।

Mayi chaananyayogena bhaktiravyabhichaarinee;
Viviktadeshasevitwamaratirjanasamsadi.

10. Exclusive devotion to Me through a constant communion, desire to resort to solitary places and a distaste for crowds...

अध्यात्मज्ञाननित्यत्वं तत्त्वज्ञानार्थदर्शनम् ।
एतज्ज्ञानमिति प्रोक्तमज्ञानं यदतोऽन्यथा ।।११।।

Adhyaatmajnaananityatwam tatwajnaanaarthadarshanam;
Etatjnaanamiti proktam ajnaanam yadatonyathaa.

11. Constant application of the mind to spiritual matters and an instinctive perception of the Truth. All these together can be called knowledge. Everything else is ignorance.

ज्ञेयं यत्तत्प्रवक्ष्यामि यज्ज्ञात्वामृतमश्नुते ।
अनादिमत्परं ब्रह्म न सत्तन्नासदुच्यते ।।१२।।

Jneyam yattatpravakshyaami yajjnaatwaamritamashnute;
Anaadimatparam brahma na sattannasaduchyate.

12. Now I shall give you that knowledge by which a person becomes immortal—the knowledge of the eternal, Supreme Brahman which is said to be neither existent nor non-existent.

सर्वतःपाणिपादं तत्सर्वतोऽक्षिशिरोमुखम् ।
सर्वतःश्रुतिमल्लोके सर्वमावृत्य तिष्ठति ।।१३।।

Sarvatah paanipaadam tat sarvatokshishiromukham;
Sarvatah shrutimalloke sarvamaavritya tishthati.

13. This Being pervades everything, with hands and
feet everywhere, with eyes, heads, mouths and ears
on all sides.

सर्वेन्द्रियगुणाभासं सर्वेन्द्रियविवर्जितम्।
असक्तं सर्वभृच्चैव निर्गुणं गुणभोक्तृ च ।।१४।।

Sarvendriyagunaabhaasam sarvendriyavivarjitam;
Asaktam sarvabhricchaiva nirgunam gunabhoktri cha.

14. Even though this Being does not possess any of
the senses, yet it is illumined by the function of the
senses. It is all-supporting yet unattached, enjoyer
of the modes of Nature even though devoid of them.

बहिरन्तश्च भूतानामचरं चरमेव च।
सूक्ष्मत्वात्तदविज्ञेयं दूरस्थं चान्तिके च तत् ।।१५।।

Bahirantashcha bhootaanaamacharam charameva cha;
Sookshmatwaat tadavijneyam doorastham chaantike cha
tat.

15. This Being constitutes all that is within us as well
as all that is experienced as being outside us. It is
both   animate and inanimate, far and near, yet
incomprehensible because of its subtlety.

अविभक्तं च भूतेषु विभक्तमिव च स्थितम् ।
भूतभर्तृ च तज्ज्ञेयं ग्रसिष्णु प्रभविष्णु च ।।१६।।

Avibhaktam cha bhooteshu vibhaktamiva cha sthitam;
Bhootabhartri cha tadjneyam grasishnu prabhavishnu
cha.

16. Though one and indivisible, It exists as if divided into many. Know It to be the sustainer, destroyer and generator.

ज्योतिषामपि तज्ज्योतिस्तमसः परमुच्यते ।
ज्ञानं ज्ञेयं ज्ञानगम्यं हृदि सर्वस्य विष्ठितम् ।।१७।।

Jyotishaamapi tajjyotistamasah paramuchyate;
Jnaanam jneyam jnaanagamyam hridi sarvasya vishthitam;

17. It is the light of all lights, totally beyond the darkness (of ignorance). It is knowledge, the object of knowledge as well as the goal of knowledge. It is seated in the hearts of all.

इति क्षेत्रं तथा ज्ञानं ज्ञेयं चोक्तं समासतः ।
मद्भक्त एतद्विज्ञाय मद्भावायोपपद्यते ।।१८।।

Iti kshetram tathaa jnaanam jneyam choktam samaasatah;
Madbhakta etadvijnaaya madbhaavaayopapadyate.

18. Thus have I briefly explained about the Field, about knowledge and the object of knowledge. My

devotee who understands this will attain to My
Being.

प्रकृतिं पुरुषं चैव विद्ध्यनादी उभावपि।
विकारांश्च गुणांश्चैव विद्धि प्रकृतिसंभवान् ।।१९।।

Prakritim purusham chaiva vidhyanaadee ubhaavapi;
Vikaaraamshcha gunaamshchaiva viddhi prakritisamb-
havaan.

19. Understand that both material Nature and Spirit
are without beginning. But the modes of Nature and
their modifications are born out of Nature.

कार्यकरणकर्तृत्वे हेतुः प्रकृतिरुच्यते।
पुरुषः सुखदुःखानां भोक्तृत्वे हेतुरुच्यते ।।२०।।

Kaaryakaranakartritwe hetuh prakritiruchyate;
Purushah sukhaduhkhaanaam bhoktritwe heturuchyate.

20. The ideas of cause and effect and doership are
all caused by Nature while the Spirit is the cause of
the experience of pleasure and pain.

पुरुषः प्रकृतिस्थो हि भुङ्क्ते प्रकृतिजान्गुणान्।
कारणं गुणसङ्गोऽस्य सदसद्योनिजन्मसु ।।२१।।

Purushah prakritistho hi bhunkte prakritijaan gunaan;
Kaaranam gunasangosya sadasadyonijanmasu.

21. The Spirit seated in Nature enjoys Her qualities and this identification with the modes is the cause of birth in either good or evil wombs.

उपद्रष्टानुमन्ता च भर्ता भोक्ता महेश्वरः।
परमात्मेति चाप्युक्तो देहेऽस्मिन्पुरुषः परः ।।२२।।

Upadrashtaanumantaa cha bhartaa bhoktaa maheshwarah;
Paramaatmeti chaapyukto dehesmin purushah parah.

22. The Supreme Spirit within this body is called the witness, the consenter, the upholder, the enjoyer and the Almighty Lord.

य एवं वेत्ति पुरुषं प्रकृतिं च गुणैः सह।
सर्वथा वर्तमानोऽपि न स भूयोऽभिजायते ।।२३।।

Ya evam vetti purusham prakritim cha gunaih saha;
Sarvathaa vartamaanopi na sa bhooyo'bhi jaayate.

23. The one who knows the truth about this Spirit, about Nature and her modes, is not born again, whatever be the way of life followed.

ध्यानेनात्मनि पश्यन्ति केचिदात्मानमात्मना।
अन्ये सांख्येन योगेन कर्मयोगेन चापरे ।।२४।।

Dhyaanenaatmani pashyanti kechidaatmaanamaatmanaa;
Anye saankhyena yogena karmayogena chaapare.

24. This knowledge can be gained through deep meditation in which the Self is perceived in the Self and by the Self, or it can come through the practice of the *Yoga* of Wisdom or the *Yoga* of Action.

अन्ये त्वेवमजानन्तः श्रृत्वान्येभ्य उपासते।
तेऽपि चातितरन्त्येव मृत्युं श्रुतिपरायणाः ।।२५।।

Anye twevamajaanantah shrutwaanyebhya upaasate;
Te'pi chaatitarantyeva mrityum shrutiparaayanaah.

25. Those who do not know these paths of *yoga*, may follow methods of worship as advocated by others. With faith and persistence they too will go beyond mortality.

यावत्संजायते किंचित्सत्त्वं स्थावरजङ्गमम्।
क्षेत्रक्षेत्रज्ञसंयोगात्तद्विद्धि भरतर्षभ ।।२६।।

Yaavat samjaayate kinchit sattwam sthavarajangamam;
Kshetrakshetrajnasamyogaat tadviddhi bharatarshabha.

26. Understand this O Arjuna (Bharatharshabha), that all beings both moving and unmoving are born of the union of the Field with the Knower of the Field (Spirit and Nature).

समं सर्वेषु भूतेषु तिष्ठन्तं परमेश्वरम्।
विनश्यत्स्वविनश्यन्तं यः पश्यति स पश्यति ।।२७।।

Samam sarveshu bhooteshu tishthantam parameshwaram;
Vinashyatswavinashyantam yah pashyati sa pashyati.

27. The true seer is one who sees the Supreme Lord
seated equally in all beings—the Imperishable within
the perishable.

समं पश्यन्हि सर्वत्र समवस्थितमीश्वरम् ।
न हिनस्त्यात्मनात्मानं ततो याति परां गतिम् ।।२८।।

Samam pashyanhi sarvatra samavasthitameeshvaram;
Na hinastyaatmanaatmaanam tato yaati paraam gatim.

28. Such a one who sees the Lord seated equally in
all things does not destroy the Self by the self and
therefore attains the supreme goal.

प्रकृत्यैव च कर्माणि क्रियमाणानि सर्वशः ।
यः पश्यति तथात्मानमकर्तारं स पश्यति ।।२९।।

Prakrityaiva cha karmaani kriyamaanaani sarvashah;
Yah pashyati tathaatmaanamakartaaram sa pashyati.

29. The true seer is one who sees all action as being
done by material Nature and the Spirit as the
inactive witness.

यदा भूतपृथग्भावमेकस्थमनुपश्यति ।
तत एव च विस्तारं ब्रह्म संपद्यते तदा ।।३०।।

Yadaa bhootaprithagbhaavamekasthamanupashyati;
Tata eva cha vistaaram brahma sampadyate tadaa.

30. When the seer perceives all these diversified existences as proceeding from and expanding from, the One alone, he attains Brahman.

अनादित्वान्निर्गुणत्वात्परमात्मायमव्ययः।
शरीरस्थोऽपि कौन्तेय न करोति न लिप्यते ।।३१।।

Anaaditwaat nirgunatwaat paramaatmaayamavyayah;
Shareerasthopi kaunteya na karoti na lipyate.

31. O Arjuna (Kaunteya)! The Supreme imperishable Self, though dwelling within the body, neither acts nor is tainted by action for It is without origin and without attributes.

यथा सर्वगतं सौक्ष्म्यादाकाशं नोपलिप्यते।
सर्वत्रावस्थितो देहे तथात्मा नोपलिप्यते ।।३२।।

Yathaa sarvagatam saukshmyaadaakaasham nopalipyate;
Sarvatraavasthito dehe tathaatmaa nopalipyate.

32. As the all-pervading ether is not tainted due to its subtlety, the Spirit, though pervading the body, is not tainted.

यथा प्रकाशयत्येकः कृत्स्नं लोकमिमं रविः।
क्षेत्रं क्षेत्री तथा कृत्स्नं प्रकाशयति भारत ।।३३।।

Yathaa prakashayatyekah kritsnam lokamimam ravih;
Kshetram kshetree tathaa kritsnam prakaashayati bhaarata.

33. O Arjuna (Bharata)! As the same sun illumines the whole world, the one Lord of all the Fields illumines the entire Field.

क्षेत्रक्षेत्रज्ञयोरेवमन्तरं   ज्ञानचक्षुषा ।
भूतप्रकृतिमोक्षं च ये विदुर्यान्ति ते परम् ।।३४।।

Kshetrakshetrajnayrevamantaram jnaanachakshushaa;
Bhootaprakritimoksham cha ye vidur yaanti te param.

34. Those who are able to perceive with the eye of wisdom the distinction between the Field and the Knower of the Field as well as the method by which people can be liberated from the bondage of Nature—they will attain the Supreme.

ॐ तत्सदिति श्रीमद्भवद्गीतासूपनिषत्सु ब्रह्मविद्यायां योगशास्त्रे श्रीकृष्णार्जुनसंवादे क्षेत्रक्षेत्रज्ञविभाग—
योगो नाम त्रयोदशो ध्यायः ।।१३।।

Om tat sat iti srimad bhagavad gitaasoopanishatsu
brahmavidyaayaam yogashaastre sri krishnaarjunasam-
vaade kshetrakshetrajnavibhaagayogo naama trayodas-
ho'dhya-ayah.

Aum Tat Sat:

Thus in the Upanishad of the Bhagavad Gita, the

Knowledge of Supreme Brahman, the Scripture of *Yoga*, the dialogue between Sri Krishna and Arjuna, ends the thirteenth chapter entitled, "The *Yoga* of the Distinction between the Field and the Knower of the Field."

Aum Sri Krishnaya Paramatmane Namah!
Aum Sri Parthasarathaye Namah!

अथ   चतुर्दशोऽध्यायः
Atha Chathurdasho'dhyayah

CHAPTER XIV

GUNATRAYA VIBHAGA YOGA
The Yoga of the Distinction
between the three Gunas

श्रीभगवानुवाच

परं भूयः प्रवक्ष्यामि ज्ञानानां ज्ञानमुत्तमम् ।
यज्ज्ञात्वा मुनयः सर्वे परां सिद्धिमितो गताः ।।१।।

Sree Bhagavaan uvaacha
Param bhooyah pravakshyaami jnaanaanaam jnaana-
muttamam;
Yajjnaatwaa munayah sarve paraam siddhimito gataah.

Thus spoke the Blessed Lord:

1. Once again I shall impart to you that Supreme knowledge, which is superior to all other types of knowledge by knowing which all the sages have been liberated from this state and have attained the highest perfection.

इदं ज्ञानमुपाश्रित्य मम साधर्म्यमागताः ।
सर्गेऽपि नोपजायन्ते प्रलये न व्यथन्ति च ।।२।।

Idam jnaanamupaashritya mama saadharmyamaagataah;
Sargepi nopajaayante pralaye na vyathanti cha.

2. Those who have acquired this wisdom and have entered into My being are not born again at the time of creation nor are they disturbed at the time of universal dissolution.

मम योनिर्महद्ब्रह्म तस्मिनगर्भं दधाम्यहम् ।
संभवः सर्वभूतानां ततो भवति भारत ।।३।।

Mama yonirmahadbrahma tasmin garbham dadhaam-
yaham;
Sambhavah sarvabhootaanaam tato bhavati bhaarata.

3. Primordial matter is My womb into which I cast
the seed O Arjuna (Bharatha), and from this comes
the birth of all beings.

सर्वयोनिषु कौन्तेय मूर्तयः संभवन्ति याः।
तासां ब्रह्म महद्योनिरहं बीजप्रदः पिता ।।४।।

Sarvayonishu kaunteya moortayah sambhavanti yaah;
Taasaam Brahma mahadyoniraham beejapradah pitaa.

4. Whatever be the forms that emerge from different wombs O Arjuna (Kaunteya), understand that I
am the seed-giving father and primordial matter, the
procreating womb.

सत्त्वं रजस्तम इति गुणाः प्रकृतिसंभवाः।
निबध्नन्ति महाबाहो देहे देहिनमव्ययम् ।।५।।

Sattwam rajastama iti gunaah prakritisambhavaah;
Nibadhnanti mahaabaaho dehe dehinamavyayam.

5. *Sattva, rajas* and *tamas* are the three modes of
Nature O Arjuna (Mahabaho), which bind the imperishable Spirit to the (perishable) body.

तत्र सत्त्वं निर्मलत्वात्प्रकाशकमनामयम् ।
सुखसङ्गेन बध्नाति ज्ञानसङ्गेन चानघ ।।६।।

Tattra sattwam nirmalatwaat prakaashakamanaamayam;
Sukhasangena badhnaati jnaanasangena chaanagha.

6.   Of these *sattva* being flawless, stainless and filled
with light, binds O Arjuna (Anagha), by creating
attachment to happiness and knowledge.

रजो रागात्मकं विद्धि तृष्णासङ्गसमुद्भ वम् ।
तन्निबध्नाति कौन्तेय कर्मसङ्गेन देहिनम् ।।७।।

Rajo raagaatmakam viddhi trishnaasangasamudbhavam;
Tannibadhnaati kaunteya karmasangena dehinam.

7.   The nature of *rajas* is passion, arising from desire
and attachment. It binds the embodied soul O Arjuna
(Kaunteya), through attachment to action.

तमस्त्वज्ञानजं विद्धि मोहनं सर्वदेहिनाम् ।
प्रमादालस्यनिद्राभिस्तन्निबध्नाति भारत ।।८।।

Tamastwajnaanajam viddhi mohanam sarvadehinaam;
Pramaadaalasyanidrabhistannibadhnaati bhaarata.

8. *Tamas* is the child of ignorance O Arjuna (Bharatha).
It deludes the embodied being and binds it through
attachment to negligence, indolence and sleep.

ॐ

सत्त्वं सुखे संजयति रजः कर्मणि भारत।
ज्ञानमावृत्य तु तमः प्रमादे संजयत्युत ।।६।।

Sattvam sukhe samjayati rajah karmani bhaarata;
Jnaanamaavritya tu tamah pramaade samjayatyuta.

9.   *Sattva* makes one attached to happiness and *rajas*
to action O Arjuna (Bharatha), while *tamas* veils
knowledge and binds us to negligence.

रजस्तमश्चाभिभूय सत्त्वं भवति भारत।
रजः सत्त्वं तमश्चैव तमः सत्त्वं रजस्तथा ।।१०।।

Rajastamashchaabhibhooya sattwam bhavati bhaarata;
Rajas sattwam tamashchaiva tamas sattwam rajastathaa.

10. O Arjuna (Bharatha)! Sometimes *sattva* predomi-
nates, having overpowered *rajas* and *tamas*. At times
rajas supersedes over *sattva* and *tamas* and sometimes *tamas* takes the upper hand over *sattva* and
rajas.

सर्वद्वारेषु देहेऽस्मिन्प्रकाश उपजायते।
ज्ञानं यदा तदा विद्याद्विवृद्धं सत्त्वमित्युत ।।११।।

Sarvadwaareshu dehe'smin prakaasha upajaayate;
Jnaanam yadaa tadaa vidyaadvivriddham sattvamityuta.

11. When all the gates of the body (the five senses)
are flooded with the light of understanding, we can
know that *sattva* is predominating.

लोभः प्रवृत्तिरारम्भः कर्मणामशमः स्पृहा।
रजस्येतानि जायन्ते विवृद्धे भरतर्षभ ।।१२।।

*Lobhah pravrittiraarambhah karmaanamashamah sprihaa;
Rajasyetaani jaayante vivriddhe bhaaratarshabha.*

12. When greed activity, restlessness, desire and the constant launching of new projects are seen O Arjuna (Bharatarshabha), know that *rajas* is predominant.

अप्रकाशो प्रवृत्तिश्च प्रमादो मोह एव च।
तमस्येतानि जायन्ते विवृद्धे कुरुनन्दन ।।१३।।

*Aprakaashopravrittishcha pramaado moha eva cha;
Tamasyetaani jaayante vivriddhe kurunandana.*

13. When nescience, inertia, negligence and delusion is seen O Arjuna (Kurunandana), know that *tamas* is predominating.

यदा सत्त्वे प्रवृद्धे तु प्रलयं याति देहभृत्।
तदोत्तमविदां लोकानमलान्प्रतिपद्यते ।।१४।।

*Yadaa sattwe pravriddhe tu pralayam yaati dehabhrit;
Tadottamavidaam lokaanamalaan pratipadyate.*

14. If death occurs when *sattva* is uppermost, the embodied soul attains the spotless regions of the knowers of the highest principles.

ॐ

रजसि प्रलयं गत्वा कर्मसङ्गिषु जायते।
तथा प्रलीनस्तमसि मूढयोनिषु जायते ।।१५।।

Rajasi pralayam gatwaa karmasangishujaayate;
Tathaa praleenastamasi moodhayonishu jaayate.

15. One who dies when *rajas* is predominant, will be
born amongst those attached to action and one who
dies when *tamas* is in ascendance, will be born in the
wombs of the dull witted.

कर्मणः सुकृतस्याहुः सात्त्विकं निर्मलं फलम्।
रजसस्तु फलं दुःखमज्ञानं तमसः फलम् ।।१६।।

Karmanah sukritasyaahuh saattvikam nirmalam phalam;
Rajasastu phalam duhkhamajnaanam tamasah phalam.

16. It is said that the fruit of good action is pure and
sattvic, pain is the consequence of *rajasic* action,
while ignorance is the result of *tamasic* action.

सत्त्वात्संजायते ज्ञानं रजसो लोभ एव च।
प्रमादमोहौ तमसो भवतो ज्ञानमेव च ।।१७।।

Sattwaatsamjaayate jnaanam rajaso lobha eva cha;
Pramaadamohau tamaso bhavato'jnaanameva cha.

17. Wisdom is born out of *sattva*, greed from *rajas*
and delusion, negligence and ignorance from *tamas*.

ऊर्ध्वं गच्छन्ति सत्त्वस्था मध्ये तिष्ठन्ति राजसाः।
जघन्यगुणवृत्तिस्था अधो गच्छन्ति तामसाः ॥१८॥

Oordhwam gacchanti sattwasthaa madhye tishthanti raajasaah;
Jaganyagunavrittisthsa adho gachchanti taamasaah.

18. Those who are established in *sattva* ascend, those in *rajas* remain in the middle and those who are steeped in the lowest mode of *tamas*, degenerate.

नान्यं गुणेभ्यः कर्तारं यदा द्रष्टानुपश्यति।
गुणेभ्यश्च परं वेत्ति मद्भावं सोऽधिगच्छति ॥१९॥

Naanyam gunebhyah kartaaram yadaa drashtaanupa-shyati;
Gunebhyashcha param vetti madbhaavam so'dhigacchati.

19. The seer who beholds no other agency (for action) than the modes and knows that which is above these modes, attains My Being.

गुणानेतानतीत्य त्रीन्देही देहसमुद्भवान्।
जन्ममृत्युजरादुःखैर्विमुक्तोऽमृतमश्नुते ॥२०॥

Gunaanetaanateetya treendehi dehasamudbhavaan;
Janmamrityujaraaduhkhairvimukto'mritamashnute.

20. When the embodied soul rises above the three modes from which the body has evolved, it gains

ॐ

freedom from birth, death, decay and sorrow and attains immortality.

अर्जुन उवाच

कैर्लिङ्गैस्त्रीन्गुणानेतानतीतो भवति प्रभो।

किमाचारः कथं चैतांस्त्रीन्गुणानतिवर्तते ।।२१।।

Arjuna uvaacha
Kairlingais treengunaanetaanateeto bhavati prabho;
Kimaachaarah katham chaitaanstreengunaanativartate.

Thus spoke Arjuna:

21. O Lord! What are the signs of one who has transcended these three modes? How does such a person act and what were the methods used to surmount these modes?

श्रीभगवानुवाच

प्रकाशं च प्रवृत्तिं च मोहमेव च पाण्डव।

न द्वेष्टि संप्रवृत्तानि न निवृत्तानि काङ्क्षति ।।२२।।

Sree bhagavaan uvaacha
Prakaasham cha pravrittim cha mohameva cha paandava;
Na dweshti sampravrittaani na nivrittaani kaankkshati.

Thus spoke the Blessed Lord:

22. O Arjuna (Pandava)! Such a person does not shun the appearance of illumination (effect of *sattva*),

activity (effect of *rajas*) or delusion (effect of *tamas*)
nor long for them when they are absent.

उदासीनवदासीनो गुणैर्यो न विचाल्यते।
गुणा वर्तन्त इत्येव योऽवतिष्ठति नेङ्गते ।।२३।।

Udaaseenavadaaseeno gunairyo na vichaalyate;
Gunaa vartanta ityeva yovatishthati nengate.

23. Such a person is not moved by the modes and
remains unconcerned, standing aloof, knowing well
that all things proceed from the operation of the
modes.

समदुःखसुखः स्वस्थः समलोष्टाश्मकाञ्चनः।
तुल्यप्रियाप्रियो धीरस्तुल्यनिन्दात्मसंस्तुतिः ।।२४।।

Samaduhkhasukhah swasthah samaloshtaashmakaan-
chanah;
Tulyapriyaapriyo dheerastulyanindaatmasamstutih.

24. Such a person abides firmly in the Self and
accepts with equanimity both agrreeable and disagreeable happenings, pleasure and pain, censure
and praise, regarding alike a clod, a stone and a
lump of gold.

मानापमानयोस्तुल्यस्तुल्यो मित्रारिपक्षयोः।
सर्वारम्भपरित्यागी गुणातीतः स उच्यते ।।२५।।

Maanaapamaanayostulyastulyo mitraaripakshayoh;
Sarvaarambhaparityaagi gunaateetah sa uchyate.

25. One who initiates no action, who is unperturbed
in the face of honour and dishonour, and alike to
friend and foe, can be said to have transcended the
modes.

मां च योऽव्यभिचारेण भक्तियोगेन सेवते।
स गुणान्समतीत्यैतान्ब्रह्मभूयाय कल्पते ।।२६।।

Maam cha yovyabhichaarena bhaktiyogena sevate;
Sa gunaan samateetyaitaan brahmabhooyaaya kalpate.

26. One who serves Me with an all-consuming and
constant devotion can also be said to have transcended the modes and befits union with Brahman.

ब्रह्मणो हि प्रतिष्ठाहममृतस्याव्ययस्य च।
शाश्वतस्य च धर्मस्य सुखस्यैकान्तिकस्य च ।।२७।।

Brahmano hi pratishthaahamamritasyaavyayasya cha;
Shaashwatasya cha dharmasya sukhasyaikaantikasya cha.

27. For verily I am the abode of Brahman and the
eternal dharma—immortal, immutable and filled
with absolute bliss.

ॐ तत्सदिति श्रीमद्भगवद्गीतासूपनिषत्सु ब्रह्मविद्यायां
योगशास्त्रे श्रीकृष्णार्जुनसंवादे गुणत्रयविभागयोगो
नाम चतुर्दशोऽध्यायः ।।१४।।

Om tat sat iti srimad bhagavad gitaasoopanishatsu brahmavidyaayaam yogashaastre sri krishnaarjunasamvaade gunatrayavibhaagayogo naama chaturdasho'dhyaayah.

Aum Tat Sat:

Thus in the Upanishad of the Bhagavad Gita, the Knowledge of Supreme Brahman, the Scripture of *Yoga*, the dialogue between Sri Krishna and Arjuna, ends the fourteenth chapter entitled, "The *Yoga* of the Distinction between the three Gunas."

Aum Sri Krishnaya Paramatmane Namah!
Aum Sri Parthasarathaye Namah!

अथ पञ्चदशोऽध्यायः
Atha Panchadasho'dhyaya

CHAPTER XV
PURUSHOTTAMA YOGA
The Yoga of the Supreme Person

श्रीभगवानुवाच

ऊर्ध्वमूलमधःशाखमश्वत्थं प्राहुरव्ययम् ।
छन्दांसि यस्य पर्णानि यस्तं वेद स वेदवित् ।।१।।

Sree Bhagavaan uvaacha
Oordhwamoolamadhasshaakhamashwattham praahu-
ravyayam;
Cchandaamsi yasya parnaani yastam veda sa vedavit.

Thus spoke the Blessed Lord:

1. It is said that the imperishable peepul tree is rooted above and branching below. The Vedas are its leaves. The one who knows this is the knower of the Vedas.

अधश्चोर्ध्वं प्रसृतास्तस्य शाखा
        गुणप्रवृद्धा विषयप्रवालाः ।
अधश्च मूलान्यनुसंततानि
        कर्मानुबन्धीनि मनुष्यलोके ।।२।।

Adhashchordhwam prasritaastasya shaakhaa
        Gunapravriddhaa vishayapravaalaah;
Adhascha moolaanyanusantataani
        Karmaanubandheeni manushyaloke.

2. The branches of this tree extend both above and below and are nourished by the modes. Sense objects are its tendrils. The (aerial) roots (of attachment) plunge down into the mortal world, creating bondage through action.

न रूपमस्येह तथोपलभ्यते
        नान्तो न चादिर्न च संप्रतिष्ठा ।
अश्वत्थमेनं सुविरूढमूलम्
        मसङ्गशस्त्रेण दृढेन छित्त्वा ॥३॥

Na roopamasyeha tadhopalabhyate
        Naanto na chaadirnacha sampratishthaa;
Ashwatthamenam suviroodhamoolam
        Asangashastrena dridhena cchitwaa.

ततः पदं तत्परिमार्गितव्यं
        यस्मिनगता न निवर्तन्ति भूयः ।
तमेव चाद्यं पुरूषं प्रपद्ये
        यतः प्रवृत्ति प्रसृता पुराणी ॥४॥

Tatah padam tat parimaargitavyam;
        Yasmin gataa na nivartanti bhooyah;
Tameva chaadyam purusham prapadye
        Yatah pravrittih prasritaa puraanee.

3&4.   Its beginning, end, foundation and its actual
form cannot be perceived here in this world. Having
cut down this firmly-rooted peepul tree with the
powerful axe of detachment, one should strive for
the highest goal from which there is no return (to the
world of birth and death). "I seek refuge in the
Primeval Person from whom has stemmed this urge
for eternal activity."

निर्मानमोहा जितसङ्गदोषा
अध्यात्मनित्या विनिवृत्तकामाः।
द्वन्द्वैर्विमुक्ताः सुखदुःखसंज्ञै-
र्गच्छन्त्यमूढाः पदमव्ययं तत् ।।५।।

Nirmaanamohaa jitasangadoshaa
Adhyaatmanityaa vinivrittakaamaah;
Dwandwairvimuktaah sukhaduhkhasamjnair
Gacchantyamoodhaah padamavyayam tat.

5. Those undeluded ones who are free from pride
and delusion, who are victorious over the evils of
attachment, whose desires have been stilled, who are
liberated from the dualities of pleasure and pain and
who dwell constantly in the Self, reach the immutable abode.

न तद्भासयते सूर्यो न शशाङ्को न पावकः ।
यद्गत्वा न निवर्तन्ते तद्धाम परमं मम ।।६।।

Na tadbhaasayate sooryo na shashaanko na paavakah;
Yadgatwaa na nivartante taddhaama paramam mama.

6. My supreme abode, having reached which there
is no return, is that which cannot be illumined by the
brilliance of the sun, moon or fire.

ममैवांशो जीवलोके जीवभूतः सनातनः ।
मनःषष्ठानीन्द्रियाणि प्रकृतिस्थानि कर्षति ।।७।।

Mamaivaamsho jeevaloke jeevabhootah sanaatanah;
Manah shashthaaneendriyaani prakritisthaani karshati.

7.   The embodied soul is an eternal portion of My
own self. When it takes birth in the world of living
beings, it attracts the six senses inclusive of the
mind, abiding in Nature.

शरीरं यदवाप्नोति यच्चाप्युत्क्रामतीश्वरः।
गृहीत्वैतानि संयाति वायुर्गन्धानिवाशयात् ॥८॥

Shareeram yadavaapnoti yacchaa pyutkraamateeshwarah;
Griheetwaitaani samyaati vaayurgandhaanivaashayaat.

8.   When the Lord (the embodied soul) takes on and
casts off a body, he carries these (the mind and
senses) as the breeze carries perfumes from their
source (the flowers).

श्रोत्रं चक्षुः स्पर्शनं च रसनं घ्राणमेव च।
अधिष्ठाय मनश्चायं विषयानुपसेवते ॥९॥

Shrotram chakshuh sparshanam cha rasanam ghraanameva
cha;
Adhishthaaya manashchaayam vishayaanupasevate.

9.   The embodied soul experiences the various objects through the medium of the ear, eye, skin,
tongue, nose and mind.

उत्क्रामन्तं स्थितं वापि भुञ्जानं वा गुणान्वितम्।
विमूढा नानुपश्यन्ति पश्यन्ति ज्ञानचक्षुषः ।।१०।।

Utkraamantam sthitham vaapi bhunjaanam vaa gunaanvitam;
Vimoodhaa naanupashyanti pashyanti jnaanachakshushah.

10. The deluded do not perceive this Spirit which is united with the modes and abides, enjoys and departs (from the body). Only they perceive who have the eye of wisdom.

यतन्तो योगिनश्चैनं पश्यन्त्यात्मन्यवस्थितम्।
यतन्ताऽप्यकृतात्मानो नैनं पश्यन्त्यचेतसः ।।११।।

Yatanto yoginashchainam pashyantyaatmanyavasthitam;
Yatantopyakritaatmaano nainam pashyantyachetasah.

11. Striving *yogis* perceive this Spirit as the ind-weller within themselves but the unrefined and the un-intelligent, even though striving do not see it.

यदादित्यगतं तेजो जगद्भासयतेऽखिलम्।
यच्चन्द्रमसि यच्चाग्नौ तत्तेजो विद्धि मामकम् ।।१२।।

Yadaadityagatam tejo jagadhbaasayatekhilam;
Yacchandramasi yacchaagnau tattejo viddhi maamakam.

12. Know that effulgence to be Mine, which dwells in the sun and illumines the entire universe—which glows in the moon and in fire.

ॐ

गामाविश्य च भूतानि धारयाम्यहमोजसा।
पुष्णामि चौषधीःसर्वाःसोमो भूत्वा रसात्मकः ॥१३॥

Gaamaavishya cha bhootaani dhaarayaamyahamojasaa;
Pushnaami chaushadheeh sarvaah somo bhootwaa
rasaatmakah.

13. Entering the earth I sustain all beings with My
energy and becoming the sapidity of the moon I
cause all medicinal herbs to thrive.

अहं वैश्वानरो भूत्वा प्राणिनां देहमाश्रितः।
प्राणापानसमायुक्तः पचाम्यन्नं चतुर्विधम् ॥१४॥

Aham vaishwaanaro bhootwaa praaninaam dehamaash-
ritah;
Praanaapaanasamaayuktah pachaamyannam chaturvi-
dham.

14. I am the flame of life dwelling in the bodies of
all living beings. Uniting with the inhalations and
exhalations, I digest the four types of food.

सर्वस्य चाहं हृदि संनिविष्टो
        मत्तः स्मृतिर्ज्ञानमपोहनं च।
वेदैश्चसर्वैरहमेव वेद्यो
        वेदान्तकृद्वेदविदेव चाहम् ॥१५॥

Sarvasya chaaham hridi sannivishto
      Mattas smritirjnaanamapohanam cha;
Vedaishcha sarvairahameva vedyo
      Vedaantakridvedavideva chaaham.

15. I abide in the heart of all living beings. From Me comes both memory, knowledge and their lack. It is I whom all the Vedas seek to know. I am indeed the knower of the Vedas as well as the author of the Vedanta.

द्वाविमौ पुरूषौ लोके क्षरश्चाक्षर एव च।
क्षरः सर्वाणि भूतानि कूटस्थोऽक्षर उच्यते ।।१६।।

Dwaavimau purushau loke ksharashchaakshara eva cha;
Kshras sarvaani bhootaani kootashthokshara uchyate.

16. There are two spiritual entities in the world—the perishable and the imperishable. The totality of creation constitutes the perishable. The immovable, unchanging foundation of the perishable is called the imperishable.

उत्तमः पुरूषस्त्वन्यः परमात्मेत्युदाहृतः।
यो लोकत्रयमाविश्य बिभर्त्यव्यय ईश्वरः ।।१७।।

Uttamah purushastwanyah paramaatmetyudaahritah;
Yo lokatrayamaavishya bibhartavyaya eeshwarah.

17. Distinct from these two is the Supreme Person

who is the highest Self, the indestructible Lord who enters the three worlds and sustains them.

यस्मात्क्षरमतीतोऽहमक्षरादपि चोत्तमः।
अतोऽस्मि लोके वेदे च प्रथितः पुरूषोत्तमः ।।१८।।

Yasmaatksharamateetohamaksharaadapi chottamah;
Ato'smi loke vede cha prathitah purushottamah.

18. Since I transcend both the perishable and the imperishable, I am called the Supreme Person by the Vedas and by the world.

यो मामेवमसंमूढो जानाति पुरूषोत्तमम्।
स सर्वविद्भजति मां सर्वभावेन भारत ।।१९।।

Yo maamevamasammoodho jaanaati purushottamam;
Sa sarvavidbhajati maam sarvabhaavena bhaarata.

19. O Arjuna (Bharatha)! The undeluded person is one who knows Me as the Supreme Person. Such a one is all-knowing and worships Me with his entire being.

इति गुह्यतमं शास्त्रामिदमुक्तं मयानघ।
एतद्बुद्ध्वा बुद्धिमान्स्यात्कृतकृत्यश्च भारत ।।२०।।

Iti guhyatamam shaastramidamuktam mayaanagha;
Etadbuddhwaa buddhimaansyaat kritakrityashcha
bhaarata.

20. O Thou sinless One (Anagha)! This most profound teaching has thus been imparted by Me.
Knowing this a person becomes truly wise and
fulfils all his duties, O Arjuna (Bharatha)!

ॐ तत्सदितिश्रीमद्भगवम्दीतासूपनिषत्सु ब्रह्मविद्यायां
योगशास्त्रे श्रीकृष्णार्जुनसंवादे पुरूषोत्तमयोगो
नाम पञ्चदशोऽध्यायः ॥१५॥

*Om tat sat iti srimad bhagavad gitaasoopanishatsu
brahmavidyaayam yogashaastre sri krishnaarjunasamvaade
purushottamyogo naama panchadasho dhyaayah.*

Aum Tat Sat:

Thus in the Upanishad of the Bhagavad Gita, the
Knowledge of Supreme Brahman, the Scripture of
Yoga, the dialogue between Sri Krishna and Arjuna
ends the fifteenth chapter entitled, "The *Yoga* of the
Supreme Person."

Aum Sri Krishnaya Paramatmane Namah!
Aum Sri Parthasarathaye Namah!

अथ षोडशोऽध्यायः
Atha Shodasho'dhyayah.

CHAPTER XVI

DAIVASURA SAMPAD VIBHAGA YOGA
The Yoga of the Distinction between the
Divine and Demonic Qualities.

श्रीभगवानुवाच

अभयं सत्त्वसंशुद्धिर्ज्ञानयोगव्यवस्थितिः ।
दानं दमश्च यज्ञश्च स्वाध्यायस्तप आर्जवम् ॥१॥

Sree Bhagavaan uvaacha
Abhayam sattwasamshuddhirjnaanayogavyavasthitih;
Daanam damashcha yajnashcha swaadhyaayastapa
aarjavam.

Thus spoke the Blessed Lord:

1. Fearlessness, purity of heart, steadfastness in *yoga* and knowledge, charity, self-control, sacrifice, study of the scriptures, austerity and rectitude...

अहिंसा सत्यमक्रोधस्त्यागः शान्तिरपैशुनम् ।
दया भूतेष्वलोलुप्त्वं मार्दवं ह्रीरचापलम् ॥२॥

Ahimsaa satyamakrodhastyaagah shaantirapaishunam;
Dayaa bhooteshvaloluptwam maardavam hreerachaapalam.

2. Non-violence, truth, absence of anger, the spirit of renunciation, serenity, not prone to fault-finding, compassion to all beings, non-covetousness, gentleness, modesty and a non-capricious nature...

ॐ

तेजः क्षमा धृतिः शौचमद्रोहो नातिमानिता ।
भवन्ति संपदं दैवीमभिजातस्य भारत ॥३॥

Tejah kshamaa ddhritih shauchamadroho naatimaanitaa;
Bhavanti sampadam daiveemabhijaatasya bhaarata.

3.   Spiritual energy, patience, fortitude, cleanliness,
absence of malice and pride—these are the marks of
one who is endowed with divine qualities O Arjuna
(Bharatha).

दम्भो दर्पोऽभिमानश्च क्रोधः पारुष्यमेव च।
अज्ञानं चाभिजातस्य पार्थ संपदमासुरीम् ।।४।।

Dambho darpobhimaanashcha krodhah paarushyameva
cha;
Ajnaanam chaabhijaatasya paartha sampadamaasureem.

4.   Ostentation, arrogance, pride, anger, brutality
and ignorance are the hallmarks of one with demonic qualities, O Arjuna (Partha).

दैवी संपद्विमोक्षाय निबन्धायासुरी मता।
मा शुचः संपदं दैवीमभिजातोऽसि पाण्डव ।।५।।

Daivee sampadvimokshaaya nibandhaayaasuree mataa;
Maa shuchah sampadam daiveemabhijaatosi paandava.

5.   Divine qualities lead to liberation and demonic
to bondage. Fear not O Arjuna (Partha), for you are
born with divine qualities.

द्वौ भूतसर्गौ लोकेऽस्मिन्दैव आसुर एव च।
दैवो विस्तरशः प्रोक्त आसुरं पार्थ मे शृणु ।।६।।

Dwau bhootasargau loke'smin daiva aasura eva cha;
Daivo vistarashah prokta aasuram paartha me shrinu.

6. There are two types of beings in the world O
Arjuna (Partha)—the divine and the demonic. The
divine has been described to you in detail. Now
learn from Me about the demonic.

प्रवृतिं च निवृत्तिं च जना न विदुरासुराः।
न शौचं नापि चाचारो न सत्यं तेषु विद्यते ।। ७।।

Pravrittim cha nivrittim cha janaa na viduraasuraah;
Na shaucham naapi chaachaaro na satyam teshu vidyate.

7. Demonic types have no idea of when to act and
when to refrain from action. They are devoid of
purity, truth and moral standards.

असत्यमप्रतिष्ठं ते जगदाहुरनीश्वरम्।
अपरस्परसंभूतं किमन्यत्कामहैतुकम् ।।८।।

Asatyamapratishtham te jagadaahuraneeshwaram;
Aparasparasambhootam kimanyat kaamahaitukam.

8. "What else is the world but a product of lust,
brought about by mutual union? It has no truth, no
moral basis and no God," is what they say.

एतां दृष्टिमवष्टभ्य नष्टात्मानोऽल्पबुद्धयः ।
प्रभवन्त्युग्रकर्माणः क्षयाय जगतोऽहिताः ।।६।।

Etaam drishtimavashtabhya nashtaatmaanolpabuddhayah;
Prabhavantyugrakarmaanah kshayaaya jagato'hitaah.

9. Holding fast to this view, these degenerate ones
of little understanding resort to violent deeds. They
are enemies of the world and are bent on its destruction.

काममाश्रित्य दुष्पूरं दम्भमानमदान्विताः ।
मोहाद्गृहीत्वासद्ग्राहान्प्रवर्तन्ते शुचिव्रताः ।।१०।।

Kaamamaashritya dushpooram dambhamaanamadaa-
nvitaah;
Mohaadgriheetvaasadgraahaan pravartanteshuchivrataah.

10. Filled with insatiable desires, arrogant, proud
and hypocritical, they cling to their wrong notions
through delusion and obstinately pursue their impure aims.

चिन्तामपरिमेयां च प्रलयान्तामुपाश्रिताः ।
कामोपभोगपरमा एतावदिति निश्चिताः ।।११।।

Chintaamaparimeyaam cha pralayaantaamupaashritaah;
Kaamopabhogaparamaa etaavaditi nichitaah.

11. They are convinced that the gratification of

desire is the highest aim in life. They are beset with innumerable worries which end only with death.

आशापाशशतैर्बद्धाः कामक्रोधपरायणाः।
ईहन्ते कामभोगार्थमन्यायेनार्थसञ्चयान् ।।१२।।

Aashaapaashashatairbaddhaah kaamakrodhaparaayanaah;
Eehante kaamabhogaarthamanyaayenaarthasanchayaan.

12. Fettered by a hundred bonds of desire, slaves of passion and anger, they resort to unjust means to amass wealth for the gratification of their sensual pleasures.

इदमद्य मया लब्धमिमं प्राप्स्ये मनोरथम्।
इदमस्तीदमपि मे भविष्यति पुनर्धनम् ।।१३।।

Idamadya mayaa labdhamimam praapsye manoratham;
Idamasteedamapi me bhavishyati punardhanam.

13. "I have gained this today and I shall surely be able to fulfil all my other fancies in future. All this is already mine and all this wealth too will be mine in due course."

असौ मया हतः शत्रुर्हनिष्ये चापरानपि।
ईश्वरोऽहमहं भोगी सिद्धोऽहं बलवान्सुखी ।।१४।।

Asau mayaa hatah shatrurhanishye chaaparaanapi;
Ishwarohamaham bhogee siddhoham balavaansukhee.

14. "I have killed this enemy today and the rest too I shall slay. I am the mighty Lord! I am the enjoyer—successful and happy."

आढ्योऽभिजनवानस्मि कोऽन्योऽस्ति सदृशोमया
यक्ष्ये दास्यामि मोदिष्य इत्यज्ञानविमोहिताः ।।१५।।

Aadyobhijanavaanasmi konyosti sadrishomayaa;
Yakshye daasyaami modishya ityajnaanavimohitaah.

15. "I am wealthy and high born. Who is there equal to me? I will perform rituals, give alms and rejoice." Thus they are deluded by ignorance.

अनेकचित्तविभ्रान्ता मोहजालसमावृताः ।
प्रसक्ताः कामभोगेषु पतन्ति नरकेऽशुचौ ।।१६।।

Anekachittavibhraantah mohajaalasamaavritaah;
Prasaktaah kaamabhogeshu patanti narakeshuchau.

16. Lost in these flights of fancy, entangled in their web of delusion, they are slaves to their desires and fall into hells of impurity.

आत्मसंभाविताः स्तब्धा धनमानमदान्विताः ।
यजन्ते नामयज्ञैस्ते दम्भेनाविधिपूर्वकम् ।।१७।।

Aatmasambhaavitaah stabdhaa dhanamaanamadaanvitaah;
Yajante naamayajnaiste dambhenaavidhipoorvakam.

17. Self-conceited, stubborn, haughty and intoxicated with their pride of wealth, they perform rituals for mere show and slight the accepted ordinances.

अहंकारं बलं दर्प कामं क्रोधं च संश्रिताः।
मामात्मपरदेहेषु प्रद्विषन्तोऽभ्यसूयकाः ।।१८।।

Ahamkaaram balam darpam kaamam krodham cha samshritaah;
Maamaatmaparadeheshu pradwishantobhyasooyakaah.

18. Filled with ego, these malicious people are powerful, insolent, lusty and wrathful. They hate Me who dwell in their own bodies as well as in the bodies of others.

तानहं द्विषतः क्रूरान्संसारेषु नराधमान्।
क्षिपाम्यजस्रमशुभानासुरीष्वेव योनिषु ।।१९।।

Taanaham dwishatah krooraan samsaareshu naraadhamaan;
Kshipaamyajasramashubhaanaasureeshweva yonishu.

19. These degenerate ones, malicious and cruel doers of evil, I cast again and again into demonic wombs.

आसुरीं योनिमापन्ना मूढा जन्मनि जन्मनि।
मामप्राप्यैव कौन्तेय ततो यान्त्यधमां गतिम् ।।२०।।

Aasureem yonimaapanna moodhaa janmani janmani;
Maamapraapyaiva kaunteya tato yaantyadhamaam gatim.

20. O Arjuna (Kaunteya)! These deluded beings who
have fallen into demonic wombs, sink down to still
lower levels and do not attain Me for many births.

त्रिविधं नरकस्येदं द्वारं नाशनमात्मनः।
कामः क्रोधस्तथा लोभस्तस्मादेतत्त्रयं त्यजेत् ।।२१।।

Trividham narakasyedam dwaaram naashanamaatmanah;
Kaamah krodhastathaa lobhastasmaadetattrayam tyajet.

21. Lust, anger and greed are the triple gates to hell
which take the embodied soul to perdition. Therefore one should avoid them.

ॐ

एतैर्विमुक्तः कौन्तेय तमोद्वारैस्त्रिभिर्नरः।
आचरत्यात्मनः श्रेयस्ततो याति परां गतिम् ।।२२।।

Etairvimuktah kaunteya tamodwaaraistribhirnarah;
Aacharatyaatmanah shreyastato yaati paraam gatim.

22. Once freed from these doors to darkness, O
Arjuna (Kaunteya), one can practise what is beneficial to oneself and thus attain the Supreme goal.

यः शास्त्रविधिमुत्सृज्य वर्तते कामकारतः।
न स सिद्धिमवाप्नोति न सुखं न परां गतिम् ।।२३।।

Yah shaastravidhimutsrijya vartate kaamakaaratah;
Na sa siddhimavaapnoti na sukham na paraam gatim.

23. One who casts aside scriptural injunctions and acts under the impulse of desire alone, will not attain happiness, perfection or the highest state.

तस्माच्छास्त्रं प्रमाणं ते कार्याकार्यव्यवस्थितौ ।
ज्ञात्वा शास्त्रविधानोक्तं कर्म कर्तुमिहार्हसि ।।२४।।

Tasmaat shaastram pramaanam te kaaryaakaaryav-
yavasthitau;
Jnaatwaa shaastravidhaanoktam karma kartumihaarhasi.

24. Therefore let the scriptures be your authority in determining right and wrong conduct. You should act in this world according to the injunctions as given in the scriptures.

ॐ तत्सदिति श्रीमद्भगवद्गीतासूपनिषत्सु ब्रह्मविद्यायां योगशास्त्रे श्रीकृष्णार्जुनसंवादे दैवासुर–संपद्विभागयोगो नाम षोडशोऽध्याय ।।१६।।

Om tat sat iti srimad bhagavad gitaasoopanishatsu
brahmavidyaayaam yogashaastre sri krishnaarjunasa-
mvaade daivaasurasampadvibhaagayogo naama shoda-
sho'dhyaa-yah.

Aum Tat Sat:

Thus in the Upanishad of the Bhagavad Gita, the Knowledge of Supreme Brahman, the Scripture of *Yoga*, the dialogue between Sri Krishna and Arjuna, ends the sixteenth chapter entitled, "The *Yoga* of the Distinction between the Divine and Demonic Qualities."

ॐ

Aum Sri Krishanaya Paramatmane Namah!
Aum Sri Parthasarathaye Namah!

अथ सप्तदशोऽध्यायः
Atha Saptadasho'dhyayah

CHAPTER XVII
SHRADDHATRAYA VIBHAGA YOGA
The Yoga of the Threefold Faith

अर्जुन उवाच

ये शास्त्रविधिमुत्सृज्य यजन्ते श्रद्धयान्विताः ।
तेषां निष्ठा तु का कृष्ण सत्त्वमाहो रजस्तमः ।।१।।

Arjuna uvaacha
Ye shaastravidhimutsrijya yajante shraddhayaanvitaah;
Teshaam nishthaa tu kaa krishna sattwamaaho rajastamah.

Thus spoke Arjuna:

1. O Krishna! What is the position of those who cast aside scriptural ordinances yet continue their spiritual observances with faith? Are they *sattvic*, *rajasic* or *tamasic*?

श्रीमगवानुवाच

त्रिविधा भवति श्रद्धा देहिनां सा स्वभावजा ।
सात्त्विकी राजसी चैव तामसी चेति तां शृणु ।।२।।

Sree Bhagavaan uvaacha
Trividhaa bhavati shraddhaa dehinaam saa swabhaavajaa;
Sattvikee raajasee chaiva taamasee cheti taam shrinu.

Thus spoke the Blessed Lord:

2. The faith of all embodied beings is moulded by *sattva, rajas, and tamas,* for they are inherent in their nature. You may now hear about it.

सत्त्वानुरूपा सर्वस्य श्रद्धा भवति भारत ।
श्रद्धामयोऽयं पुरुषो यो यच्छ्रद्धः स एव सः ।।३।।

Sattvaanuroopaa sarvasya shraddhaa bhavati bhaarata;
Sraddhaamayoyam purusho yo yacchraddhah sa eva sah.

3.   Each one's faith depends on his natural dispo-
sition O Arjuna (Bharatha). A person's nature will be
coloured by his faith. As the belief, so the person.

यजन्ते सात्त्विका देवान्यक्षरक्षांसि राजसाः।
प्रेतान्भूतगणांश्चान्ये यजन्ते तामसा जनाः ।।४।।

Yajante saattvikaa devvaanyaksharakshaamsi raajasaah;
Pretaanbhootaganaamschaanye yajante taamasaa janaah.

4.   *Sattvic* people make offering to the gods, *rajasic*
people to the *yakshas* and *rakshasas,* while the *tamasic*
ones worship spirits and other elemental powers.

अशास्त्रविहितं घोरं तप्यन्ते ये तपो जनाः।
दम्भाहंकारसंयुक्ताः कामरागबलान्विताः ।।५।।

Ashaastravihitam ghoram tapyante ye tapo janaah;
Dambhaahamkaarasamyuktaah kaamaraagabalaanvitaah.

कर्षयन्तः शरीरस्थं भूतग्राममचेतसः।
मां चैवान्तःशरीरस्थं तान्विद्ध्यासुरनिश्चयान् ।।६।।

Karshayantah shareerastham bhootagraamamachetasah;
Maam chaivaantahshareerastham taanvidhyaasuranish-
chayaan.

5&6.   Those arrogant and egoistic people who perform severe austerities which are not recognised by the scriptures, impelled by the force of their desires and passions, tormenting the elements which constitute their bodies as well as Me, the indweller, can be called demonic in resolve.

आहारस्त्वपि सर्वस्य त्रिविधो भवति प्रियः।
यज्ञस्तपस्तथा दानं तेषां भेदमिमं शृणु ॥ ७ ॥

Aahaarastwapi sarvasya trividho bhavati priyah;
Yajnastapastathaa daanam yeshaam bhedamimam srinu.

7.   These triple modes are the root cause of the differences in tastes found in people in food, rituals, austerities and the practice of charity. Hear now of the distinction between these.

आयुःसत्त्वबलारोग्यसुखप्रीतिविवर्धनाः।
रस्याः स्निग्धाः स्थिरा हृद्या आहाराः सात्त्विकप्रियाः ॥ ८ ॥

Aayuh sattvabalaarogyasukhapreetivivardhanaah;
Rasyaah snigdhaah sthiraa hridyaa ahaaraah saattvikapriyaah.

8.   Foods which promote life, vitality, strength and health, which give joy and satisfaction, which are tasty, succulent, nourishing and agreeable are preferred by the *sattvic* types.

ॐ

कट्वम्ललवणात्युष्णतीक्ष्णरूक्षविदाहिनः ।
आहारा राजसस्येष्टा दुःखशोकामयप्रदाः ॥६॥

Katvamlalavanaatyushnateekshnarookshavidaahinah;
Aahaarah raajasasyeshtaa duhkhashokaamayapradaah.

9. The *rajasic* temperament prefers foods which are strong-tasting, bitter, sour, pungent, salty, excessively hot, acrid and burning, giving rise to pain, grief and ill-health.

यातयामं गतरसं पूति पर्युषितं च यत् ।
उच्छिष्टमपि चामेध्यं भोजनं तामसप्रियम् ॥१०॥

Yaatayaamam gatarasam pooti paryushitam cha yat;
Ucchishtamapi chaamedhyam bhojanam taamasapriyam.

10. The *tamasic* temperament likes cold, tasteless, stale, rotten foods, refuse, and other impure eatables.

अफलाकाङ्क्षिभिर्यज्ञो विधिदृष्टो य इज्यते ।
यष्टव्यमेवेति मनः समाधाय स सात्त्विकः ॥११॥

Aphalaakaankhsibhiryajno vidhidrishto ya ijyate;
Yashtavyameveti manah samaadhaaya sa saattvikah.

11. *Sattvic* offerings are those which are made according to scriptural injunctions, with no desire for personal gain, because of a strong sense of duty.

अभिसंधाय तु फलं दम्भार्थमपि चैव यत्।
इज्यते भरतश्रेष्ठ तं यज्ञं विद्धि राजसम् ।।१२।।

Abhisandhaaya tu phalam dambhaarthamapi chaiva yat;
Ijyate bharatashreshtha tam yajnam viddhi raajasam.

12. O Arjuna (Bharathashreshta)! That sacrifice which
is performed with ostentation with a view to personal gain alone, is *rajasic.*

विधिहीनमसृष्टान्नं मन्त्रहीनमदक्षिणम्।
श्रद्धाविरहितं यज्ञं तामसं परिचक्षते ।।१३।।

Vidhiheenamasrishtaannam mantraheenamadakshinam;
Shraddhaavirahitam yajnam taamasam parichakshate.

13. That sacrifice which is not in conformity with the
accepted code, performed without faith, in which no
food offerings are made, no *mantras* chanted and no
gifts given, can be termed *tamasic.*

देवद्विजगुरुप्राज्ञपूजनं शौचमार्जवम्।
ब्रह्मचर्यमहिंसा च शारीरं तप उच्यते ।।१४।।

Devadwijagurupraajnapoojanam shauchamaarjavam;
Brahmacharyamahimsaa cha shaareeram tapa uchyate.

14. Worship of the gods, of Brahmins, preceptors
and the wise, cleanliness, straightforwardness, sexual
purity and non-violence constitute the austerity of
the body.

अनुद्वेगकरं वाक्यं सत्यं प्रियहितं च यत्।
स्वाध्यायाभ्यसनं चैव वाङ्मयं तप उच्यते ।।१५।।

Anudwegakaram vaakyam satyam priyahitam cha yat;
Swaadhyaayaabhyasanam chaiva vaangmayam tapa
uchyate.

15. Speech which is truthful, pleasant and beneficial
and which does not hurt anyone, as well as the
regular recitation of the scriptures, constitute austerity
of speech.

मनःप्रसादः सौम्यत्वं मौनमात्मविनिग्रहः।
भावसंशुद्धिरित्येतत्तपो मानसमुच्यते ।।१६।।

Manah prasaadah saumyatwam maunamaatmavinigrahah;
Bhaavasamshuddhirityetattapo maanasamuchyate.

16. Serenity of the mind, gentleness, silence, self-
control and purity of motive, constitute the austerity
of the mind.

श्रद्धया परया तप्तं तपस्तत्त्रिविधं नरैः।
अफलाकाङ्क्षिभिर्युक्तैः सात्त्विकं परिचक्षते ।।१७।।

Shraddhayaa parayaa taptam tapastattrividham naraih;
Aphalaakaankshibhiryuktaih saattvikam parichakshate.

17. These three types of austerities, practised with
faith by those of balanced mind without expectation
of reward, can be termed _sattvic._

सत्कारमानपूजार्थं तपो दम्भेन चैव यत् ।
क्रियते तदिह प्रोक्तं राजसं चलमध्रुवम् ।।१८।।

Satkaaramaanapoojaartham tapo dambhena chaiva yat;
Kriyate tadiha proktam raajasam chalamadhruvam.

18. Austerities which are performed with ostentation in order to get respect, honour and reverence, which yield unstable and perishable results are called *rajasic*.

मूढग्राहेणात्मनो यत्पीडया क्रियते तपः ।
परस्योत्सादनार्थं वा तत्तामसमुदाहृतम् ।।१९।।

Moodhagraahenaatmano yat peedayaa kriyate tapah;
Parasyotsaadanaartham vaa tattaamasamudaahritam.

19. Austerities which are practised foolishly by torturing one's own body or with the aim of inflicting harm on others, are termed *tamasic*.

दातव्यमिति यद्दानं दीयतेऽनुपकारिणे ।
देशे काले च पात्रे च तद्दानं सात्त्विकं स्मृतम् ।।२०।।

Daatavyamiti yaddaanam deeyate'nupakaarine;
Deshe kaale cha paatre cha taddaanam saattvikam smritam.

20. That gift which is made to a worthy person from whom no service is expected in return, which is

given at the groper time and place, from a strong
sense of duty, is *sattvic.*

यत्तु प्रत्युपकारार्थं फलमुद्दिश्य वा पुनः।
दीयते च परिक्लिष्टं तद्दानं राजसं स्मृतम ।।२१।।

Yattu pratyupakaaraartham phalamuddishya vaa punah;
Deeyate cha pariklishtam taddaanam raajasam smritam.

21. That gift which is given grudgingly, hoping for
some return or reward, is said to be *rajasic.*

अदेशकाले यद्दानमपात्रेभ्यश्च दीयते।
असत्कृतमवज्ञातं तत्तामसमुदाहृतम् ।।२२।।

Adeshakaale yaddaanamapaatrebhyashcha deeyate;
Asatkritamavajnaatam tattaamasamudaahritam.

22. That gift which is made disrespectfully and
contemptuously to an unworthy person at the wrong
time and place is called *tamasic.*

ॐ तत्सदिति निर्देशो ब्रह्मणस्त्रिविधः स्मृतः।
ब्राह्मणास्तेन वेदाश्च यज्ञाश्च विहिताः पुरा ।।२३।।

Om Tatsaditi nirdesho brahmanas trividhah smritah;
Braahmanaastena vedaashcha yajnaashcha vihitaah puraa.

23. The *mantra—Aum Tat Sat,* is the triple definition

of Brahman by which the Brahmins, the Vedas and
the *yajnas* were created of old.

तस्मादोमित्युदाहृत्य   यज्ञदानतपःक्रियाः ।
प्रवर्तन्ते विधानोक्ताः सततं ब्रह्मवादिनाम्   ।।२४।।

Tasmaadomityudaahritya yajnadaanatapahkriyaah;
Pravartantte vidhaanoktaah satatam brahmavaadinaam.

24. Thus the knowers of the Vedas always com-
mence all acts of sacrifice, charity and austerity as
enjoined in the Vedas, with the utterance of the
mantra, Aum.

तदित्यनभिसंधाय फलं यज्ञतपःक्रियाः ।
दानक्रियाश्च विविधाः क्रियन्ते मोक्षकाङ्क्षिभिः   ।।२५।।

Tadityanabhisandhaaya phalam yajnatapahkriyaah;
Daanakriyaashcha vividhaah kriyante mokshakaankh-
shibhih.

25. The seekers of liberation who have no expectation of rewards, perform all acts of sacrifice, penance
and charity with the utterance of the word *Tat.*

सद्भावे साधुभावे च सदित्येतत्प्रयुज्यते ।
प्रशस्ते कर्मणि तथा सच्छब्दः पार्थ युज्यते   ।।२६।।

Sadbhaave saadhubhaave cha sadityetatprayujyate;
Prashaste karmani tathaa sacchabdah paartha yujyate.

26. O Arjuna (Partha)! The word *Sat* is used to denote reality as well as worth. It can also be used for all noble acts.

यज्ञे तपसि दाने च स्थितिः सदिति चोच्यते।
कर्म चैव तदर्थीयं सदित्येवाभिधीयते ।।२७।।

Yajne tapasi daane cha sthitih saditi chochyate;
Karma chaiva tadartheeyam sadityevaabhidheeyate.

27. Steadfastness in sacrifice, charity and austerity as well as all action done for the sake of the Supreme, can be termed *Sat*.

अश्रद्धया हुतं दत्तं तपस्तप्तं कृतं च यत्।
असदित्युच्यते पार्थ न च तत्प्रेत्य नो इह ।।२८।।

Ashraddhayaa hutam dattam tapastaptam kritam cha yat;
Asadityuchyate paartha na cha tatpretya no iha.

28. Whenever something is done without faith—the offering of an oblation, or the giving of charity or the practice of austerity, it is termed *asat*, O Arjuna (Partha), because it is of no use either here or in the hereafter.

ॐ तत्सदिति श्रीमद्भगवद्गीतासूपनिषत्सु ब्रह्मविद्यायां योगशास्त्रे श्रीकृष्णार्जुनसंवादे श्रद्धात्रयविभाग—योगो नाम सप्तदशोऽध्यायः ।।१७।।

Om tat sat iti srimad bhagavad gitaasoopanishatsu brahmavidyaayaam yogashaastre sri krishnaarjunasamvaade shraddhaatrayavibhaagayogo naama saptadasho'dhyaayah.

Aum Tat Sat:

Thus in the Upanishad of the Bhagavad Gita, the Knowledge of Supreme Brahman, the Scripture of *Yoga*, the dialogue between Sri Krishna and Arjuna, ends the seventeenth chapter entitled, "The *Yoga* of the Threefold Faith."

ॐ

Aum Sri Krishnaya Paramatmane Namah!
Aum Sri Parthasarathaye Namah!

अथाष्टादशोऽध्यायः
Atha Ashtadasho'dhyayah

CHAPTER XVIII
MOKSHA SANNYASA YOGA
The Yoga of Liberation and Renunciation

अर्जुन उवाच

संन्यासस्य महाबाहो तत्त्वमिच्छामि वेदितुम्।
त्यागस्य च हृषीकेश पृथक्केशिनिषूदन ।।१।।

Arjuna uvaacha
Sannyaasasya mahaabaaho tattwamicchaami veditum;
Tyaagasya cha hrisheekesha prithakkeshinishoodana.

Thus spoke Arjuna:

1. O Krishna (Mahabaho, Hrishikesha, Kesinis-
hoodana)! I wish to know the principles and differences between renunciation (*sannyasa* or Sankhya
yoga) and relinquishment (*tyaga* or Karma *yoga*.)

श्रीभगवानुवाच

काम्यानां कर्मणां न्यासं संन्यासं कवयो विदुः।
सर्वकर्मफलत्यागं प्राहुस्त्यागं विचक्षणाः ।।२।।

Sree Bhagavaan uvaacha
Kaamyaanaam karmanaam nyaasam sannyaasam kavayo
viduh;
Sarvakarmaphalatyaagam praahustyaagam vichakshanaah.

Thus spoke the Blessed Lord:

2. The sages declare that *sannyasa* is the renunciation of actions prompted by desire and the wise are
of the opinion that *tyaga* is the relinquishment of
attachment to the fruit of action.

ॐ

त्याज्यं दोषवदित्येके कर्म प्राहुर्मनीषिणः।
यज्ञदानतपःकर्म न त्याज्यमिति चापरे ।।३।।

Tyaajyam doshavadityeke karma praahurmaneeshinah;
Yajnadaanatapahkarma na tyaajyamiti chaapare.

3.   Some wise people say that all actions should be
given up as they are all defective, while others
declare that acts of sacrifice, charity and austerity
should not be abandoned.

निश्चयं शृणु मे तत्र त्यागे भरतसत्तम।
त्यागो हि पुरुषव्याघ्र त्रिविधः संप्रकीर्तितः ।।४।।

Nishchayam shrinu me tatra tyaage bharatasattama;
Tyaago hi purushavyaaghra trividhah samprakeertitah.

4.   Hear My final word on *tyaga* O Arjuna
(Bharathasattama, Purushavyagrah)! It is said to be
of three kinds.

यज्ञदानतपःकर्म न त्याज्यं कार्यमेव तत्।
यज्ञो दानं तपश्चैव पावनानि मनीषिणाम् ।।५।।

Yajnadaanatapahkarma na tyaajyam kaaryameva tat;
Yajno daanam tapashchaiva paavanaani maneeshinaam.

5.   Acts of sacrifice, charity and austerity should be
performed and not abandoned. Sacrifice, charity
and austerity purify even the wise.

एतान्यपि तु कर्माणि सङ्गत्यक्त्वा फलानि च।
कर्तव्यानीति मे पार्थ निश्चितं मतमुत्तमम् ॥६॥

Etaanyapi tu karmaani sangam tyaktwaa phalaani cha;
Kartavyaaneeti me paartha nishchitam matamuttamam.

6. It is My firmly held belief O Arjuna (Partha), that
these actions should be performed but without attachment to the fruits.

नियतस्य तु संन्यासः कर्मणो नोपपद्यते।
मोहात्तस्य परित्यागस्तामसः परिकीर्तितः ॥७॥

Niyatasya tu sannyaasah karmano nopapadyate;
Mohaattasya parityaagastaamasah parikeertitah.

7. Renunciation of one's obligatory duties is not
considered proper. To give them up through delusion is said to be *tamasic*.

दुःखमित्येव यत्कर्म कायक्लेशभयात्त्यजेत्।
स कृत्वा राजसं त्यागं नैव त्यागफलं लभेत् ॥८॥

Duhkhamityeva yat karma kaayakleshabhayaat tyajet;
Sa kritwaa raajasam tyaagam naiva tyaagaphalam labhet.

8. One who gives up these actions because they are
difficult or because they entail bodily discomfort is
rajasic and will not gain the benefit of renunciation.

ॐ

कार्यमित्येव यत्कर्म नियतं क्रियतेऽर्जुन।
सङ्गंत्यक्त्वा फलं चैव स त्यागः सात्त्विको मतः ।।६।।

Kaaryamityeva yatkarma niyatam kriyate'rjuna;
Sangam tyaktwaa phalam chaiva sa tyaagah saattviko
matah.

9.   One who performs all obligatory actions as a
bounden duty, without attachment to the fruits, is
sattvic.

न द्वेष्ट्यकुशलं कर्म कुशले नानुषज्जते।
त्यागी सत्त्वसमाविष्टो मेधावी छिन्नसंशयः ।।१०।।

Na dweshtyakushalam karma kushale naanushajjate;
Tyaagee sattvasamaavishto medhaavee chchinnasam-
shayah.

10. The *sattvic* renouncer is wise. He has no doubts
and no aversion to disagreeable actions and no
attachment to agreeable ones.

न हि देहभृता शक्यं त्यक्तुं कर्माण्यशेषतः।
यस्तु कर्मफलत्यागी स त्यागीत्यभिधीयते ।।११।।

Na hi dehabhritaa shakyam tyaktum karmaanyasheshatah;
Yastu karmaphalatyaagi sa tyaageetyabhidheeyate.

11. Indeed it is impossible for an embodied being to relinquish action altogether, so the one who gives up the fruit of action is known as a renunciate (*tyagi*).

अनिष्टमिष्टं मिश्रं च त्रिविधं कर्मणः फलम्।
भवत्यत्यागिनां प्रेत्य न तु संन्यासिनां क्वचित् ।।१२।।

Anishtamishtam mishram cha trividham karmanah phalam;
Bhavatyatyaaginaam pretya na tu sannyaasinaam kwachit.

12. Those who have not given up desire for the fruit of action, can expect three types of result when they depart (die)—pleasant, unpleasant and mixed but for the renouncer there is none.

पञ्चैतानि महाबाहो कारणानि निबोध मे।
सांख्ये कृतान्ते प्रोक्तानि सिद्धये सर्वकर्मणाम् ।।१३।।

Panchaitaani mahaabaaho kaaranaani nibodha me;
Saamkhye kritaante proktaani siddhaye sarvakarmanaam.

13. Hear from Me O Arjuna (Mahabaho), of the five factors which are necessary for the accomplishment of any action as stated in the doctrine of the Sankhya.

अधिष्ठानं तथा कर्ता करणं च पृथग्विधम्।
विविधाश्च पृथक्चेष्टा दैवं चैवात्र पञ्चमम् ।।१४।।

Adhishthaanam tathaa kartaa karanam cha prithagvidham;
Vividhaashcha prithakcheshtaa daivam chaivaatra
panchamam.

14. These five are the body, the agent, the sense
organs, the different types of effort and finally the
fifth—divine providence.

शरीरवाङ्मनोभिर्यत्कर्म प्रारभते नरः।
न्याय्यं वा विपरीतं वा पञ्चैते तस्य हेतवः ।।१५।।

Shareeravaangmanobhiryat karma praarabhate narah;
Nyaayyam vaa vipareetam vaa panchaite tasya hetavah.

15. These five are necessary factors in whatever
action either proper or improper which a person
performs with his body, mind and speech.

तत्रैवं सति कर्तारमात्मानं केवलं तु यः।
पश्यत्यकृतबुद्धित्वान्न स पश्यति दुर्मतिः ।।१६।।

Tatraivam sati kartaaramaatmaanam kevalam tu ya;
Pashyatyakritabuddhitwaanna sa pashyati durmatih.

16. Such being the case, the immature mind with
little understanding which thinks itself to be sole
agent, does not see at all.

यस्य नाहंकृतो भावो बुद्धिर्यस्य न लिप्यते।
हत्वापि स इमाँल्लोकान्न हन्ति न निबध्यते ।।१७।।

Yasya naahamkrito bhaavo buddhiryasya na lipyate;
Hatwaapi sa immaamlokaan na hanti na nibadhyate.

17. One who is free from egoism and whose intellect is not tainted (with the feeling of doership), does not slay and is not bound (by the action), even if he were to slay all these people.

ज्ञानं ज्ञेयं परिज्ञाता त्रिविधां कर्मचोदना।
करणं कर्म कर्तेति त्रिविधः कर्मसंग्रहः ।।१८।।

Jnaanam jneyam parijnaataa trividhaa karmachodanaa;
Karanam karma karteti trividhah karmasangrahah.

18. Knowledge, the object of knowledge and the knower are the three incentives to action. The three-fold bases for action are, the instruments, the action and the agent.

ज्ञानं कर्म च कर्ता च त्रिधैव गुणभेदतः।
प्रोच्यते गुणसंख्याने यथावच्छृणु तान्यपि ।।१९।।

Jnaanam karma cha kartaa cha tridhaiva gunabhedatah;
Prochyate gunasankhyaane yathaavacchrinu taanyapi.

19. According to the Sankhya doctrine, knowledge, action and agent are of three kinds, distinguished by the difference in their modes. Hear of these also.

सर्वभूतेषु येनैकं भावमव्ययमीक्षते ।
अविभक्तं विभक्तेषु तज्ज्ञानं विद्धि सात्त्विकम् ।२० ।

Sarvabhooteshu yenaikam bhaavamavyayameekshate;
Avibhaktam vibhakteshu tadjnaanam viddhi saattvikam.

20. *Sattvic* knowledge is that which sees the One Immutable Being in all becomings; the One indivisible whole in all divisions.

पृथक्त्वेन तु यज्ज्ञानं नानाभावान्पृथग्विधान् ।
वेत्ति सर्वेषु भूतेषु तज्ज्ञानं विद्धि राजसम् ।।२१।।

Prithaktwena tu yajjnaanam naanaabhaavaanprit-hagvidhaan;
Vetti sarveshu bhooteshu tajjnaanam viddhi raajasam.

21. *Rajasic* knowledge sees only the multiplicity and variety in all beings, all totally different from each other.

यत्तु कृत्स्नवदेकस्मिन्कार्ये सक्तमहैतुकम् ।
अतत्त्वार्थवदल्पं च तत्तामसमुदाहृतम् ।।२२।।

Yattu kritsnavadekasmin kaarye saktamahaitukam;
Atattwaarthavadalpam cha tattaamasamudaahritam.

22. *Tamasic* knowledge clings to some trivial part as
if it were the whole even though such a premise has
no rational validity and no foundation in truth.

नियतं सङ्गरहितमरागद्वेषतः कृतम् ।
अफलप्रेप्सुना कर्म यत्तत्सात्त्विकमुच्यते ।।२३।।

Niyatam sangarahitam araagadweshatah kritam;
Aphalaprepsunaa karma yattatsaathwikamuchyate.

23. *Sattvic* action is that which has been rightly
ordained, free from attachment and performed with
neither desire nor aversion or expectation of reward.

यत्तु कामेप्सुना कर्म साहंकारेण वा पुनः।
क्रियते बहुलायासं तद्राजसमुदाहृतम् ।।२४।।

Yattu kaamepsunaa karma saahankaarena vaa punah;
Kriyate bhulaayaasam tadraajasamudaahritam.

24. *Rajasic* action is impelled by desire and egoism
and is done with great strain.

अनुबन्धं क्षयं हिंसामनवेक्ष्य च पौरुषम्।
मोहादारभ्यते कर्म यत्तत्तामसमुच्यते ।।२५।।

Anubandham kshayam himsaamanavekshya cha paurusham;
Mohaadaarabhyate karma yattat taamsamuchyate.

25. *Tamasic* action is undertaken in a mechanical fashion without taking into consideration the consequences, or loss or injury to others or even of one's own ability to accomplish it.

मुक्तसङ्गोऽनहंवादी   धृत्युत्साहसमन्वितः ।
सिद्ध्यसिद्ध्योर्निर्विकारः कर्ता सात्त्विक उच्यते ।।२६।।

Mukatasangonahamvaadi dhrityutsaahasamanvitah;
Sidhyasidhyornirvikaarah kartaa saattvika uchyate.

26. The *sattvic* worker (agent) is detached, non-egoistic, resolute, enthusiastic and unaffected by success and failure.

रागी कर्मफलप्रेप्सुर्लुब्धो हिंसात्मकोऽशुचिः ।
हर्षशोकान्वितः कर्ता राजसः परिकीर्तितः ।।२७।।

Raagee karmaphalaprepsurlubdho himsaatmako'shuchih;
Harshashokaanvitah kartaa raajasah parikeertitah.

27. The *rajasic* worker is passionately attached to the fruit of action, impure, greedy, resorting to violence and easily elated and depressed (by success and failure).

अयुक्तः प्राकृतःस्तब्धः शठो नैष्कृतिकोऽलसः ।
विषादी दीर्घसूत्री च कर्ता तामस उच्यते ।।२८।।

Ayuktah praakritah stabdhah shatho naishkritikolasah;
Vishaadee deerghasootree cha kartaa taamasa uchyate.

28. The *tamasic* worker is unreliable, vulgar, stubborn, cunning, insolent, lazy, and procrastinating.

बुद्धेर्भेदं धृतेश्चैव गुणतस्त्रिविधं शृणु ।
प्रोच्यमानमशेषेण पृथक्त्वेन धनंजय ।।२९।।

Buddherbhedam dhriteshchaiva gunatastrividham shrinu;
Prochyamaanamasheshena prithaktwena dhananjaya.

29. O Arjuna (Dhananjaya)! You may now listen to an exhaustive account of the differences in intelligence and perseverance according to the three modes.

प्रवृत्तिं च निवृत्तिं च कार्याकार्ये भयाभये ।
बन्धं मोक्षं च या वेत्ति बुद्धिः सा पार्थ सात्त्विकी ।।३०।।

Pravrittim cha nivrittim cha karyaakaarye bhayaabhaye;
Bandham moksham cha yaa vetti buddhih saa paartha
saattvikee.

30. O Arjuna (Partha)! The *sattvic* intellect knows to differentiate between action and renunciation, what should be done and what avoided, what to fear and

what not to fear as well as the truth about bondage
and liberation.

यया धर्ममधर्मं च कार्यं चाकार्यमेव च।
अयथावत्प्रजानाति बुद्धिः सा पार्थ राजसी ।।३१।।

*Yayaa dharmamadharmam cha kaaryam chaakaaryameva
cha;*
Ayathaavat prajaanaati buddhih saa paartha raajasee.

31. O Arjuna (Partha)! The *rajasic* intellect misjudges
between right and wrong (*dharma* and *adharma*),
what aught to be done and what ought not to be
done.

अधर्मं धर्ममिति या मन्यते तमसावृता।
सर्वार्थान्विपरीतांश्च बुद्धिः सा पार्थ तामसी ।।३२।।

Adharmam dharmamiti yaa manyate tamasaavritaa;
*Sarvaarthaan vipareetaamscha buddhih saa paartha
taamasee.*

32. Enveloped in darkness, the *tamasic* intellect has
a distorted view of everything and sees wrong as
right.

धृत्या यया धारयते मनःप्राणेन्द्रियक्रियाः।
योगेनाव्यभिचारिण्या धृतिः सा पार्थ सात्त्विकी ।।३३।।

Dhrityaa yayaa dhaarayate manahpraanendriyakriyaah;
Yogenaavyabhichaarinyaa dhritih saa paartha saattvikee.

33. The unswerving firmness by which one controls
the functions of the mind, breath and senses through
yoga, is *sattvic* firmness.

यया तु धर्मकामार्थान्धृत्या धारयतेऽर्जुन।
प्रसङ्गेन फलाकाङ्क्षी धृतिः सा पार्थ राजसी ।।३४।।

Yayaa tu dharmakaamarthaan dhrityaa dhaarayaterjuna;
Prasangena phalaakaankshee dhritih saa paartha rajasee.

34. That persistence with which one hangs on to
duty, wealth and pleasure only because of attachment to the fruit, that firmness is *rajasic*.

यया स्वप्नं भयं शोकं विषादं मदमेव च।
न विमुञ्चति दुर्मेधा धृतिः सा पार्थ तामसी ।।३५।।

Yayaa swapnam bhayam shokam vishaadam madameva
cha;
Na vimunchati durmedhaa dhritih saa paartha taamasee.

35. That firmness by which the stupid person clings
on to sleep, fear, grief, depression and pride, is
tamasic.

सुखं त्विदानीं त्रिविधं शृणु मे भरतर्षभ।
अभ्यासाद्रमते यत्र दुःखान्तं च निगच्छति ।।३६।।

Sukham twidaaneem trividham shrinu me bharatarshabha;
Abhyaasaadramate yatra duhkhaantam cha nigacchati.

36. O Arjuna (Bharatharshabha)! Now hear from Me of the three types of happiness, which gains joy with practice and puts an end to suffering.

यत्तदग्रे विषमिव परिणामे मृतोपमम् ।
तत्सुखं सात्त्विकं प्रोक्तमात्मबुद्धिप्रसादजम् ।।३७।।

Yattadagre vishamiva parinaamemritopamam;
Tatsukham saattvikam proktamaatmabuddhiprasaadajam.

37. That which appears like poison at first but turns out to be like nectar in the end, which springs from a clear understanding of the Self is *sattvic*.

विषयेन्द्रियसंयोगाद्यत्तदग्रेऽमृतोपमम् ।
परिणामे विषमिव तत्सुखं राजसं स्मृतम् ।।३८।।

Vishayendriyasamyogaadyattadagre'mritopamam;
Parinaame vishamiva tatsukham raajasam smritam.

38. That happiness is *rajasic* which is derived from the contact of the senses with their objects and therefore it is like nectar in the beginning and poison at the end.

यदग्रे चानुबन्धे च सुखं मोहनमात्मनः ।
निद्रालस्यप्रमादोत्थं तत्तामसमुदाहृतम् ।।३९।।

Yadagre chaanubandhe cha sukham mohanamaatmanah;
Nidraalasyapramaadottham tattaamasamudaahritam.

39. That happiness which begins and ends in self-delusion, and arises from sleep, sloth and miscomprehension, is said to be *tamasic*.

न तदस्ति पृथिव्यां वा दिवि देवेषु वा पुनः ।
सत्त्वं प्रकृतिजैर्मुक्तं यदेमिः स्यात्त्रिमिर्गुणैः ।।४०।।

Na tadasti prithivyaam vaa divi devesheu vaa punah;
Sattvam prakritijairmuktam yadebhih syaattribhirgunaih.

40. There is no being, either on earth or in heaven amongst the gods that is free from the workings of these three modes of Nature.

ब्राह्मणक्षत्रियविशां शूद्राणां च परंतप ।
कर्माणि प्रविभक्तानि स्वभावप्रभवैर्गुणैः ।।४१।।

Braahmanakshatriyavishaam shoodraanam cha paramtapa;
Karmaani pravibhaktaani swabhaavaprabhavairgunaih.

41. O Arjuna (Paramtapa)! The duties of the Brahmins, Kshatriyas, Vaishyas and Shudras are also apportioned according to their own inborn qualities (*gunas*).

शमो दमस्तपः शौचं क्षान्तिरार्जवमेव च।
ज्ञानं विज्ञानमास्तिक्यं ब्रह्मकर्म स्वभावजम् ।।४२।।

Shamo damastapah shaucham kshaantiraarjavameva cha;
Jnaanam vijnaanamaastikyam brahmakarma swbhaavajam.

42. Serenity, self-control, austerity, purity, endurance, candour, knowledge, wisdom and belief in God are the duties of the Brahmins, born of their innate nature.

शौर्यं तेजो धृतिर्दाक्ष्यं युद्धे चाप्यपलायनम्।
दानमीश्वरभावश्च क्षात्रं कर्म स्वभावजम् ।।४३।।

Shauryam tejo dhritirdaakshyam yuddhe chaapyapalaa-
yanam;
Daanameeshwarabhaavashcha kshaatram karma
swabhaavajam.

43. Heroism, majesty, resolution, dexterity, not shirking from battle, generosity and ability to command, are the duties of the Kshatriyas which are part of their nature (these are the signs of the Kshatriya).

कृषिगौरक्ष्यवाणिज्यं वैश्यकर्म स्वभावजम्।
परिचर्यात्मकं कर्म शूद्रस्यापि स्वभावजम् ।।४४।।

Krishigorakshyavaanijyam vaishyakarma swabhaavajam;
Paricharyaatmakam karma shoodrasyaapi swabhaavajam.

44. Agriculture, rearing of cattle and trade are the duties of the Vaishyas, born of their own nature. The duty of the Shudras which is natural to them is service.

स्वे स्वे कर्मण्यभिरतः संसिद्धिं लभते नरः।
स्वकर्मनिरतः सिद्धिं यथा विन्दति तच्छृणु ॥४५॥

Swe swe karmanyabhiratah samsiddhim labhate narah;
Swakarmaniratah siddhim yathaa vindati tacchrinu.

45. A person can attain perfection through the performance of his own duty. Now hear from Me how such a one who is devoted to duty attains perfection.

यतः प्रवृत्तिर्भूतानां येन सर्वमिदं ततम्।
स्वकर्मणा तमभ्यर्च्य सिद्धिं विन्दति मानवः ॥४६॥

Yatah pravrittirbhootaanaam yena sarvamidam tatam;
Swakarmanaa tamabhyarchya siddhim vindati maanavah.

46. One can attain perfection by worshipping Him, from Whom all beings originate and by Whom all this is pervaded, through the performance of one's own duty.

श्रेयान्स्वधर्मो विगुणः परधर्मात्स्वनुष्ठितात्।
स्वभावनियतं कर्म कुर्वन्नाप्नोति किल्बिषम् ॥४७॥

ॐ

*Shreyaanswadharmo vigunah paradharmaatswanu-
shthitaat;
Swabhaavaniyatam karma kurvannaapnoti kilbisham.*

47. One who performs duties as dictated by his own
nature incurs no sin. Therefore it is better to do one's
own duty, however imperfectly than the duty of
another however well executed.

सहजं कर्म कौन्तेय सदोषमपि न त्यजेत्।
सर्वारम्भा हि दोषेण धूमेनाग्निरिवावृताः ।।४८।।

*Sahajam karma kaunteya sadoshamapi na tyajet;
Sarvaarambhaa hi doshena dhoomenaagnirivaavritaah.*

48. O Arjuna (Kaunteya)! One should not give up
one's inborn duty however (apparently) defective. In
any case, all undertakings are enveloped by evil as
fire by smoke.

असक्तबुद्धिः सर्वत्र जितात्मा विगतस्पृहः।
नैष्कर्म्यसिद्धिं परमां संन्यासेनाधिगच्छति ।।४९।।

*Asaktabuddhih sarvatra jitaatmaa vigatasprihah;
Naishkarmyasiddhim paramaam sannyaasenaadhigacchati.*

49. One whose intellect is not attached to anything,
who has subdued his self (lower) and has no desires,
attains the state of perfect non-action through renunciation.

सिद्धिं प्राप्तो यथा ब्रह्म तथाप्नोति निबोध मे।
समासेनैव कौन्तेय निष्ठा ज्ञानस्य या परा ।।५०।।

Siddhim praapto yathaa brahma tathaapnoti nibodha me;
Samaasenaiva kaunteya nishthaa jnaanasya yaa paraa.

50. Now I shall briefly tell you O Arjuna (Kaunteya),
how one who has reached perfection also attains
Brahman who is the summit of wisdom.

बुद्ध्या विशुद्धया युक्तो घृत्यात्मानं नियम्य च।
शब्दादीन्विषयांस्त्यक्त्वा रागद्वैषौ व्युदस्य च ।।५१।।

Buddhyaa vishuddhayaa yukto dhrityaatmaanam niyamya
cha;
Shabdaadeenvishayaanstyaktwaa raagadweshau vyudasya
cha.

51. Purifying the intellect and firmly subduing the
(lower) self, casting off attraction and repulsion to
sound and other sense objects.

विविक्तसेवी लघ्वाशी यतवाक्कायमानसः।
ध्यानयोगपरो नित्यं वैराग्यं समुपाश्रितः ।।५२।।

Viviktasevee laghwaashee yatavaakkaayamaanasah;
Dhyaanayogaparo nityam vairaagyam samupaashritah.

52. Dwelling in sequestered places, eating sparingly,
controlling speech, body and mind, constantly en-

gaging in the *yoga* of meditation, strengthened through dispassion.

अहंकारं बलं दर्पं कामं क्रोधं परिग्रहम्।
विमुच्य निर्ममः शान्तो ब्रह्मभूयाय कल्पते ।।५३।।

Ahamkaaram balam darpam kaamam krodham parigraham;
Vimuchya nirmamah shaanto brahmabhooyaaya kalpate.

53. Giving up egoism, violence, arrogance, lust, wrath and possessiveness, calm and unselfish—such a person is fit to attain unity with Brahman.

ब्रह्मभूतः प्रसन्नात्मा न शोचति न काङ्क्षति।
समः सर्वेषु भूतेषु मद्भक्तिं लभते पराम् ।।५४।।

Brahmabhootah prasannaatmaa na shochati na kaankshati;
Samah sarveshu bhooteshu madbhaktim labhate paraam.

54. The serene Self who is one with Brahman does not grieve or yearn. The same to all beings, he attains supreme devotion to Me.

भक्त्या मामभिजानाति यावान्यश्चासि तत्त्वतः।
ततो मां तत्त्वतो ज्ञात्वा विशते तदनन्तरम् ।।५५।।

Bhaktyaa maamabhijaanaati yaavanyashchaasmi tattwatah;

Tato maam tattwato jnaatwaa vishate tadanantaram.

55. Through devotion he comes to know who and what I am in reality. One who knows Me in truth, forthwith enters into Me.

सर्वकर्माण्यपि सदा कुर्वाणो मद्व्यपाश्रयः ।
मत्प्रसादादवाप्नोति शाश्वतं पदमव्ययम् ।।५६।।

Sarvakarmaanyapi sadaa kurvaano madvyapaashrayah;
Matprasaadaadavaapnoti shaashwatam padamavyayam.

56. Though continuing to perform all actions, one who takes refuge in Me, will attain the eternal, imperishable abode, by My grace.

चेतसा सर्वकर्माणि मयि संन्यस्य मत्परः ।
बुद्धियोगमुपाश्रित्य मच्चित्तः सततं भव ।।५७।।

Chetasaa sarvakarmaani mayi sannyasya matparah;
Buddhiyogamupaashritya macchittah satatam bhava.

57. Mentally surrendering all actions to Me and regarding Me as the Supreme, take recourse to the *yoga* of the intelligent will and constantly think of Me.

मच्चित्तः सर्वदुर्गाणि मत्प्रसादात्तरिष्यसि ।
अथ चेत्त्वमहंकारान्न श्रोष्यसि विनङ्क्ष्यसि ।।५८।।

Macchittah sarvadurgaani matprasaadaat tarishyasi;
Atha chettwamahankaaraanna shroshyasi vinankshyasi.

58. Fix your mind on Me and you will be able to overcome all obstacles by My grace but if through egoism you refuse to listen to Me, you will surely perish.

यदहंकारमाश्रित्य न योत्स्य इति मन्यसे।
मिथ्यैष व्यवसायस्ते प्रकृतिस्त्वां नियोक्ष्यति ।।५९।।

Yadahamkaaramaashritya na yotsya iti manyase;
Mithyaisha vyavasaayaste prakritistwaam niyokshyati.

59. If out of conceit you say, "I shall not fight", your resolve will be in vain for your own nature will compel you.

स्वभावजेन कौन्तेय निबद्धः स्वेन कर्मणा।
कर्तुं नेच्छसि यन्मोहात्करिष्यस्यवशोऽपि तत् ।।६०।।

Swabhaavajena kaunteya nibaddhah swena karmanaa;
Kartum necchasi yanmohaat karishyasyavashopi tat.

60. O Arjuna (Kaunteya)! You will be helplessly driven to do that same action which out of delusion you have decided against doing, bound as you are by your *karma*, born of your own nature.

ईश्वरः सर्वभूतानां हृद्देशेऽर्जुन तिष्ठति।
भ्रामयन्सर्वभूतानि यन्त्रारूढानि मायया ।।६१।।

Ishwarah sarvabhootaanaam hriddeshe'rjuna tishthati;
Bhraamayan sarvabhootaani yantraaroodhaani maayayaa.

61. O Arjuna! The Lord dwells in the hearts of all
beings causing them to revolve as if mounted on a
giant wheel, through the power of His cosmic illusion (*maya*).

तमेव शरणं गच्छ सर्वभावेन भारत।
तत्प्रसादात्परां शान्तिं स्थानं प्राप्स्यसि शाश्वतम् ।।६२।।

Tameva sharanam gaccha sarvabhaavena bhaarata;
Tatprasaadaatparaam shantim sthaanam praapsyasi
shaashwatam.

62. Seek refuge in Him alone O Arjuna (Bharatha),
with your entire being, for by His grace you will be
able to attain supreme peace and the eternal abode.

इति ते ज्ञानमाख्यातं गुह्याद्गुह्यतरं मया।
विमृश्यैतदशेषेण यथेच्छसि तथा कुरु ।।६३।।

Iti te jnaanamaakhyaatam guhyaadguhyataram mayaa;
Vimrishyaitadasheshena yathechchasi tathaa kuru.

63. Thus has wisdom more profound than all pro-

ॐ

fundities been declared to you by Me. Reflect fully
upon it and then act as you please.

सर्वगुह्यतमं भूयः शृणु मे परमं वचः।
इष्टोऽसि मे दृढमिति ततो वक्ष्यामि ते हितम् ।।६४।

Sarvaguhyatamam bhooyah shrinu me paramam vachah;
Ishtosi me dridhamiti tato vakshyaami te hitam.

64. Listen again to My supreme word—the most
profound! You are extremely dear to Me, hence I
shall tell you what is best for you.

ॐ मन्मना भव मद्भक्तो मद्याजी मां नमस्कुरु।
मामेवैष्यसि सत्यं ते प्रतिजाने प्रियोऽसि मे ।।६५।।

Manmanaa bhava madbhakto madyaajee maam
namaskuru;
Mamevaishyasi satyam te pratijaane priyo'si me.

65. Fix your mind on Me, be devoted to Me, sacrifice
unto Me and prostrate before Me. I give you My
solemn pledge that you will indeed come to Me for
you are dear to Me.

सर्वधर्मान्परित्यज्य मामेकं शरणं व्रज।
अहं त्वा सर्वपापेभ्यो मोक्षयिष्यामि मा शुचः ।।६६।।

Sarvadharmaan parityajya maamekam sharanam vraja;
Aham twaa sarvapaapebhyo mokshayishyaami maa
shuchah;

66. Abandoning all duties (*dharmas*), take refuge in
Me alone. Do not worry for I shall deliver you from
all evils.

इदं ते नातपस्काय नाभक्ताय कदाचन।
न चाशुश्रूषवे वाच्यं न च मां योऽभ्यसूयति ।।६७।।

Idam te naatapaskaaya naabhaktaaya kadaachana;
Na chaashushrooshave vaachyam na cha maam
yobhyasooyati.

67. You should not speak of this to one who is
devoid of austerity or to one without devotion, or
to one who is not service-minded or who does not
care to listen or to one who belittles Me.

य इमं परमं गुह्यं मद्भक्तेष्वभिधास्यति।
भक्तिं मयि परां कृत्वा मामेवैष्यत्यसंशयः ।।६८।।

Ya imam paramam guhyam madbhakteshvabhidhaasyati;
Bhaktim mayi paraam kritwaa maamevaishyatyasam-
shayah.

68. One who is greatly devoted to Me and who
imparts this profound teaching to My devotees, will
undoubtedly come to Me.

न च तस्मान्मनुष्येषु कश्चिन्मे प्रियकृत्तमः।
भविता न च मे तस्मादन्यः प्रियतरो भुवि ।।६९।।

Na cha tasmaanmanushyeshu kashchinme priyakrittamah;
Bhavitaa na cha me tasmaadanyah priyataro bhuvi.

69. There shall be none among mortals who does a
more loving service to Me than such a one and there
shall be none on earth who is dearer to Me.

अध्येष्यते च य इमं धर्म्यं संवादमावयोः।
ज्ञानयज्ञेन तेनाहमिष्टः स्यामिति मे मतिः ।।७०।।

Adhyeshyate cha ya imam dharmyam samvaadamaavayoh;
Jnaanayajnena tenaahamishtah syaamiti me matih.

70. I aver that those who study this sacred dialogue
of ours will be worshipping Me through the performance of the sacrifice of knowledge (*jnana yajna*).

श्रद्धावाननसूयश्च शृणुयादपि यो नरः।
सोऽपि मुक्तः शुभाँल्लोकान्प्राप्नुयात्पुण्यकर्मणाम् ।।७१।।

Shraddhaavaananasooyashcha srinuyaadapi yo narah;
So'pi muktah shubhaamlokaanpraapnuyaatpunyak-
armanaam.

71. Even those who listen to this (discourse)
uncritically and with full faith, will attain the pure
worlds of the righteous, after liberation (from this
body).

कच्चिदेतच्छ्रुतं पार्थ त्वयैकाग्रेण चेतसा।
कच्चिदज्ञानसंमोहः प्रनष्टस्ते धनंजय ।।७२।।

Kacchidetacchrutam paartha twayaikaagrena chetasaa;
Kacchidajnaanasammohah pranashtaste dhananjaya.

72. O Arjuna (Partha, Dhananjaya)! Have you been listening to this with full concentration? Has your delusion born out of ignorance been destroyed?

अर्जुन उवाच
नष्टो मोहः स्मृतिर्लब्धा त्वत्प्रसादान्मयाच्युत।
स्थितोऽस्मि गतसन्देहः करिष्ये वचनं तव ।।७३।।

Arjuna uvaacha
Nashto mohah smritirlabdhaa twatprasaadaanmayaa-
chyuta;
Sthito'smi gatasandehah karishye vachanam tava.

Thus spoke Arjuna:

73. O Krishna (Achyutha)! By Your grace my delusion has been dispelled and I have regained my senses. My doubts have vanished and I stand firm to obey Your command.

संजय उवाच
इत्यहं वासुदेवस्य पार्थस्य च महात्मनः।
संवादमिममश्रोषमद्भुतं रोमहर्षणम् ।।७४।।

Sanjaya uvaacha
Ityaham vaasudevasya paarthasya cha mahaatmanah;
Samvaadamimamashraushamadbhutam romaharshanam.

Thus spoke Sanjaya:

74. Thus have I heard this remarkable discourse between Krishna (Vaasudeva) and the high-souled Arjuna (Partha) which has thrilled me.

व्यासप्रसादाच्छुतवानेतद्गुह्यमहं परम् ।
योगं योगेश्वरात्कृष्णात्साक्षात्कथयतः स्वयम् ॥७५॥

Vyaasaprasaadaacchrutavaanetadguhyamaham param;
Yogam yogeshwaraat krishnaat saakshaat kathayatah swayam.

75. By the grace of Vyasa I have heard this supreme and most profound *yoga* directly from the mouth of Lord Krishna — the Master of the masters of *yoga*.

राजन्संसृत्य संसृत्य संवादमिममद्भुतम् ।
केशवार्जुनयोः पुण्यं हृष्यामि च मुहुर्मुहुः ॥७६॥

Raajan samsmritya samsmritya samvaadamimamad-
bhutam;
Keshavaarjunayoh punyam hrishyaami cha muhurmuhuh.

76. O King (Dritarashtra)! Repeatedly recalling this wonderful and sacred dialogue between Krishna (Keshava) and Arjuna, I rejoice over and over again.

तच्च संस्मृत्य संस्मृत्य रूपमत्यद्भुतं हरे: ।
विस्मयो मे महान्राजन्हृष्यामि च पुनः पुनः ।।७७।।

Taccha samsmritya samsmritya roopamatyadbhutam hareh;
Vismayo me mahaan rajan hrishyaami cha punah punah.

77. Repeatedly recalling that most wonderful form of Krishna (Hari), I am filled with awe and I rejoice over and over again.

यत्र योगेश्वरः कृष्णो यत्र पार्थो धनुर्धरः ।
तत्र श्रीर्विजयो भूतिर्ध्रुवा नीतिर्मतिर्मम ।।७८।

Yatra yogeshwarah krishno yatra paartho dhanurdharah;
Tatra shreervijayo bhootirdhruvaa neetirmatirmama.

78. I am convinced that prosperity, victory, glory and righteousness shall reign wherever Krishna, the master *yogi*, and Arjuna, the wielder of the bow stand united.

ॐ तत्सदिति श्रीमद्भगवद्गीतासूपनिषत्सु ब्रह्मविद्यायां
योगशास्त्रे श्रीकृष्णार्जुनसंवादे मोक्षसंन्यासयोगो
नामाष्टादशोऽध्यायः ।।१८।।

Hari om tat sat iti srimad bhagavad gitaasoopanishatsu brahmavidyaayaam yogashaastre sri krishnaarjunasamvaade mokshasannyaasyogo naama ashtaadasho'dhyaayah.

Aum Tat Sat:

Thus in the Upanishad of the Bhagavad Gita, the Knowledge of Supreme Brahman, the Scripture of *Yoga*, the dialogue between Sri Krishna and Arjuna, ends the eighteenth chapter entitled, "The *Yoga* of Liberation and Renunciation."

Hari Aum Tat Sat

GLOSSARY OF SANSKRIT TERMS

GLOSSARY OF SANSKRIT TERMS

adhibhuta	the world of phenomena.
adhyatma	the Spirit within the embodied person.
adidaiva	the Spirit in Nature.
Adityas	sun gods.
adiyajna	Lord of all sacrifices (action).
asat	non-existence.
asuras	demons.
Ashvins	twin physicians of the gods.
atman	the immortal Spirit within the human being.
Aum	mantra (sound), denoting the Supreme.
Brahman	the supreme unmanifest Absolute.
Brahmins	members of the priestly caste.
buddhi yoga	yoga of the intelligent will.
dharma	duty, religion, morality, ethics.
gunas	the three essential modes of energy of the three primeval qualities that form the nature of things.
Gandharvas	celestial musicians.
japa	repetition of God's names.

jnana yajna	the sacrifice of knowledge.
jnana yoga	the yoga of knowledge.
jnani	a wise person.
kalpa	eon; age.
karma	action entailing reaction.
karma yoga	the yoga of action.
Kshatriya	one belonging to the warrior and ruling caste.
kshetra	field.
Kshetrajna	the knower of the field; the Supreme Lord.
kusha	type of grass used in rituals.
Mahat Brahma	the procreating father of creation.
Maruts	wind gods.
maya	the Lord's power of illusion.
nirvana	state of bliss; liberation.
Prakriti	material nature; the active principle of Purusha.
Purusha	The Lord; the pure witnessing consciousness.
rajas	kinesis; the quality of activity; passion.
rakshasas	hostile beings with cannibalistic habits.
Rudras	type of gods.

samadhi	super-conscious state.
Sankhya	the philosophy of wisdom; one of the six systems of Indian philosophy.
sannyasa	renunciation.
sannyasin	a renunciate.
sat	existence; reality.
sattva	the quality of harmony; goodness.
Shudras	members of the fourth caste engaged in service.
siddhas	perfected souls.
soma	sacred medicinal plant found in the Himalayas used in sacrifices.
swadharma	action governed by the essential quality of our nature.
tamas	the quality of darkness; inertia.
Tat	That; denoting the Supreme.
tyaga	relinquishment; mental renunciation.
tyagi	a renouncer.
Upanishads	the final portions of all the Vedas containing highest philosophical truths.
Vaishyas	members of the merchant

ॐ

	class; the third caste.
Vasus	demigods.
Vedas	the most ancient books on spirituality known to humanity (four in number).
Vedanta	the philosophy based on the Upanishads which are found in the last portion of the Vedas.
Yakshas	demigods; keepers of treasure.
yajna	Vedic fire sacrifice; ritual.
yoga	union or oneness of the subjective being with the Supreme; any activity which leads to this oneness.
yoga maya	the Lord's power of illusion.
yogi	one who practises yoga; one who is in union with God.

Names and Titles given to Lord Krishna in the Srimad Bhagavad Gita

Achyutha	The One who has no fall. The ever constant One.
Aadideva	The first of the gods.
Aja	The Unborn.
Akshara	The Imperishable One.
Anaadi	The One without a beginning.
Ananta	The One without an end.
Anantabahu	The One with endless arms.
Ananta roopa	The One with endless forms.
Anantaveerya	The One with unlimited valour.
Aprabhava	The One with incomparable glory.
Aprameya	The immeasurable One.
Arisudana	The slayer of enemies.
Avyaya	The immutable One.
Bhagavan	The blessed One with the eight divine qualities.
Bhavan	The holy One.
Bhutesha	The Lord of all beings.
Deva	A divine being; a shining being.
Devadeva	God of gods.

Devavara	Best among gods.
Devesha	Lord of gods.
Dharmagoptha	The custodian of dharma.
Divyam	The effulgent.
Govinda	The Chief of herdsmen; Protector of jivas and cattle.
Hari	The remover of sorrows.
Hrishikesha	The bristling-haired One; The Lord of the senses.
Isa; Iswara	God.
Jagannivasa	The abode of the universe.
Jagathpathi	The Lord of the universe.
Janardana	The agitator; The One who removes the sorrows of birth and death.
Kamalapatraksha	The One with eyes like a lotus petal.
Keshava	The One with thick hair.
Keshinishoodana	The slayer of the demon Keshi.
Krishna	The One who is dark in complexion; The enticer.
Madhava	Consort of Madhavi or Mahalakshmi.
Madhusudana	Destroyer of the demon Madhu.

Mahabaahu	The mighty-armed One.
Mahatman	The great-souled One.
Mahayogeeswara	The great Lord of yoga.
Mahayogi	The great yogi
Paramam	The transcendent.
Parabrahman	The supreme, transcendental Brahman.
Param dhama	The supreme abode.
Parameshwara	The supreme God.
Paramnidhanam	The supreme refuge.
Pavitram	The pure One.
Prabhu	The splendid One.
Prajapati	Lord of creatures.
Purusha	The pure witnessing consciousness.
Purushapurana	The ancient person.
Purushottama	The supreme Person or Spirit.
Sahasrabahu	The thousand-armed One.
Sakha	Friend.
Sarva	The all-encompassing One.
Sri Bhagavan	The blessed One filled with auspiciousness.
Vaasudeva	The son of Vasudeva; the omnipresent being.
Varshneya	Belonging to the Vrishni clan.
Vedidavyam	The supreme knowable.
Vishnu	The all-pervading One.
Vishwamoorthi	The One whose form is the

ॐ

	universe.
Vishwaroopa	The One with the cosmic form.
Vishveshvara	God of the universe.
Yadava	The descendent of King Yadu.
Yogin; yogi	The One who is ever united with the Supreme.
Yogeeshwara	The Master yogi.

Names and Titles given to Arjuna in the
Srimad Bhagavad Gita.

Anagha	The sinless one.
Arjuna	The pure one; the white one.
Bharatha	The descendent of King Bharatha.
Bharathasattama	Most virtuous among the descendents of Bharatha.
Bharatharshabha	Bull of the Bhaarathaas.
Bharathashreshta	Best of the Bhaarathaas.
Dhananjaya	Conqueror of wealth.
Gudakesha	Curly-haired one; the conqueror of sleep.
Kapidwaja	The ape-bannered one.
Kaunteya	Son of Kunti.
Kiritin	The diademed one.
Kurunandana	Joy of the Kurus.
Kurupraveera	Hero of the Kurus.
Kurusattama	Noblest of the Kurus.
Kurushreshta	Best among the Kurus.
Mahabaho	The mighty-armed one.
Pandava	The son of Pandu.

Paramtapa	The scorcher of foes.
Partha	The son of Pritha or Kunti.
Purusharshabha	Bull among men.
Purushavyagrah	Tiger among men.
Savyasachin	The ambidextrous one.

List of other characters appearing in the Srimad
Bhagavad Gita according to their
order of appearance.

Dritarashtra	Blind king of the Kurus. Father of the Kauravas.
Sanjaya.	The king's companion.
Duryodana	Eldest of the Kauravas.
Dronaacharya	Preceptor of the Kauravas and Pandavas.
Drupada	Father-in-law of the Pandavas.
Drishtadyumna	Drupada's eldest son; brother-in-law of the Pandavas.
Arjuna	Third among the five Pandavas.
Bhima; Vrikodara	Second among the Pandavas.
Yuyudhana; Satyaki	Kinsman of Krishna.
Virata	King of the Matsyas.
Dhrishtaketu	King of the Chedis.
Chekitana	Ally of the Pandavas.
Purujit	Ally of the Pandavas.
Kuntibhoja	Ally of the Pandavas; adopted father of Kunti, the mother of the Pandavas.
Shaibya	King of the Shibis.
Yudhamanyu	Ally of the Pandavas.
Uttamaujas	Ally of the Pandavas.